APOCALYPSE DEFERRED

APOCALYPSE DEFERRED

Girard and Japan

EDITED BY
JEREMIAH L. ALBERG

University of Notre Dame Press
Notre Dame, Indiana

University of Notre Dame Press
Notre Dame, Indiana 46556
undpress.nd.edu

Copyright © 2017 by the University of Notre Dame

All Rights Reserved

Published in the United States of America

Library of Congress Cataloging-in-Publication Data

Names: Alberg, Jeremiah, 1957– editor.
Title: Apocalypse deferred : Girard and Japan / edited by Jeremiah L. Alberg.
Description: Notre Dame : University of Notre Dame Press, 2017. | Includes bibliographical references and index.
Identifiers: LCCN 2017001228 (print) | LCCN 2017009532 (ebook) | ISBN 9780268100162 (hardcover : alk. paper) | ISBN 0268100160 (hardcover : alk.paper) | ISBN 9780268100179 (pbk. : alk. paper) | ISBN 0268100179 (pbk. : alk. paper) | ISBN 9780268100186 (pdf) | ISBN 9780268100193 (epub)
Subjects: LCSH: Girard, Renée, 1923-2015—Influence. | Violence—Religious aspects. | Eschatology. | Japan. | Disasters—Japan.
Classification: LCC B2430.G494 A66 2017 (print) | LCC B2430.G494 (ebook) | DDC 205/.697—dc23
LC record available at https://lccn.loc.gov/2017001228

∞ *This paper meets the requirements of ANSI/NISO Z39.48-1992 (Permanence of Paper).*

This book is dedicated to the memory of René Girard.

CONTENTS

Acknowledgments ix

A Light Shall Appear in the East: An Introduction
to This Volume 1
Jeremiah L. Alberg

PART 1. CATASTROPHE, APOCALYPSE, AND JAPAN

1. The Nuclear Menace—A New Sacrament for Humanity:
   Catastrophes and Near Misses 19
   Jean-Pierre Dupuy

2. World War II and the Victimary Era 41
   Eric Gans

3. Undifferentiation Reconsidered 55
   Anthony D. Traylor

4. A Reading of the Atomic Bombing of Nagasaki-Urakami
   with Nagai and Girard 66
   Yoko Irie Fayolle

PART 2. MIMETIC THEORY AND JAPANESE CULTURE

5. Girardian Structure and Dionysian Components 89
   Shoichiro Iwakiri

6. The Sacrifice of the Mediator: The Murder on Gifu's
   Sugou Plateau and Folk Performing Art 106
   Mizuho Kawasaki

viii Contents

7. Decadence and Conversion: On the Thought
   of Ango Sakaguchi   118
   Kunio Nakahata

8. Living in a State of Abandonment: The Anime *Vexille*'s
   Supplementary Apocalypse   136
   Andreas Oberprantacher

9. Subculture, Conformity, and Sacrifice: *Kamikaze Girls*
   through a Mimetic Lens   149
   Matthew Taylor

PART 3. MIMETIC THEORY AND THEOLOGY

10. Back to the Future: The Prophetic and the Apocalyptic
    in Jewish and Christian Settings   171
    Sandor Goodhart

11. Reading the Antichrist Type: Christian Apocalyptic
    Typology and Girardian Mimesis   186
    Thomas Ryba

12. The Place of Mimesis and the Apocalyptic: Toward
    a Topology of the "Far and Near," or Is René Girard
    a Postmodernist?   215
    Richard Schenk

CONCLUSION

13. The Drum, the *Gaita*, and the Desert: Thoughts
    on How to Approach Conflicts with Mimetic Theory   245
    Mario Roberto Solarte Rodríguez
    and Mery Edith Rodríguez Arias

    List of Contributors   261
    Index   266

ACKNOWLEDGMENTS

All of the essays in this collection, save one, were originally offered as oral presentations at a conference titled, "Apocalypse Revisited: Japan, Hiroshima, and the Place of Mimesis." While the introduction provides more background about this conference and the reason for the difference in the title of the conference and this volume, here is the place to acknowledge that without that event this particular book would never have come into being. Thus, our thanks must go, first of all, to those who made the conference possible.

International Christian University, through the office and the person of the vice president for academic affairs (at the time Professor Junko Hibiya, who is now president of the university), contributed much to the realization of this gathering of people interested in revisiting the theme of the apocalypse in a Japanese setting. Also, the staff of the Institute for the Study of Christianity and Culture contributed many hours of hard work both in preparing for and in ensuring the smooth running of the conference itself. Our thanks go out to these people.

Many others contributed in a variety of ways, but two people must be explicitly named. Ms. Naoko Wakatake labored long and hard, coordinating many different facets of the organization. Without her the conference simply would not have taken place. Ms. Nozomi Uematsu directed the student workers so that all the various venues operated smoothly. Without her the conference might have taken place, but it would not have been the success that it was. I am personally very grateful to both of them.

Financially, both the nonprofit organization Imitatio and the Raven Foundation were very generous in their support for a meeting of this sort to be held in Asia, the first time such a conference was held outside of North America or Europe.

I thank William Johnsen, the editor of *Contagion*, for permission to reprint Richard Schenk's contribution, which originally appeared in its pages. I thank Eric Gans for his permission to use his contribution, which can also be found on the Generative Anthropology website. Finally, I thank Sandor Goodhart for permission to print his essay, an earlier version of which appeared in his 2014 volume of essays, *The Prophetic Law*.

A LIGHT SHALL APPEAR IN THE EAST

An Introduction to This Volume

JEREMIAH L. ALBERG

When a book has multiple authors, and when these authors come from several different continents with diverse training and expertise, and when they are addressing such dramatically diverse topics as Japanese anime and typology in the Bible—all of which are true of this volume—then readers can have a difficult time finding their way. To aid readers in their quest, I offer two perspectives in this introduction. First, I will provide some background as to how this particular collection of essays came into existence, or the story of this collection. Second, I will give an account of my own rationale for the structure of the book, or the story this collection tells.

The Story of This Collection

Many of these essays, as can be seen in even a brief perusal, have been deeply affected not only by the place in which the meeting was held, Tokyo, Japan, but also the time at which it was held, the summer of 2012, when memories of the devastating earthquake, tsunami, and nuclear disaster of Eastern Japan which had occurred in March 2011, nearly a year and a half earlier, were still very fresh in everyone's mind. There was a period in preparing for the conference when we worried whether it could take place in the planned venue at all. It is not surprising, then, that several of the contributors, both Japanese and non-Japanese, touch upon this disaster in their reflections and use it as a touchstone for thinking about apocalyptic realities.

At the time that the conference was first being planned by the Colloquium on Violence and Religion (COV&R), we obviously had no idea of the disasters that Japan would go through. Instead, the desire was to break out of the tradition of always holding the conferences either in Europe or North America. There was a hope to hear new voices and to see things from a different perspective. The association of Japan with the apocalyptic through the events of World War II in general and the atomic bombing of Hiroshima and Nagasaki in particular were very much at the forefront of our minds. The events of March 2011 put it all in a much stronger light.

Some more remote background contributed to making Japan an appropriate place for holding a conference that treated such things as the thought of René Girard, mimetic theory, apocalyptic catastrophes, and possible salvation. Although Girard has never been to Japan, his thought has exerted a steady influence in that country through his writings, both in their original languages and in translation.

With a few exceptions, Girard's works were translated into Japanese here in the order of their publication. At first there was a ten-year lag between the appearance of a work in French and its translation into Japanese. *Mensonge romantique et vérité Romanesque* (published in English as *Deceit, Desire, and the Novel*), published in 1961, came out (translated literally) as *A Phenomenology of Desire: Romantic Lie and Romanesque Truth* in 1971. *La violence et le sacré* originally appeared in 1972, with its Japanese translation coming out in 1982. Then things began to speed up a bit. There is a lag of only six years between the original publication of *Things Hidden since the Foundation of the World* (1978) and its translation. A translation of *The Scapegoat* was published in 1985, only three years after the original. Girard's book on Job was published in Japanese in 1989, around four years after the original. Even his massive book on Shakespeare, *A Theater of Envy*, was translated after only a space of four years. There are even two books translated into Japanese well before their English translation: *The One by Whom Scandal Comes* and *When These Things Begin: Conversations with Michel Treguer*. The translations of these works were carried out by Japanese scholars in French, British, and American literature, as well as by a sociologist.

In addition, several significant secondary works by such people as Jean-Pierre Dupuy, Paul Dumouchel, and Andrew McKenna have also appeared in Japanese. In 2015 Mark Ansprach's *Á charge de Revance: Figures d'elementare de la réciprocité* was also translated. There has been one book-length study of Girard's thought by Yoshinari Nishinaga, a professor of French literature, titled *The Direction of the "Individual": René Girard and Modern Society*. Finally, Girard's thought has also been employed not just in literary theory but by Japanese historians and ethnologists as well. Thus, scholars in Japan have shown a continual interest in Girard's thought since it first emerged in the early 1960s and have drawn on it in a variety of studies.

This widespread interest received a more concrete institutional form thanks, in part, to funding from a foundation, Imitatio, which supports efforts to expand the reach of mimetic theory. A small group of scholars living in Japan were thus able to meet in 2010 and 2011 to prepare for the conference. By happy coincidence, another scholarly association, the Generative Anthropology Society and Conference (GASC), was also planning to hold its conference in Japan, and so it was decided that the groups should join forces. Eric Gans, the founder of generative anthropology, had been an early student of Girard's, and their thought has much in common.

The actual conference took place from July 5 to July 8 on the campus of International Christian University (ICU) in Tokyo. The university is located on what was, up until the end of the war, the site of the Nakajima Aircraft Company. During the war, the company was developing and testing designs for advanced long-range bombers. Given its location, ICU identified a crucial part of its educational mission as the conscious effort to "beat spears into plowshares." Mimetic theory's focus on the causes of violence and violence's role in the constitution of culture aligns well with this mission.

The original conference bore the title Apocalypse Revisited: Japan, Hiroshima, and the Place of Mimesis. The title of this book, however, better reflects the content of the papers. The "deferral" of violence plays an important role in both mimetic theory and the generative anthropology of Eric Gans. In the former, greater violence is deferred through controlled violence, or "bad" violence is deferred through "good" violence. In the latter, the object that is both desired and unavailable gives birth to an originary love and resentment that will mark all further development. From a Christian perspective we might say, especially in reference to the Apocalypse, that deferral may be the best that we can hope for.

The Story the Collection Tells

Reviews of an edited collection often contain a moment in which the reviewer confesses to having failed to find the logical key that would grant access to the unity of the various papers collected between the covers of the book being reviewed. Thus, she is reduced to commenting on the few papers that strike her as particularly outstanding or criticizing those papers that fail to achieve what they set out to do. I hope that the *logos* of this collection will stand out on its own. Still, I would like to provide a few signposts to help the reader on his or her way.[1]

Catastrophe, Apocalypse, and Japan

The essays of Part 1 are mostly, but not exclusively, rooted in the various events of World War II. The first paper, appropriately enough by Jean-Pierre Dupuy, sets the frame and the premise of this collection. Dupuy focuses on a struggle within Girard's system. He sees that for Girard, human *méconnaisance* (the misrecognition of the victim as responsible for a given society's problems) plays a central role in mimetic theory. The generative scapegoat mechanism works only so long as we don't know what we are doing when we scapegoat the victim. Our increased knowledge of its working contributes to its inability to function. Dupuy points out how the Bomb is known and is, indeed, recognized by Girard as being known. He avers that "nuclear peace" is a new form of the sacred informed by knowledge that the power of destruction that threatens us also protects us and that this power comes, not from God, but from ourselves. But this, Dupuy astutely points out, undermines the postulate of *méconnaisance*, which is necessary for the sacrificial mechanism to function. Accordingly, Dupuy wants to clarify the situation of the sacred Bomb and our recognition of it, a situation that Girard has termed "intermediary and complex." At the same time that Dupuy points out our recognition of the reality of nuclear weapons and their destructive potential, he is astounded that "we do not see the moral horror" of the situation. It seems that *méconnaisance* is still operative. Dupuy detects a weakness in every person when his capacity for inventive destruction becomes disproportionate to the human condition. Thus, he recognizes the basis for the *méconnaisance*—the growing gap between the human capacity for making and the capacity for imagining what they have made.

Dupuy concretizes the problem by looking at the writings of Günther Anders and asking, with him, how it is that the Japanese can speak of the atomic bombing of Hiroshima by characterizing it as if it were a natural catastrophe, as if there were no malice involved. He equates this absence of hatred with an absence of scruple, which becomes the most inhuman form of all. Dupuy's question gets a fuller context and an indirect response from the essays that follow. I will point this out below.

The next contributor, Eric Gans, much like the German novelist G. W. Sebald, lives in the shadow of the war and sees our present existence as the period of the deferral of World War III. Gans makes the case that the Holocaust establishes the basis for our condemnation of all other practices that affirm ontological differences among groups of human beings. Even those whose grievances predate the Holocaust, such as the victims of colonialism, must symbolically pass through it to conclude that such practices are dehumanizing.

Yet Gans is cognizant of the reality that the apocalyptic aspects of World War II were not limited to Europe and to the Jews. He helpfully summarizes and analyzes Girard's scattered statements about the atomic bomb. He echoes what Dupuy in his essay has already pointed to: Girard's conviction that the existence of the Bomb raises human awareness about its own power to destroy itself. Thus, we confront the mad paradox of guaranteeing nonviolence through the threat of absolute destruction. In effect the Bomb has the capacity, as violence often does, of returning us to an original state: mutual destruction or deferral of violence, a kind of brutal equality in which each can destroy the whole. Up until the emergence of weapons of mass destruction, the originary dynamic was such that it diminished violence by channeling it toward the common good, but now, as Gans points out, the advantage goes to whichever group is willing to accept suicide.

Thus, Gans points out the West's vulnerability to any group that rejects forbearance and a concern for the victim and asserts its own unique religious validity. He also posits that the most successful anthropology is the one that serves as a foundation for the most successful society because this is the highest proof that it grasps the fundamental truth behind human social organization. This is the ultimate test of the struggle between the logos of violence and the logos of peace.

One possible answer to Dupuy's questioning comes to us in the form of a survivor's almost immediate response in faith to the suffering of Nagasaki. But in order to clearly perceive this response *as* an answer to Dupuy, I have placed Anthony D. Traylor's on "Undifferentiation" as a bridge between Dupuy's question and Yoko Irie Fayolle's answer. Traylor's essay is an exegetical offering on one of Girard's last works, *Achever Clausewitz* or, in English, *Battling to the End*. In this argumentative reconstruction of Girard's work, Taylor finds new considerations on the apocalyptic significance of undifferentiation. Girard's earlier view, of which Dupuy is cognizant, was that undifferentiation was the necessary condition for a new, sacrificially generated differentiation to emerge lest the society be destroyed. Girard saw ritual reenactments of the undifferentiated as attempts "to replicate the conditions proven by past experience to be effective in generating communal harmony and renewal." But with *Achever Clausewitz*, Traylor sees a new possibility developing out of an idea that is already present in *Things Hidden*, namely, that there are two forms of undifferentiation—"at once very close and radically opposed." One form is the mimetic crisis that we have already mentioned, in which mimetic doubles escalate their violence to an extreme, thus rendering themselves more and more identical, all the while continuing to assert their metaphysical autonomy from their rival. But there is also a benevolent reciprocity in the unilateral refusal to retaliate. In this state of affairs, both the dangers of failure and the chances of success are maximal: either violent meltdown or conversion. Violence and love share in the abolition of differences, abolition of difference being a constitutive element of both love and violence.

In *Achever Clausewitz*, the question is how the claim of autonomy will be resolved. An undifferentiation that realizes that it is, in fact, the peaceful identity of the potential rivals is the "secret possibility" at the heart of violent identity. Thus, reconciliation becomes the flip side of violence.[2]

While the common ground of violent and peaceful identity is undifferentiation, their fundamental difference is in the self's investment in autonomy. Paradoxically, the violent situation contains the possibility of allowing the protagonists to see "what violence does not want to see." "What violence does not wish to see is precisely the nothingness which (strangely enough) under normal circumstances succeeds in dividing and distancing us from our fellow human beings." With this recognition, the other becomes my other self. This involves the elimination of false differences and the giving up of any claims to metaphysical autonomy: "Thus, this divide separating violent from peaceful identity is marked by the presence or absence of autonomous self-assertion." Girard's thinking is now focused on the "*continuous* . . . the *mysterious kinship between violence and reconciliation*, negative and positive undifferentiation, the mimetic crisis and . . . the 'mystical body.'" The only way from the one to the other is through an internal transformation of mimetism itself.

In her essay on Dr. Takashi Nagai's funeral oration, Yoko Irie Fayolle gives us the opportunity to intuit the telos of violence that goes beyond a return to differentiation and is predicated on a certain self-effacement. Three months after the bombing, Dr. Nagai's funeral address was given at the service for the 8,500 Christians of the Urakami Church in Nagasaki who died instantly in the blast. At first it does not seem very promising material for a Girardian reading unless that is meant in a critical sense. Dr. Nagai speaks of a Holocaust offered through the Providence of God. Fayolle's aim is to understand "both the truth of Christianity and Girard's theories in the secular context of Japan."

The atomic bomb that killed so many of the Catholic community of Nagasaki did not inflict death on a random group of believers. This was an ancient community rooted in the Hidden Christians of Japan, that incredible group of lay faithful who for two hundred and fifty years secretly kept the faith in Christ and his Church and in the prophecies they had heard only to emerge into a world that treated them exactly as it had treated their ancestors before they went into hiding—it persecuted them. This time, however, the persecution posed negative consequences for the world of trade and diplomacy, and so Japan adopted a "freedom of religion" clause to its Constitution in the Meiji period. Still, prejudice and hatred do not die out so quickly. The Christians of Urakami were considered "impure" and were judged by at least some of their Japanese co-citizens as having deserved their fate. The gods were angry because these Japanese did not love their country and worshipped a foreign God. Into this situation, Nagai's funeral oration proclaims their innocence and our guilt. They were the ones that God found worthy to come into his presence. They were all *alter Christi*, standing in the place of Christ.

What Nagai saw in the flames of the fires caused by the Bomb is what Girard posited one might see: "the light of peace, . . . something beautiful, something pure, something sublime." Nagai mourns their death while also rejoicing that they have entered eternal life.

There are voices who accuse Nagai of exempting both the Japanese and the United States from responsibility and thereby opening the way for future use of nuclear weapons. They see in Nagai's speech the exact opposite of what it is. They see a logic of sacrifice when in fact it is a logic of mercy. Nagai, in good Christian tradition, is rehabilitating the victims, relieving them of their reputation for impurity, restoring to both those who perished and the Christians who survived their human worth and dignity. He frees the survivors of resentment.

It is here that the idea of *méconnaissance*, which Dupuy had questioned, returns: "Nagai reveals the *méconnaissance* of Japanese society by calling the victims of the atomic bomb 'pure lambs' and appealing to their innocence in public." He puts the victims in Christ's place and thus he becomes their Paraclete. As Fayolle astutely points out, in Japanese society there have been many martyrs, many witnesses, "but no one had ever come to their defense." Nagai, by witnessing to their innocence and the truth of Christianity, became united to the victims in this witnessing. His witness has a power—the power "to persuade survivors to abandon all plans of mimetic retaliations." This may help to explain the behavior of the citizens of Hiroshima and Nagasaki after the war as noted above by Dupuy and Anders.

At this point, our essays branch off into two streams. The first stream explores Japanese culture using mimetic theory as well as tests mimetic theory using Japanese culture. The second stream develops some of the theological implications of mimetic theory.

Mimetic Theory and Japanese Culture

The essays in this part cover a wide range of topics within Japanese cultural history. The first essay, by Shoichiro Iwakiri, goes back to the source of Japanese literature in reading the *Tale of Genji* with an awareness of mimetic theory. At the same time, Iwakiri challenges Girard not so much on the grounds that mimetic theory does not apply to Japanese culture as on the grounds that Girard is too negative about the Dionysian elements of culture and that the Christian emphasis in his thought limits his appreciation of non-Christian values.

Mizuho Kawasaki's essay represents the kind of reading many Girardians engage in when they look to their own culture, guided by the insights of mimetic theory. Kawasaki analyzes a ritual dance that takes place annually in Hide city in Gifu prefecture. What is fascinating about this study is not so much the discovery of traces of the stereotypes of persecution such as scapegoating, accusations, and violence in the ritual, but how close to the surface the historical events that underlie the ritual are. Kawasaki's research has ramifications for our understanding of traditional Japanese mythical figures such as Tengu. If one digs a little deeper, beyond the mythical figures and the comparative analysis that mimetic theory makes possible, one also finds real victims. Although Japanese culture is quite old, many of its myths, even the oldest, only go back in their written form to the eighth century CE. Many of the stories and rituals are much more recent. This allows historical references to be much more easily traced and lends credence to Girard's somewhat controversial claim that behind our myths lie real victims, real violence.

Kawasaki is able to record the oral tradition in the community in which the ritual dance is practiced that preserves the name of the victim. The oral tradition that accompanies the ritual speaks of mimetic rivalry, growing antagonism between two groups, and a murder. Further, the place of the murder became a shrine. Kawasaki suggests that the relationship between the murder of Gorube and the ritual dance, the *Sugoishishi*, "is identical to the relation between generative violence and ritual as sacrifice in Girard's usage."

Kunio Nakahata turns to the work of the Japanese novelist and essayist Ango Sakaguchi as a way of bringing mimetic theory and Japanese culture together. Nakahata sees that one of the difficulties with mimetic theory in terms of ethics is the following: if sacrificial structures are the matrix of the cultural world, then how is it ethically possible for someone to step out of that matrix? In *Things Hidden since the Foundation of the World*, Girard makes clear that he thinks it is not possible without help from outside, without having someone who "owes nothing to violence." In fact, this comes in the context of Girard's "proof" that Jesus Christ is of divine origin. Conversion thus becomes a leaving or going out of the structure of sacred violence. Nakahata finds an analogous thought in Ango's work on *karakuri*. This is a difficult term to translate, and so Nakahata leaves it in the original but explains that *karakuri* are systems in a broad sense which include not only visible but also invisible systems, or a sort of second nature realized in the mind of Japanese, for example, which they transform into the external realities surrounding them. It is similar to Hegel's notion of "objective mind." Ango's point is that although *karakuri* are constructed and therefore are, in a sense, arbitrary, they are not experienced as such. For most people most of the time it is simply reality. For the Japanese, the Imperial system is one such *karakuri*.

This is not a form of conspiracy theory in which evil priests or politicians have consciously constructed a false reality to control the masses. However, Ango nevertheless sees these *karakuri* as historical realities.

It was the experience of the total violence of the war that broke through the *karakuri* for Ango. It freed him to glimpse the truth. Unfortunately, after the war ended, Ango experienced not a communal or national facing up to the truth but the quick and silent reconstruction of *karakuri* as another way of ignoring the moral horror, referred to above by Dupuy. The pressing question for Ango became how one avoids such self-deception. The path for Ango was not Christian conversion but "the possibility of finding a root of humanity," which "means to fall outside of the '*karakuri*' at the same time." Ango calls this consciousness "a radical intentionality toward life."

Ango saw the falling away from "wholesome morals" of prewar and wartime Japan as being a hopeful sign. It was a fall into decadence he could support because it represented a recovery of true humanity.

Whether the recovery occurred is contested in the next essay. Andreas Oberprantacher turns first to an analysis of Jean-Luc Nancy's concept of the state of abandonment and the uses the dystopian Japanese anime *Vexille* as a vehicle for exploring the apocalyptic possibility awaiting us. *Vexille* presents the end not as an apocalyptic bang but as a slow-motion, violent contagion. In addition to the usual scenario of escalating mimetic rivalries resolved through a double sacrificial gesture that both restores order and veils the violence, *Vexille* also presents the nameless Tokyo slum dwellers as living in a state of abandonment. The slum dwellers' lives are a representation of Agamben's notion of "base-life"—life that is both unworthy of being saved and unworthy of being sacrificed.

Again in this essay we come to the point of undifferentiation. The sacrificial crisis is such that "purification is no longer possible and impure, contagious, reciprocal violence spreads throughout the community." What Oberprantacher observes is that our latest art forms as well as our latest theoretical considerations represented in such figures as Nancy and Agamben both suggest that the sacrificial crisis may not resolve itself. It may, in fact, give way to a "lasting crisis." Like Traylor, Oberprantacher calls for a reexamination of the focus in mimetic theory on typical scapegoat mechanisms. Oberprantacher raises the question of whether the preference for the scapegoat "may distort one's critical attention and sensibility to the extent that one hardly notices all the excessive violence that is not bound and structured by mimetic rivalry." Thus, a new strategy of concealment is revealed. Not only is the truth of the scapegoat mechanism being concealed, the bloodless, but nonsacrificial bio-political violence involved in slumification and desertification is equally blocked from view. Oberprantacher calls us to direct our attention to the margins to understand that when we move the scapegoat mechanism to the center of our attention, we have not done away with the phenomenon of *méconnaissance*, since the margin of our attention, where the surplus of violence may be playing out, still exists.

It is at the moment when these essays reach the point at furthest remove from "mainstream" culture, be it Japanese or Western, that we find ourselves paradoxically before the most revelatory—Matthew Taylors's analysis of the cult film *Kamikaze Girls* (*Shimotsuma Monogatari*). This analysis of the film is revelatory in several ways, one being that it reveals what a supple instrument mimetic theory and generative anthropology are for analyzing contemporary Japanese culture. It also demonstrates that mimetic theory and generative anthropology call for no less attentive viewing, critical response, and background knowledge than any other method of cultural analysis. Taylor's analysis shows the way in which such things as scapegoating, myth, and sacrifice are handled in contemporary Japanese film, and by extension in Japanese culture itself.

Perhaps uniquely in this volume, Taylor gives us real insight into Gans's theory that not just sacrificial violence, but also symbolic representation in myth or as language itself can *defer* violence. If the original myth allows for and covers up violence, its reworking is more capacious, saving the intended victim while allowing everyone to feel purged of the need to sacrifice.

Taylor's exploration is not a hazy mimetic analysis. He goes beyond Girard's "brilliant interpretative concept" of pseudo-narcissism—that is, a narcissism that is de-established once the admiration is cut off, to explore in the film the relationship between the narcissism and the sacred. The reader learns from Taylor how the Lolita figure, the rococo style, and much else in the film and in the subculture go back to a popular manga series, *The Rose of Versailles*. As is often the case, the key to understanding this phenomenon is both present and absent from the film. Massively, if implicitly, present through the images and colors, *The Rose of Versailles* is never explicitly mentioned in the film. Taylor's striking conclusion is that the subcultural Lolitas are modeling their identities on Marie Antoinette through the mediation of *The Rose of Versailles* while denying the influence of these mediators. The hidden mediation of Marie Antoinette is significant because it moves the Lolita's identity from being pseudo-narcissistic to being pseudo-sacrificial. The sacred ultimate saves.

Taylor's analysis not only shows that mimetic theory does not allow the interpreter to slight the hard work of becoming conversant in another culture and understanding the culture's subcultures, but also has the added advantage of showing precisely that mimetic theory allows one to put such knowledge to significant use. Who would have thought that knowledge of a 1970s manga could be used to show how a twenty-first-century Japanese cult continues to hide its own sacred and sacrificial tendencies?

Mimetic Theory and Theology

The following three essays, especially the second one, by Thomas Ryba, should be read as a kind of retrospective view of all that has gone before. In other words, these essays tell us something more about all the articles that precede them and cast the light of the Judeo-Christian tradition over the whole collection in a more intense form.

We turn, then, from Japan to a more familiar conceptual landscape for Western readers—the Judeo-Christian one. The first essay, by Sandor Goodhart, not only illuminates in a new way the relationship between the prophetic and the apocalyptic in their Jewish and Christian setting, but also allows a backward glance or even a hopeful glimpse at the Japanese writings that are examined.

Goodhart succeeds in a reading of the prophetic that combines a prospective viewpoint with an absolute and specific interpretation that frees the prophetic text to be fulfilled and yet not completed. I want to cash out this notion of "not completed" in a more robust manner.

Goodhart claims that Girard's strong apocalyptic reading of Clausewitz's understanding of reciprocity "conforms to the deepest prophetic insights of Christian scripture." In an analogous way, I would propose that the analysis of Japanese culture in terms of mimetic theory shows that it too is open to both receiving and being received by this same prophetic insight. Goodhart concludes his essay by saying that Girard's reading "opens new doors for us." He specifies these doors as being not only a renewed appreciation for Judaism, Christianity, the prophetic, and the apocalyptic but also for their interaction throughout the history of Western Europe, because it is there that the dynamics of mimetic behavior, sacrificial violence, and their exposure in the religious texts of *our culture* play themselves out. Earlier essays have opened other doors in the same way, showing that in the history and culture of Japan, these same dynamics have been operative.

Goodhart suggests that "Girardian research of the future" orient itself to this Western European history of "the mimetic, the sacrificial, and their violent conflation in the context of biblical scripture and their prophetic and apocalyptic understanding," but in our conference setting and in this volume we have opened a new door to a different culture, different religion, and possibly different scriptures. The next two essays show us ways in which this might be possible.

Ryba's essay is a master class in how to read biblical "type" in general and the Antichrist in particular. He delineates the way in which a scriptural type is "in dialectical relation to the salvation history that contextualizes it." The fulfillment of an apocalyptic announcement is the emergence of new meaning so that types predict vaguely and are fulfilled concretely. The apocalyptic is a call to anti-idolatry in the hope that we might defer its fulfillment. In this sense it becomes a perennial optic for social criticism, that is, for anti-idolatry.

Ryba sees the possibility of a correct reading of the type, Antichrist, in the recognition of what he calls the negative mimetic double of Christ. This consists in recognizing the kind of perverse imitation of Christ that does the opposite of what he does and so is completely reactive toward Christ. Not surprisingly, this kind of perverse mime is traditionally associated with Satan. A reading of this type implies that one is situated in a history in which these things have occurred in the past and are occurring now, with the ultimate fulfillment yet to happen.

Our reading of scripture equips us to read reality. Thus, it is not just a question of how to read the apocalyptic in scripture (Goodhart and Ryba) but how to understand this place, Japan, which for so many of us is so far away, and to be drawn near to it through its apocalyptic sufferings, that is, how to come near to Japan without rivalry—"a kind of nearness . . . prepared by preliminary distance," as Richard Schenk so eloquently puts it. What Schenk is gesturing toward is a way to understand a world that has such diverse places but are still connected, even radically connected, via suffering, and to avoid nationalism and racism.

First, the real primordial distance is the path to true nearness, whether you live in Japan or not. This involves an opening to other, non-Christian, religions. Girard teaches a "path to a kind of closeness" that still allows for a limited rivalry of allies and friends because it presupposes the initial distancing of lasting acknowledgment of the other as other. This reverence of the other requires self-restraint as a sacrifice, a sacrifice that is at once an affirmation of and an intercession for the other that can be fulfilled only by a coexistent.

This implies a conversion, a conversion that is a completion of Heidegger; it consists in finding "the real primordial distance that the human in his transcendence establishes for all beings," which in turn is the path to the true nearness of things: a nearness without rivalry, a nearness of forgiveness. As Schenk sees it, it is Girard rather than Vattimo who acknowledges the greater distance that is needed for the path to genuine newness.

How do we draw close to the Apocalypse without bringing it on? How do we draw close to Japan without obliterating its uniqueness? The two questions seem unrelated but are not. Schenk gives us some reasons why mimetic theory might not so much provide a definitive answer to the questions but rather illuminate the path one must travel in answering them and in this way extend the illumination by faith from the standpoint of the ending. "By faith" because, as Schenk points out, it is faith that provides the "opportunities of productive non-contemporaneity" so necessary for this distance. Only this, "at first more distant faith could still today generate new rationality, the proximity of new experience, and the widespread renewal of social change." This new rationality is not completely discontinuous with the old; rather, it allows for the morally troubling aspects of our society, the remnants of sacrificial structures to become visible and, as they become visible, to be done away with.

Thus, Schenk's approach can leave one troubled. Sacrifice is not totally done away with, but rather is as limited as can be: limited both in practice and in imagery. Limited up to the point where its evasion leads to great harm or the forfeit of a greater good.

Conclusion

The collection ends with an essay that is intended to open up even more horizons, both geographically and conceptually. Mario Roberto Solarte Rodríguez and Mery Edith Rodríguez Arias reflect and theorize on the experience of conflict resolution in their native Colombia. The developing world has in many ways been the missing element in the story being told so far. Very few voices from those places that suffer the "state of war," not as an apocalyptic anime but as hard reality, are heard in this collection. This last essay is not meant to "make up" for that so much as to underscore it—whole regions of the world have been left out in this story and they too need to be heard. Many native cultures and peoples have been implicitly ignored in our focus on Japan and mimetic theory and that fact should be acknowledged.

It is in this spirit that the last essay comes to us as a kind of challenge to look at our neighbor who is suffering. Mario Solarte and Mery Rodríguez's work is rooted in the particular but speaks a universal language and issues a universal call. Their work shows both a great respect for the culture of Colombia and a willingness to examine the violent roots not just of the dominating powers but also the indigenous cultures. The cumulative result is that Solarte and Rodríguez lead us to the desert and its silence. It seems to me an appropriate place, and state, with which to end this story.

René Girard died during the time that I was doing the final preparation of these pages for publication. Accordingly, the book is being dedicated to his memory. This book is just one example of the fruitful way his theories can be used to help us understand people, places, and events that are otherwise either too near and thus lead to rivalry, or too distant and thus lead to indifference. Girard's thought provides the "*proximity that places us at a distance.*"[3] The more closely we imitate him the less we will be in rivalry.

Notes

1. As will be seen, I use quotations from the essays in this collection (including the authors' quotes of other sources) in explaining them. All quotations are taken from the essay that is being commented upon.

2. René Girard, *Battling to the End: Conversations with Benoit Chantre* (East Lansing: Michigan State University, 2010), 72.

3. Ibid., 120.

PART I

CATASTROPHE, APOCALYPSE, AND JAPAN

CHAPTER 1

THE NUCLEAR MENACE—A NEW SACRAMENT FOR HUMANITY

Catastrophes and Near Misses

JEAN-PIERRE DUPUY

Nuclear Peace as the Mock Version of the Gospel

René Girard's "hypothesis," as he calls it himself, asserts that the sacred is produced by a mechanism of self-externalization that, in transforming violence into ritual practices and systems of rules, prohibitions, and obligations, allows violence to contain itself. In this view, the sacred is identified with a "good" form of institutionalized violence that holds in check "bad" anarchic violence. The de-sacralization of the world that modernity has brought about is driven by a kind of knowledge, or suspicion perhaps, that has gradually insinuated itself into human thinking: could it be that good and bad violence are not opposites, but actually the same thing; that, at bottom, there is no difference between them?

There is no doubt that we now know that "Satan casts out Satan," as the Bible says; we know that evil is capable of self-transcendence, and by virtue of just this, is capable of containing itself within limits—and so, too, of averting total destruction. The most striking illustration is to be found in the history of the decades that made up the Cold War. Throughout this period, it was as though the bomb protected us from the bomb—an astonishing paradox that some of the most brilliant minds have sought to explain, with only mixed success. The very existence of nuclear weapons, it would appear, has prevented the world from disappearing in a nuclear holocaust. That evil should have contained evil is therefore a possibility, but plainly it is not a necessity, as the nuclear situation today shows us with unimprovable clarity. The question is no longer: why has an atomic war not taken place since 1945? Now the question has become: when will it take place in the future?

It used to be said of the atomic bomb, especially during the years of the Cold War, that it was our new sacrament. Very few among those who were given to saying this sort of thing saw it as anything more than a vague metaphor. But in fact there is a very precise sense in which nuclear apocalypse can be said to bear the same relation to strategic thought that the sacrificial crisis, in René Girard's mimetic theory, bears to the human sciences: it is the absent—yet radiant—center from which all things emerge; or perhaps, to change the image, a black—and therefore invisible—hole whose existence may nonetheless be detected by the immense attraction that it exerts on all the objects around it.

In the section "Science and Apocalypse" of *Des choses cachées depuis la fondation du monde* (book 2, chapter 3), Girard makes important observations on what has been called in an improbable oxymoron, "nuclear peace."[1] This, according to him, shows clearly that we are already living under the spell of the Book of Revelation. The Bomb has become like the "Queen of the world"; we live under Her protection, but we also know that Her destructive power is purely human. Girard writes, "Dans un monde toujours plus désacralisé, seule la menace permanente d'une destruction totale et immédiate empêche les hommes de s'entredétruire. C'est toujours la violence, en somme, qui empêche la violence de se déchaîner" (In a world more and more desacralized, only the permanent threat of total and immediate destruction stops human beings from destroying one another. As always, violence is that which prevents the unleashing of violence) (*Des choses cachées*, 279). What is remarkable at this stage of his analysis is that Girard feels the need to tell us that nuclear peace is not the sign that the Kingdom of God is already with us (*Des choses cachées*, 281). He goes so far as to say that the "puissance de destruction [de la bombe], . . . sous certains rapports, . . . fonctionne de façon analogue au sacré" (the power of destruction of the bomb, . . . under certain aspects, . . . functions in a way similar to the logic of the sacred) (*Des choses cachées*, 278–79). Thus, according to Girard himself, nuclear peace is a new form of the sacred informed by the knowledge that the power of destruction which threatens us with complete annihilation and, at the same time, protects us against that tragic end, comes from us and not from God. That raises an important issue regarding the internal consistency of Girard's anthropology of violence and the sacred. A central postulate of the theory is that the misrecognition (*méconnaissance*) of sacrificial mechanisms is a necessary condition for their functioning. The misrecognition issue is one of the major keystones in the edifice built up by Girard. Remove it and much of the theory of cultural evolution post Revelation—that is, the dynamics of modernity—is in serious danger of collapsing. *Ante apocalypsis* (before the Revelation), according to the theory, the participants in the collective victimage "know not what they do"—that may be the reason why they should be forgiven. They do not know their victim for what he is: a victim, the unlucky center of an arbitrary process of convergence. This misrecognition is not accidental, since it is an essential part of the mechanism. It is necessary to its proper functioning. The convergence of all against one rests on the common conviction that this one, the victim, carries an ultimate responsibility in the ongoing violence. The peace that follows the victim's death confirms everyone in their previous belief.

If Christianity can be said to be "the religion of the end of religion," it is because the Christian message slowly corrodes sacrificial institutions and progressively gives rise to a radically different type of society. The mechanism for manufacturing sacredness in the world has been irreparably disabled by the body of knowledge constituted by Christianity. Instead, it produces more and more violence—a violence that is losing the ability to self-externalize and contain itself. Thus, Jesus's enigmatic words suddenly take on unsuspected meaning: "Do not think that I have come to bring peace on earth; I have not come to bring peace, but a sword" (Matthew 10:34). The Christian *revelation* appears to be a snare, the knowledge it carries, a kind of trap, since it deprives humanity of the only means it had to keep its violence in check, namely the violence of the sacred. As Girard puts it,

> Every advance in knowledge of the victimage mechanism, everything that flushes violence out of its lair, doubtless represents, at least potentially, a formidable advance for men in an intellectual and ethical respect but, in the short run, it is all going to translate as well into an appalling resurgence of this same violence in history, in its most odious and most atrocious forms, *because the sacrificial mechanisms become less and less effective and less and less capable of renewing themselves.* . . . Humanity in its entirety already finds itself confronted with an ineluctable dilemma: men must reconcile themselves for evermore without sacrificial intermediaries, or they must resign themselves to the coming extinction of humanity. (*Des choses cachées*, 150, 160, emphasis mine)

The fact that there has been neither any nuclear war nor, even more significantly, any direct conventional confrontation between nuclear powers since the advent of the atomic bomb, seems to give the lie to the assertion that *méconnaissance* is a necessary condition for the mechanisms of the sacred to function—if, indeed, the bomb is a new form of the sacred. What kind of sacred compatible with the end of misrecognition are we dealing with here? Girard sees the complexity of the issue but seems to be satisfied with the remark that "C'est donc à une situation intermédiaire et complexe qu'on a affaire" (We are dealing here with a situation that is intermediary and complex) (*Des choses cachées*, 281). Unfortunately, he does not try to go further in the clarification of the "intermediary" status of our situation. That is what I will endeavor to do now.

I will draw on three major interpretations of the status of the bomb: a post-Heideggerian approach to be found in the work of German philosopher Günther Anders; a strategic analysis that starts with a game-theoretical account and is soon obliged to transcend it towards an heterodox conception of rationality; and, last but not least, René Girard's anthropology. The fact that those three interpretations converge toward similar conclusions is deeply striking and constitutes the major result of my own research.

Blindness in the Face of Apocalypse

On August 6, 1945, an atomic bomb reduced the Japanese city of Hiroshima to radioactive ashes. Three days later, Nagasaki was struck in its turn. In the meantime, on August 8, the International Military Tribunal at Nuremberg provided itself with the authority to judge three types of crime: crimes against peace, war crimes, and crimes against humanity. In the space of three days, then, the victors of World War II inaugurated an era in which unthinkably powerful arms of mass destruction made it inevitable that wars would come to be judged criminal by the very norms that these victors were laying down at the same moment. This "monstrous irony" was forever to mark the thought of the most neglected German philosopher of the twentieth century, Günther Anders.

Anders was born on July 12, 1902, as Günther Stern, to German Jewish parents in Breslau (now the Polish city of Wroclaw). His father was the famous child psychologist Wilhelm Stern, remembered for his concept of Intelligence Quotient (or IQ). Günther worked in the 1930s as an art critic in Berlin. His editor, Bertolt Brecht, suggested that he call himself something different, and from then on he wrote under the name Anders ("Different" in German). This was not the only thing that distinguished him from others. There was also his manner of doing philosophy, which he had studied at Freiburg with Husserl and Heidegger. Anders once said that to write moral philosophy in a jargon-laden style accessible only to other philosophers is as absurd and as contemptible as a baker's making bread meant only to be eaten by other bakers. He saw himself as practicing "occasional philosophy," a kind of philosophy that "arises from concrete experiences and on concrete occasions." Foremost among those "concrete occasions" was the conjunction of Auschwitz and Hiroshima, which is to say the moment when the destruction of humanity on an industrial scale entered the realm of possibility for the first time.

Anders seems not to have been very well liked, at least not by his first wife, Hannah Arendt, who had been introduced to him by their classmate at Freiburg, Hans Jonas—each of them a former student of Heidegger, as he was; each of them Jewish, as he was; each of them destined to become a more famous philosopher, and a far more influential one, than he would ever be. The memory of Günther Anders matters because he is one of the very few thinkers who have had the courage and the lucidity to link Hiroshima with Auschwitz, without in any way depriving Auschwitz of the sad privilege it enjoys as the incarnation of bottomless moral horror. He was able to do this because he understood (as Arendt herself did, though probably somewhat later) that even if moral evil, beyond a certain threshold, becomes too much for human beings to bear, they nonetheless remain responsible for it, and that no ethics, no standard of rationality, no norm that human beings can establish for themselves has the least relevance in evaluating its consequences.

It takes courage and lucidity to link Auschwitz and Hiroshima, because still today in the minds of many people—including, it would appear, a very large majority of Americans—Hiroshima is the classic example of a necessary evil. Having invested itself with the power to determine, if not the best of all possible worlds, then at least the least bad among them, America placed on one of the scales of justice the bombing of civilians and their murder in the hundreds of thousands and, on the other, an invasion of the Japanese archipelago that, it was said, would have cost the lives of a half-million American soldiers. Moral necessity, it was argued, required that America choose to put an end to the war as quickly as possible, even if this meant shattering once and for all everything that until then had constituted the most elementary rules of just war. Moral philosophers call this a consequentialist argument: when the issue is one of surpassingly great importance, deontological norms—so called because they express a duty to respect absolute imperatives, no matter what the cost or effects of doing this may be—must yield to the calculus of consequences. But what ethical and rational calculation could justify sending a million Jewish children from every part of Europe to be gassed? There lies the difference, the chasm, the moral abyss that separates Auschwitz from Hiroshima.

In the decades since, however, persons of great integrity and intellect have insisted on the intrinsic immorality of atomic weapons, in general, and the ignominy of bombing Hiroshima and Nagasaki, in particular. In 1956 the Oxford philosopher and Catholic thinker Elizabeth Anscombe made an enlightening comparison that threw into stark relief the horrors to which consequentialist reasoning leads when it is taken to its logical conclusion. Let us suppose, she said, that the Allies had thought at the beginning of 1945 that, in order to break the Germans' will to resist and to compel them to surrender rapidly and unconditionally, thus sparing the lives of a great many Allied soldiers, it was necessary to carry out the massacre of hundreds of thousands of civilians, women and children included, in two cities in the Ruhr. Two questions arise. First, what difference would there have been, morally speaking, between this and what the Nazis did in Czechoslovakia and Poland? Second, what difference would there have been, morally speaking, between this and the atomic bombing of Hiroshima and Nagasaki?[2]

In the face of horror, moral philosophy is forced to resort to analogies of this sort, for it has nothing other than logical consistency on which to base the validity of its arguments. In the event, this minimal requirement of consistency did not suffice to rule out the nuclear option nor to condemn it afterwards. Why? One reply is that because the Americans won the war against Japan, their victory seemed in retrospect to justify the course of action they followed. This argument must not be mistaken for cynicism. It involves what philosophers call the problem of moral luck. The moral judgment that is passed on a decision made under conditions of radical uncertainty depends on what occurs *after* the relevant action has been taken—something that may have been completely unforeseeable, even as a probabilistic matter.

Robert McNamara memorably describes this predicament in the extraordinary set of interviews conducted by the documentarian Errol Morris and released as a film under a most Clausewitzian title, *The Fog of War* (2003). Before serving as secretary of defense under Presidents Kennedy and Johnson, McNamara had been an advisor during the war in the Pacific to General Curtis LeMay, who was responsible for the firebombing of sixty-seven cities of Imperial Japan, a campaign that culminated in the dropping of the two atomic bombs. On the night of March 9–10, 1945, alone, one hundred thousand civilians perished in Tokyo, burned to death. McNamara approvingly reports LeMay's stunningly lucid verdict: "If we'd lost the war, we'd all have been prosecuted as war criminals."

Another possible reply is that consequentialist morality served in this instance only as a convenient pretext. A revisionist school of American historians led by Gar Alperovitz has pleaded this case with great conviction, arguing that in July 1945, Japan was on the point of capitulation.[3]

Two conditions would have had to be satisfied in order to obtain immediate surrender: first, that President Truman agree to an immediate declaration of war on Japan by the Soviet Union, and second, that Japanese surrender be accompanied by an American promise that the emperor would be allowed to continue to sit on his throne. Truman refused both conditions at the conference at Potsdam, a few days after July 16, 1945. On that day, the president received "good news." The bomb was ready—as the successful test at Alamogordo had brilliantly demonstrated.

Alperovitz concludes that Truman sought to steal a march on the Soviets before they were prepared to intervene militarily in the Japanese archipelago. The Americans played the nuclear card, in other words, not to force Japan to surrender but to impress the Russians. In that case, the Cold War had been launched on the strength of an ethical abomination and the Japanese reduced to the level of guinea pigs, since the bomb was not in fact necessary to obtain the surrender. Other historians reckon that whether or not necessary, it was not a sufficient condition of obtaining a surrender.

The historian Barton J. Bernstein has proposed a "new synthesis" that departs from both the official and the revisionist accounts.[4] The day after Nagasaki, the war minister, General Korechika Anami, and the vice chief of the Naval General Staff, Admiral Takijiro Ōnishi, urged the emperor to authorize a "special attack [kamikaze] effort," even though this would mean putting as many as twenty million Japanese lives at risk, by their own estimate, in the cause of ultimate victory. In that case, two bombs would not suffice. So convinced were the Americans of the need to detonate a third device, Bernstein says, that the announcement of surrender on August 14—apparently the result of chance and of reversals of alliance at the highest level of the Japanese government, still poorly understood by historians—came as an utter surprise. But Bernstein takes the argument a step further. Of the six options available to the Americans to force the Japanese to surrender without an invasion of the archipelago, five had been rather cursorily analyzed, singly and in combination, and then rejected by Truman and his advisors: continuation of the conventional bombing campaign, supplemented by a naval blockade; unofficial negotiations with the enemy; modification of the terms of surrender, including a guarantee that the emperor system would be preserved; awaiting Russian entry into the war; and a noncombat demonstration of the atomic bomb. As for the sixth option, the military use of the bomb, it was never discussed—not even for a moment: it was simply taken for granted. The bombing of Hiroshima and Nagasaki followed from the bomb's very existence. From the ethical point of view, Bernstein's findings are still more terrible than those of Alperovitz: dropping the atomic bomb, perhaps the gravest decision ever taken in modern history, was not something that had actually been decided.

These revisionist interpretations do not exhaust the questions that need to be asked. There are at least two more. First, how are we to make sense of the bombing of Hiroshima—and, more troubling still, of Nagasaki, which is to say the monstrously absurd determination to persist in infamy? Second, how could the consequentialist veneer of the official justification for these acts—that they were extremely regrettable, but a moral necessity just the same—have been accepted as a lawful pretext when it should have been seen instead as the most execrable and appalling excuse imaginable?

Not only does the work of Günther Anders furnish an answer to these questions, but it does so by relocating them in another context. Anders, a German Jew who had emigrated to France and then to America and then come back to Europe in 1950—everywhere an exile, the wandering Jew—recognized that on August 6, 1945, human history had entered into a new phase, its last. Or rather that the sixth day of August was only a *rehearsal* for the ninth—what he called the "Nagasaki syndrome." The dropping of the first atomic bomb over civilian populations, once it had occurred, thereby introduced the impossible into reality and opened the door to more atrocities, in the same way that an earthquake is followed by a series of aftershocks. History became obsolete that day, as Anders put it. Now that humanity was capable of destroying itself, nothing would ever cause it to lose this "negative all-powerfulness," not even a general disarmament, not even a total denuclearization of the world's arsenals. *Now that apocalypse has been inscribed in our future as fate, the best we can do is to indefinitely postpone the final moment.* We are living under a suspended sentence, as it were, a stay of execution. In August 1945, Anders says, humanity entered into the era of the "reprieve" (*die Frist*) and the "second death" of all that had existed: since the meaning of the past depends on future actions, the obsolescence of the future, its programmed end, signifies not that the past no longer has any meaning, but that it never had one.[5]

To ascertain the rationality and the morality of the destruction of Hiroshima and Nagasaki amounts to treating nuclear weapons as a means in the service of an end. A means loses itself in its end as a river loses itself in the sea and ends up being completely absorbed by it. But the bomb exceeds all the ends that can be given to it, or found for it. The question whether the end justifies the means suddenly became obsolete, like everything else. Why was the bomb used? Because it *existed*. The simple fact of its existence is a threat, or rather a promise that it will be used. Why has the moral horror of its use not been perceived? What accounts for this "blindness in the face of apocalypse"? Because beyond certain thresholds, our power of doing infinitely exceeds our capacity for feeling and imagining. It is this irreducible gap that Anders called the "Promethean discrepancy." Thus, Hannah Arendt, for example, was to diagnose Eichmann's psychological disability as a "lack of imagination." Anders showed that this is not the weakness of one person in particular; it is the weakness of every person when his capacity for invention, and for destruction, becomes disproportionately enlarged in relation to the human condition.

"Between our capacity for making and our capacity for imagining," Anders says, "a gap is opened up that grows larger by the day." The "too great" leaves us cold, he adds. "No human being is capable of imagining something of such horrifying magnitude: the elimination of millions of people.

The Paradox of Nuclear Deterrence: Away from Strategic Thinking, Back to the Sacred

A pacifist would say that surely the best way for humanity to avoid a nuclear war is not to have any nuclear weapons. This argument, which borders on the tautological, was irrefutable before the scientists of the Manhattan Project developed the atomic bomb. Alas, it is no longer valid today. Such weapons exist, and even supposing that they were to cease to exist as a result of universal disarmament, they could be recreated in a few months. Errol Morris, in *The Fog of War*, asks McNamara what he thinks protected humanity from extinction during the Cold War, when the United States and the Soviet Union permanently threatened each other with mutual annihilation. Deterrence? Not at all, McNamara replies: "We lucked out." Twenty-five or thirty times during this period, he notes, humankind came within an inch of apocalypse.

I have tried in my own work to enlarge the scope of Günther Anders's analysis by extending it to the question of nuclear deterrence. For more than four decades during the Cold War, the discussion of "mutual assured destruction" (MAD) assigned a major role to the notion of *deterrent intention*, on both the strategic and the moral level. And yet the language of intention can be shown to constitute the principal obstacle to understanding the logic of deterrence.

In June 2000 Bill Clinton, meeting with Vladimir Putin in Moscow, made an amazing statement that was echoed almost seven years later by Secretary of State Condoleezza Rice, speaking once again to the Russians. The antiballistic shield that we are going to build in Europe, they explained in substance, is only meant to defend us against attacks from rogue states and terrorist groups. *Therefore be assured*: even if we were to take the initiative of attacking you in a first nuclear strike, you could easily get through the shield and annihilate our country, the United States of America.

Plainly, the new world order created by the collapse of Soviet power in no way made the logic of deterrence any less insane. This logic requires that each nation expose its own population to certain destruction by the other's reprisals. Security becomes the daughter of terror. For if either nation were to take steps to protect itself, the other might believe that its adversary considers itself to be invulnerable, and so, in order to prevent a first strike, hastens to launch this strike itself. It is not for nothing that the doctrine of mutually assured destruction came to be known by its acronym, MAD. In a nuclear regime, nations are at once vulnerable and invulnerable: vulnerable because they can die from attack by another nation; invulnerable because they will not die before having killed their attacker—something they will always be capable of doing, no matter how powerful the strike that will have brought them to their knees.

There is another doctrine, known as NUTS (Nuclear Utilization Target Selection), which calls for a nation to use nuclear weapons in a surgical fashion for the purpose of eliminating the nuclear capabilities of an adversary while protecting itself by means of an antimissile shield. It will be obvious that MAD and NUTS are perfectly contradictory, for what makes a type of weapon or vector valuable in one case robs it of much utility in the other. Consider submarine-launched missiles, which have imprecise trajectories and whose mobile hosts are hard to locate. Whereas nuclear-equipped submarines hold little or no theoretical interest from the perspective of NUTS, they are very useful—indeed, almost ideal—from the perspective of MAD since they have a good chance of surviving a first strike and because the very imprecision of their guidance systems makes them effective instruments of terror. The problem is the Americans say that they would like to go on playing MAD with the Russians and perhaps the Chinese, while practicing NUTS with the North Koreans, the Iranians, and, until a few years ago, the Iraqis. This obliged them to show that the missile defense system they had been hoping to build in Poland and the Czech Republic would be penetrable by a Russian strike while at the same time capable of stopping missiles launched by a "rogue state."

That the lunacy of MAD, whether or not it was coupled with the craziness of NUTS, should have been considered the height of wisdom, and that it should have been credited with having kept world peace during a period whose return some people wish for today, passes all understanding. Few persons were at all troubled by this state of affairs, however, apart from American bishops—and President Reagan. Once again, we cannot avoid asking the obvious question: why?

For many years, the usual reply was that what is at issue here is an intention, not the carrying out of an intention. What is more, it is an intention of an exceedingly special kind, so that the very fact of its being formed has the consequence that the conditions that would lead to its being acted on are not realized. Since, by hypothesis, one's enemy is dissuaded from attacking first, one does not have to preempt his attack by attacking first, which means that no one makes a move. One forms a deterrent intention, in other words, precisely in order not to put it into effect. Specialists speak of such intentions as being inherently "self-stultifying."⁶ But this plainly does no more than give a name to an enigma. It does nothing to resolve it.

No one who inquires into the strategic and moral status of deterrent intention can fail to be overwhelmed by paradox. What seems to shield deterrent intention from ethical rebuke is the very thing that renders it useless from a strategic point of view, since deterrent intention cannot be efficient without the meta-intention to act on it if the circumstances require doing so. Deterrent intention, like primitive divinities, appears to unite absolute goodness, since it is thanks to this intention that nuclear war has not taken place, with absolute evil, since the act of which it is the intention is an unutterable abomination.

Throughout the Cold War, two arguments were made that seemed to show that nuclear deterrence in the form of MAD could not be effective.[7] The first argument has to do with the noncredible character of the deterrent threat under such circumstances: if the party threatening a simultaneously lethal and suicidal response to aggression that endangers its "vital interests" is assumed to be at least minimally rational, calling its bluff—say, by means of a first strike that destroys a part of its territory—ensures that it will not carry out its threat. The very purpose of this regime, after all, is to issue a guarantee of mutual destruction in the event that either party upsets the balance of terror. What chief of state having in the aftermath of a first strike only a devastated nation to defend would run the risk, by launching a retaliatory strike out of a desire for vengeance, of putting an end to the human race? In a world of sovereign states endowed with this minimal degree of rationality, the nuclear threat has no credibility whatever. Jonathan Schell summarizes this argument beautifully: "Since in nuclear deterrence theory, the whole purpose of having a retaliatory capacity is to deter a first strike, one must ask what reason would remain to launch the retaliation once the first strike had actually arrived. It seems that the logic of the deterrence strategy is dissolved by the very event—the first strike—that it is meant to prevent. Once the action begins, the whole doctrine is self-canceling. It would seem that the doctrine is based on a monumental logical mistake: one cannot credibly deter a first strike with a second strike whose raison d'être dissolves the moment the first strike arrives."[8]

Another, quite different argument was put forward that likewise pointed to the incoherence of the prevailing strategic doctrine. To be effective, nuclear deterrence must be absolutely effective. Not even a single failure can be allowed, since the first bomb to be dropped would already be one too many. But if nuclear deterrence is absolutely effective, it cannot be effective. As a practical matter, deterrence works only if it is not 100 percent effective. One thinks, for example, of the criminal justice system: violations of the law must occur and be punished if citizens are to be convinced that crime does not pay. But in the case of nuclear deterrence, the first transgression is fatal.

The most telling sign that nuclear deterrence did not work is that it did nothing to prevent an unrestrained and potentially catastrophic arms buildup. If indeed it did work, nuclear deterrence ought to have been the great equalizer. As in Hobbes's state of nature, the weakest nation—measured by the number of nuclear warheads it possesses—is on exactly the same level as the strongest, since it can always inflict "unacceptable" losses, for example by deliberately targeting the enemy's cities. France enunciated a doctrine ("deterrence of the strong by the weak") to this effect. Deterrence is therefore a game that can be played—indeed, that must be able to be played—with very few armaments on each side.

Belatedly, it came to be understood that in order for deterrence to have a chance of succeeding, it was absolutely necessary to abandon the notion of deterrent *intention*. The idea that human beings, by their conscience and their will, could control the outcome of a game as terrifying as deterrence was manifestly an idle and abhorrent fantasy. In principle, the mere existence of two deadly arsenals pointed at each other, without the least threat of their use being made or even implied, is enough to keep the warheads locked away in their silos.

This solution came with a name: *existential* deterrence. The intention or threat to retaliate and launch a counterattack that will lead to the Apocalypse is said to be the problem. Well, let us get rid of the intention. A major philosopher, Gregory Kavka, has said, "The existence of a nuclear retaliatory capability suffices for deterrence, regardless of a nation's will, intentions, or pronouncements about nuclear weapons use." A second major philosopher, David K. Lewis, similarly puts it, "It is our military capacities that matter, not our intentions or incentives or declarations." If deterrence is existential, it is because the existence of the weapons alone deters. Deterrence is inherent in the weapons because "the danger of unlimited escalation is inescapable." As Bernard Brodie put it in 1973, "It is a curious paradox of our time that one of the foremost factors making deterrence really work and work well is the lurking fear that in some massive confrontation crisis it may fail. Under these circumstances *one does not tempt fate.*"[9] The kind of rationality at work here is not a calculating rationality, but rather the kind of rationality in which the agent contemplates the abyss and simply decides never to get too close to the edge. As Lewis says, "*You don't tangle with tigers—it's that simple.*" The probability of error is what makes deterrence effective. But error, failure, or mistake is not strategic here. It has nothing to do with the notion that a nation, by irrationally running unacceptable risks, can limit a war and achieve advantage by inducing restraint in the opponent. Thomas Schelling popularized this idea—known as the "rationality of irrationality" theory—in his landmark *Strategy of Conflict*, published in 1960. Here, by contrast, the key notion is "*Fate*" The error is inscribed in the future. In other terms, the game is no longer played between two adversaries. It takes on an altogether different form. Neither is in a position to deter the other in a credible way. However, both want and need to be deterred. The way out of this impasse is brilliant. It is a matter of creating jointly a fictitious entity that will deter both at the same time. The game is now played between one actor, humankind, whose survival is at stake, and its double, namely its own violence exteriorized in the form of fate. The fictitious and fictional "tiger" we'd better not tangle with is nothing other than the violence that is in us but that we project outside of us: it is as if we were threatened by an exceedingly dangerous entity, external to us, whose intentions toward us are not evil, but whose power of destruction is infinitely superior to all the earthquakes or tsunamis that Nature has in store for us. Günther Anders and Hannah Arendt were right: we are living under a new regime of evil—an evil without harmful intent.

Heidegger famously said, "Nur noch ein Gott kann uns retten" (Only a God can still save us). In the nuclear age, this (false) God is the self-externalization of human violence into a nuclear holocaust inscribed in the future as destiny. This is what the fictitious tiger stands for.

In this light, to say that deterrence works means simply this: so long as one does not recklessly tempt the fateful tiger, there is a chance that it will forget us—for a time, perhaps a long, indeed a very long time; but not forever. From now on, as Günther Anders had already understood and announced from a philosophical perspective at the antipodes of rational choice theory, we are living on borrowed time.

In his *Memoirs*, Robert McNamara asserts that several dozen times during the Cold War humanity came ever so close to disappearing in a radioactive cloud. Was this a failure of deterrence? Quite the opposite: it is precisely these unscheduled expeditions to the edge of the black hole that gave the threat of nuclear annihilation its dissuasive force. "We lucked out," McNamara says. Quite true—but in a very profound sense it was this repeated flirting with apocalypse that saved humanity. Those "near-misses" were the condition of possibility of the efficiency of nuclear deterrence. Accidents are needed to precipitate an apocalyptic destiny. Yet unlike fate, an accident is not inevitable: it *can* not occur.

The key to the paradox of existential deterrence is found in this dialectic of fate and accident: nuclear apocalypse must be construed as something that is at once necessary and improbable. But is there anything really new about this idea? Its kinship with tragedy, classical or modern, is readily seen. Consider Oedipus, who kills his father at the fatal crossroads, or Camus's "stranger," Meursault, who kills the Arab under the blazing sun in Algiers—these events appear to the Mediterranean mind both as accidents and as acts of fate, in which chance and destiny are merged and become one.

Accident, which points to chance, is the opposite of fate, which points to necessity; but without this opposite, fate cannot be realized. A follower of Derrida would say that accident is the *supplement* of fate, in the sense that it is both its contrary and the condition of its occurring.

If we reject the Kingdom—that is, if violence is not universally and categorically renounced—all that is left to us is a game of immense hazard and jeopardy that amounts to constantly playing with fire: we cannot risk coming too close, lest we perish in a nuclear holocaust; nor can we risk standing too far away, lest we forget the danger of nuclear weapons. In principle, the dialectic of fate and chance permits us to keep just the *right distance* from the black hole of catastrophe: since apocalypse is our fate, we are bound to remain tied to it; but since an accident has to take place in order for our destiny to be fulfilled, we are kept separate from it.

Notice that the logical structure of this dialectic is exactly the same as that of the sacred in its primitive form, as elucidated by Girard. I am not speaking of an analogy here. It is the very same thing. One must not come too near to the sacred, for fear of causing violence to be unleashed; nor, however, should one stand too far away from it, for it protects us from violence. I repeat, once again: the sacred *contains* violence, in the two senses of the word.

There is a fundamental difference, though, between the sacred embodied in nuclear deterrence and the old sacred. We the Moderns know that the wild cat is a ruse, an artifice, an artful stratagem. We pretend to believe that it is real in the same way that we pretend to believe that the story we are being told or shown is true. This "suspension of disbelief" is essential for fiction to bring about real effects in us and the world.[10]

Nuclear deterrence in its existential interpretation appears to be a self-reflexive, self-organized, self-externalized social system—neither blind, spontaneous collective phenomenon nor formal, carefully crafted set of procedures as in a ritual. It is indeed, as Girard wrote, an "intermediary case." At the very least, it shows that the mechanisms of the sacred are perfectly compatible with a good measure of *connaissance*—that is, of self-knowledge.

The Good News in Reverse: The End of Hatred and Resentment

It is probably owing to the influence of Christianity that evil has come to be most commonly associated with the intentions of those who commit it. And yet the evil of nuclear deterrence in its existential form is an evil disconnected from any human intention, just as the sacrament of the bomb is a sacrament without a god. In this context, worse news than the imminent end of hatred and resentment cannot be imagined.

In 1958, Günther Anders went to Hiroshima and Nagasaki to take part in the Fourth World Conference against Atomic and Hydrogen Bombs. After many exchanges with survivors of the catastrophe, he noted in his diary, "Their steadfast resolve not to speak of those who were to blame, not to say that the event had been caused by human beings; *not to harbor the least resentment, even though they were the victims of the greatest of crimes*—this really is too much for me, it passes all understanding." And he adds, "They constantly speak of the catastrophe as if it were an earthquake or a tidal wave. They use the Japanese word, *tsunami*."[11]

The evil that inhabits the nuclear peace is not the product of any malign intention. It is the inspiration for passages of terrifying insight in Anders's book, *Hiroshima Is Everywhere*, words that send a chill down the spine: "The fantastic character of the situation quite simply takes one's breath away. At the very moment when the world becomes apocalyptic, and this owing to our own fault, it presents the image . . . of a paradise inhabited by murderers without malice and victims without hatred. Nowhere is there any trace of malice, there is only rubble."[12] And Anders prophesies that "no war in history will have been more devoid of hatred than the war by tele-murder that is to come. . . . This absence of hatred will be the most inhuman absence of hatred that has ever existed; absence of hatred and absence of scruples will henceforth be one and the same."[13]

Violence without hatred is so inhuman that it amounts to a transcendence of sorts—perhaps the only transcendence yet left to us.

Appendix: From Hiroshima to Fukushima via Chernobyl

As we saw, both Günther Anders and Hannah Arendt probed the scandalous reality that immense harm may be caused by a complete absence of malignity; that a monstrous responsibility may go hand in hand with an utter absence of malice.[14] Our moral categories, they discovered, are powerless to describe and judge evil when it exceeds the inconceivable. "A great crime offends nature," Arendt observed, quoting the legal scholar Yosal Rogat, "so that the very earth cries out for vengeance; that evil violates a natural harmony that only retribution can restore." The fact that European Jews have substituted for "holocaust" the Hebrew word "shoah," which signifies a natural catastrophe—specifically, a tidal wave, or tsunami—attests to the urge to naturalize evil when human beings become incapable of imagining the very thing of which they are the victims and the cause.

The tragedy that has struck Japan seems suddenly to have stood this image on its head: an actual tidal wave, the most tangible and unmetaphorical wave imaginable, now awakens the nuclear tiger. In this case, of course, the tiger is caged. An electronuclear reactor is not an atomic bomb; indeed, it is in a sense the opposite of one, since it is meant to control a chain reaction that it itself has triggered. In the realm of the imagination, however, a negation affirms what it denies. In reality, the other realm that we inhabit, the tiger escapes from its cage from time to time. And in Japan, more than elsewhere, the military and peaceful uses of nuclear energy cannot help but be linked in the public mind. "The earthquake, tsunami, and the nuclear incident have been the biggest crisis Japan has encountered in the sixty-five years since the end of World War II," the prime minister, Naoto Kan, told the nation. Sixty-five years ago, there were no nuclear reactors. But two atomic bombs had already been used against civilian populations. In uttering the word "nuclear," this, no doubt, is what the prime minister meant his listeners to recall.

It is as though nature rose up before mankind and said to it, from the terrible height of its forty-five-foot surge, "You sought to conceal the evil that lives inside you by likening it to my violence. But my violence is pure, impervious to your conceptions of good and evil. How should I punish you? By taking you at your word when you dare to compare your instruments of death with my immaculate force. By tsunami, then, you shall perish!"

The human and physical destruction in Japan has not come to an end. To a large extent, the tragedy is being played out on the stage of symbols and images. Among the places first to be evacuated in the Pacific were the Mariana Islands. The name of one of these, Tinian, should remind us that it was from there, in the early hours of August 6, 1945, that the B-29s took off on their mission to reduce Hiroshima to radioactive ashes, followed three days later by another wave of bombers that was to visit the same devastation on Nagasaki—as if the gigantic tide unleashed by the earthquake last month was sent to wreak vengeance on this speck of land for having given sanctuary to the sacred fire.

The special fascination of the tragedy that continues to unfold in Japan today derives from the fact that it joins together three types of catastrophe that we have long been accustomed to keep separate: natural disaster, industrial and technological disaster, and moral disaster—Tsunami, Chernobyl, and Hiroshima, as one might say. This blurring of traditional distinctions, which can now be seen as the outstanding characteristic of our age, is a consequence of two countervailing tendencies that have collided in the Japanese archipelago. One of them, the naturalization of extreme evil that I mentioned in connection with Arendt and Anders, grew up with the horrors of the previous century. The other arose in the wake of the first great tsunami to leave its mark on the history of Western philosophy, the deluge following the earthquake that struck Lisbon on All Saints Day in 1755. Of the various attempts to make sense of an event that astounded the world, Rousseau's reply to Voltaire ultimately prevailed. No, Rousseau said, it is not God who punishes men for their sins; and yes, he insisted, a human, quasi-scientific explanation can be given in the form of a connected series of causes and effects. In *Émile* (1762), Rousseau stated the lesson of the disaster: "Man, look no further for the author of evil: you are he. There is no evil but the evil that you do and that you suffer, and both come from you."

Proof of Rousseau's triumph is to be found in the world's reaction to two of the greatest natural disasters in recent memory: the Asian tsunami of Christmas 2004 and Hurricane Katrina in August of the following year. For it is precisely their status as natural catastrophes that was immediately challenged. The *New York Times* reported news of the hurricane under the headline "A Man-Made Disaster." The same thing had already been said about the tsunami, and with good reason: had Thailand's coral reefs and coastal mangroves not been ruthlessly destroyed by urbanization, tourism, aquaculture, and climate change, they would have slowed the advance of the deadly tidal wave and significantly reduced the scope of the disaster. In the case of New Orleans, it turned out that the levees constructed to protect the city had not been properly maintained for many years and that troops of the Louisiana National Guard who might have helped after the storm were unavailable because they had been called up for duty in Iraq. The same people who later questioned the wisdom of building a city on marshland next to the sea now wonder why the Japanese should have thought they could safely develop civilian nuclear power, since geography condemned them to do this in seismic zones vulnerable to massive flooding. The lesson is plain: humanity, and only humanity, is responsible, if not also to blame, for the misfortunes that beset it.

In addition to moral catastrophes and natural catastrophes, there are industrial and technological catastrophes. Here human beings are quite obviously responsible, unlike in the case of natural disaster; but in contrast to the case of moral calamity, it is because they wish to do good that they bring about evil. Ivan Illich gave the name "counterproductivity" to this ironic reversal. Illich foresaw that the greatest threats are now likely to come, not from the wicked, but from those who make it their business to protect the general welfare. Evil intentions are less to be dreaded than the good works of organizations like the International Atomic Energy Agency, whose mission is to promote "peace, health, and prosperity throughout the world." Antinuclear activists who believe they must accuse their adversaries of malevolence and perfidy fail to grasp the true situation facing the world. It is a matter of far graver concern that the managers of the immensely powerful systems and machines that threaten humankind are able and honest people. They cannot understand why anyone would think of attacking them or blame them for doing anything wrong.

I have reserved for last the most grotesque of these catastrophes, which is economic and financial. The vast global market that dominates nations today is a dumb and craven beast that takes fright at the slightest noise and in this way brings about the very thing that it shrinks from in terror. The monster has already seized Japan in its grip. It knows Japan well. In the late 1980s, Japan's market capitalization accounted for half of the market capitalization of the world's economies. Some feared at the time that the land of the rising sun would soon rule over the entire planet. Yet the monster would not allow it, and two decades passed before its victim could lift its head again. Today it senses that the nuclear industry, perhaps the only industry on earth incapable of recovering from a major catastrophe, has been thrown back on its heels. The monster will not let go.

Notes

1. René Girard, *Des choses cachées depuis la fondation du monde* (Paris: B. Grasset, 1978). All English translations are mine.

2. G. E. M. Anscombe, "Mr. Truman's Degree," in *Collected Philosophical Papers*, vol. 3, *Ethics, Religion, and Politics* (Minneapolis: University of Minnesota Press, 1981), 62–71.

3. Gar Alperovitz, *The Decision to Use the Atomic Bomb and the Architecture of an American Myth* (New York: Knopf, 1995).

4. Barton J. Bernstein, "Understanding the Atomic Bomb and the Japanese Surrender: Missed Opportunities, Little-Known Near Disasters, and Modern Memory," *Diplomatic History* 19, no. 2 (March 1995): 227–73.

5. Günther Anders, *Die Atomare Drohung* (Munich: C. H. Beck, 1981).

6. Gregory Kavka, *Moral Paradoxes of Nuclear Deterrence* (Cambridge: Cambridge University Press, 1987).

7. See the excellent synthesis of the debate by Steven P. Lee, *Morality, Prudence, and Nuclear Weapons* (Cambridge: Cambridge University Press, 1996).

8. Jonathan Schell, *The Fate of the Earth* (New York: Knopf, 1982), 307.

9. Bernard Brodie, *War and Politics* (New York: Macmillan, 1973), 370–71.

10. "Fiction" comes from the Latin *fingere*, to make up, to make believe, to invent, to feign (and not from *facere*, to make, which gave "fact").

11. Günther Anders, *Hiroshima ist überall* (Munich: C. H. Beck, 1982), 84–85.

12. Ibid., 87.

13. Ibid., 114.

14. This appendix was first published as an editorial comment in French by *Le Monde*, March 20, 2011, and was translated by M. B. DeBevoise.

CHAPTER 2

WORLD WAR II AND THE VICTIMARY ERA

ERIC GANS

Deferring World War III

Speaking as an American in Japan, I am very much aware of the opening and closing moments of the great conflict between our two countries, the first of which took place in 1941, the year of my birth. It is not mere nostalgia that makes me recall World War II; nearly seventy years after its conclusion, we still live in its shadow. Or, to put it another way, human life on earth, until its hopefully indefinitely postponed extinction, will henceforth be defined by the deferral of World War III.

Our postmodern predicament is bound up with the obsession with victims and victimage that has characterized the postwar era. The era's accomplishments include the end of colonialism, apartheid, and segregation as well as the many triumphs of feminism and, more recently, of the nonheterosexual community. They also include the anthropological reflections of deconstruction, and especially Girard's mimetic theory, which generative anthropology attempts to bring together in a minimalist synthesis.[1]

The historical explanation of this extraordinary phenomenon has always seemed to me to begin with the Holocaust. The Nazi race policies were so contrary to the most fundamental principles of human solidarity, as embodied in what I call the originary moral model of the reciprocal exchange of signs, that they provoked the reaction that in the future all policies that affirm, even tacitly, ontological difference among groups of human beings would be unacceptable. Michael Rothberg's recent *Multidirectional Memory* (2009), which insistently connects, in a French cultural context, the Holocaust to the "rival" victimizations of colonialism and slavery, only proves my point.[2] For when Rothberg remarks on Aimé Césaire's use of the term *choc en retour* to explain the Holocaust as the "boomerang effect" of applying dehumanizing colonial practices within Europe itself, the crucial point is that Césaire is speaking after the war and that his energetic condemnation of racial-colonial policies, which he affirms to be as deserving of condemnation as the Holocaust, is in fact dependent on the prior reality of the Holocaust. Even if we stipulate (as was of course far from the case) that the Holocaust was "no more than" the translation to the internal relations of the "white race" of attitudes that had previously been all but taken for granted between the races, the fact remains that it was only after the Holocaust that garden-variety racism came to be considered as not simply slightly disreputable but wholly unacceptable, to the extent that today no accusation is more stigmatizing than that of racism.

But one cannot come to Japan without recalling the other apocalyptic manifestation of human violence that made World War II the last real war that humanity will be able to fight and survive with a functioning level of culture intact, or perhaps even survive at all. The Holocaust was arguably the most extreme example in history of man's inhumanity to man. But what is yet more undeniable is that Hiroshima and Nagasaki provided examples of a technology that poses a far more direct threat to humanity's survival. The gas chambers and killing fields of what Timothy Snyder calls the Bloodlands in Eastern Europe over a period of twelve years (1933–1945) destroyed some fourteen million civilians—Ukrainian, Polish, Russian, and of course, Jewish.[3] But these deaths are scarcely a blip on the chart of world population, which today exceeds seven billion. No doubt this is statistically even truer of the few hundred thousand deaths from the two atomic bombs. But within a few years of the war, the technology was already producing far more powerful weapons—hydrogen bombs—and this progression can easily be extrapolated to the point where our entire species is in danger. In their current state, nuclear bombs and their fallout pose an undoubted threat to humanity as a whole. And their potential danger is increased by the fact that their use, based on the example of World War II, would not require a monstrous, ideologically based technology on the model of the Nazi death camps, but rather merely the "normal" strategizing of war such as that which led the Allies to bomb German and Japanese cities with the aim of forcing surrender. Today, as the West weighs the possibility that Iran will acquire nuclear weapons, such questions obtrude on our consciousness.

With these preliminary points in mind, it seemed to me appropriate to take René Girard's reflections on the historical meaning of these phenomena as my points of departure. Girard discusses the Bomb in *Des choses cachées depuis la fondation du monde* (*Things Hidden since the Foundation of the World*), which appeared in 1978. For a discussion of the Holocaust, we must wait until 1999, when in *Je vois Satan tomber comme l'éclair* (*I See Satan Fall Like Lightning*), Girard explains the Holocaust as Hitler's implementation of Nietzsche's deadly combination of insight that our Judeo-Christian civilization is dominated by the concern for victims (*le souci des victimes*) with his aberrant judgment that this care exemplifies a decadent slave morality that must be eradicated at all cost.

The Bomb

The following quotations are from *Des choses cachées*:[4]

> Quand les hommes parlent des moyens nouveaux de destruction, ils disent "la bombe" comme s'il n'y en avait qu'une et qu'elle appartenait à tout le monde et à personne, ou plutôt comme si le monde entier lui appartenait. Et elle apparaît en effet comme la Reine de ce monde. Elle trône au-dessus d'une foule immense de prêtres et de fidèles. (278)

> (When men speak of the new means of destruction, they say "the Bomb" as if there were only one and that it belonged to everyone and to no one,

or rather as if the whole world belonged to *it*. And it seems indeed to be the Queen of the World, reigning over an immense number of priests and believers. [255])

Ce qui rend nos conduites actuelles analogues aux conduites religieuses, ce n'est pas une terreur vraiment sacrée, c'est une crainte parfaitement lucide des périls qu'un duel nucléaire ferait courir à l'humanité. (280)

(What makes our present conduct analogous to religious practice is not really a sacred terror, it is a perfectly lucid fear of the dangers that a nuclear duel would pose to humanity. [257])

Pour ce qui est des terreurs apocalyptiques, nul ne peut mieux faire désormais que le journal quotidien. . . . Ce qui est révélé n'est rien de nouveau, c'est une violence qui a toujours été dans l'homme. . . .

Il faut que la situation mondiale coïncide avec l'annonce évangélique pour nous faire entendre, finalement, que c'est de cela et pas d'autre chose qu'il s'agit dans le thème apocalyptique. Ce n'est pas la perspicacité individuelle qui est à l'œuvre dans ce que nous disons, c'est un ensemble de données historiques qui fait pression sur nous. . . .

Dire que nous sommes en situation d'apocalypse objective, ce n'est nullement "prêcher la fin du monde," c'est dire que les hommes, pour la première fois, sont vraiment les maîtres de leur destin. La planète entière se retrouve, face à la violence, dans une situation comparable à celle des groupes humains les plus primitifs, à ceci près, cette fois, que c'est en connaissance de cause; nous n'avons plus de ressources sacrificielles et de malentendus sacrés pour détourner de nous cette violence. Nous accédons à un degré de conscience et de responsabilité jamais encore atteint par les hommes qui nous ont précédés. (283–84)

(When it comes to apocalyptic terrors, no one can do better any more than the daily newspaper. . . . What is revealed is nothing new, it is a violence that has always been within the human being. . . .

Only when the world situation coincides with the Gospel message are we able to understand, finally, that it is this [violence] and nothing else that is the point of the apocalyptic theme. It is not individual perspicacity that is the source of our observations, but a multiplicity of historical realities that presses on us. . . .

To say that we are in an objectively apocalyptic situation is not at all to "preach the end of the world," it is to claim that human beings, for the first time, are really masters of their own destiny. The whole planet finds itself, in the face of violence, in a comparable situation to that of the most primitive human groupings, with this difference, that this time, it is *knowingly*; we no longer have at our disposition sacrificial resources and sacred misunderstandings to turn this violence away from us. We have reached a degree of conscience and responsibility never before attained by our predecessors. [260–61])

Ce n'est pas la faute du texte évangélique, assurément, si la bonne nouvelle dont nous croyions à jamais débarrassés revient vers nous dans un contexte aussi redoutable. C'est nous qui l'avons voulu; ce contexte, c'est nous qui l'avons élaboré. Nous voulions que notre demeure nous soit laissée, eh bien, elle nous est laissée (Luke 13:35). (285)

(It is not the fault of the Gospel text, certainly, if the good news that we thought we had rid ourselves of forever returns upon us in such a formidable context. It is we who wanted it; this context, it is we who created it. We wanted our house to be left unto us, well then, it is left unto us. [Luke 13:35] [262])

Thus, the violence of the Bomb confronts us with the drastic choice either to learn to love each other or die. Girard's notion of modern history, stripped of the details that he would be the first to dismiss as secondary, is that Jesus's revelation works through history by exposing the inefficacy of sacrificial scapegoating, which for him yet remains, in the absence of any consideration of other modes of human exchange, earthbound humanity's sole means for deferring violence. The revelation of the Bomb is that we can no longer "make peace" by expelling violence outside our community. Our former sacrificial means for expelling violence from our midst can no longer be used because our "midst" is no longer protected from them, and the destruction of our enemies will also be our own. Henceforth we can only perform humanity's most fundamental operation and *defer* violence. At least until some glitch occurs, the existence of these ultimate weapons guarantees the absence of war. But as Jean-Pierre Dupuy has been demonstrating, the hair-trigger logic of MAD is fraught with paradox; the most rigorous guarantee of deterrence, and therefore of nonviolence, is the most inexorable threat of retaliatory violence.

This is a revelation not unique to Girard, and its paradoxical nature has been expressed in various forms: in film in *Dr. Strangelove* (1964), to give an early example. As an application of what we might call Christian anthropology to the modern world, it is in effect a reductio ad absurdum. By demonstrating that the existence of the Bomb imposes the same decision between peace and violence as Jesus's revelation, it can be said to fulfill that revelation but also to render it null and void. Jesus's revelation of the violent arbitrariness of the old sacred on which the world depended is no longer necessary, since the Bomb is the *Aufhebung* (transcendence) of this arbitrariness. Just one single "arbitrary" use of it, rather than killing one to save the others, or even killing the enemy to save "ourselves," would lead to the *universal* annihilation of our species.

Thus, the Bomb returns us to our originary state, in which we choose between mutual annihilation and the deferral of violence. But the option of sacrificial religion is no longer operative, for the relation between the members of the human community is the inverse of that which prevailed at the birth of humanity. According to the originary hypothesis, the human, that is, language, religion, and representation generally, emerged because no so-called Alpha individual could dominate the entire group once mimetic desire had reached the level where the entire group felt equally entitled to the central object. That is, the most powerful is brought to the level of equality by the community as a whole, who all become his peers, since the Alpha's assertion of superiority cannot be sustained against all the others. But if each member of the group possesses a weapon powerful enough to destroy the entire group, the cohesion of the others against each no longer conduces to the unity of the group as a whole. Each is in principle as powerful as all the others together, equally capable of bringing about the end of the world; each must consequently exercise restraint on his own.

To act in Girard's universe is to cast the first stone, a phrase that, as Girard rightly points out, has become a universally accepted formula for deferring violence by focusing on its component of *firstness*. Jesus's insight is to prevent this from happening, as Girard demonstrates in his very fine analysis of the "woman taken in adultery" passage in John. The Bomb pushes this reasoning to its limit by making the first act of violence not merely the beginning of a sacrificial expulsion, but potentially of mutual destruction. Thus, the world of the Bomb leads to wars less and less "total" like World War II, in which survival depends on maintaining as a conscious choice not to use the ultimate weapons, not to act by instinct, not to engage in the violence-discharging firstness of the one who casts the first stone. "No first use" is not accidentally a variant of this turn of phrase.

The originary dynamic was biased toward a diminution of violence in that the community as a whole could enforce its will on any violent individual and channel the mimetic violence of all toward a common goal, whether it be scapegoating, or what seems to me more realistic, the equal sharing of meat. The Bomb scenario, in contrast, gives an advantage to whichever member of the group can intimidate the others most credibly with a threat of using the ultimate weapon, that is, the group that best appears able to accept suicide. In the current world, I think we all know for which societies this is true. This suggests that allowing Iran and its rhetorically—at least—apocalyptic leadership to obtain nuclear arms may be a tipping point. Let us hope that this does not occur.

The Holocaust

Girard's remarks on the Holocaust situate it in the context of his vision of Western society as increasingly reflecting the Judeo-Christian concern for victims (*le souci des victimes*). Thus, he understands the Nazis as in essence disciples of Nietzsche, reflecting the latter's original and perverse insight into the victimary vocation of the West. For Girard, Nazi antisemitism is a reaction to Nietzsche's revelatory understanding that post-Enlightenment Western society, while secular in appearance, remains dominated by the Christian, victimary values whose "decadence" he denounces. This revelation of the victimary, whatever we think of it, is the source of a new "degree of freedom": once we become aware that the victimary is indeed the direction the world is taking, and if this world, as Germans after World War I were likely to find, is going badly, then a political doctrine designed explicitly for combating the concern for victims—which was to adopt over time Mussolini's term of "fascism," sticking together without concern for outsiders—became a political possibility.

Girard's analysis strikes me as an excellent starting point for the explanation of the Holocaust, provided we integrate into it the notion of Jewish firstness. Nietzsche saw clearly enough that it was Jewish monotheism, with its insistence on universal moral equality among human beings under One God, that was at the origin of the Christian care for victims. (Girard too has always insisted on this. In a moving passage in *Des choses cachées*, he insists that Judaism is the ultimate worldly religion, of which Christianity is more the deconstruction than the successor—that there can be no religion superior to that of the Pharisees, which is indeed the basis of modern, "Talmudic" Judaism.) By morally equating the Jews with "vermin," Hitler could claim to be purging the human race of egalitarian-victimary sensibilities that were in effect extraneous to the human essence, so to speak rewriting the originary event. Nietzsche's analysis was of particular value for Hitler because in describing Christian "slave morality" as of Jewish origin, Nietzsche, despite his repudiation of antisemitism, performs the classic antisemitic gesture of denying the Jewish claim to firstness. Unconcerned with chronology, Nietzsche presents the Jews and their Christian heirs as usurpers of what should have remained a heroic mode of centrality; for Nietzsche, Achilles' noble "rage" has nothing in common with *le ressentiment*. Hence the myth that presents the "Aryan race" as the truly "first" authors of Western civilization, corrupted by Jewish-Christian slave morality, and whose values the Nazis will restore. Ominously, the Nazi denial of the historical firstness of the Jews eliminates the witnessing role they had played within Christian society and that protected them at least in principle from genocide.

Here are the chief points about the Holocaust in *Je vois Satan tomber comme un éclair*:[5]

Le but spirituel de l'hitlérisme, à mon avis, était d'arracher l'Allemagne d'abord, l'Europe ensuite à la vocation que lui assigne sa tradition religieuse, le souci des victimes. (264)

(The spiritual aim of Hitlerism, in my opinion, was to free first Germany and then all of Europe from the vocation assigned to it by its religious tradition, the concern for victims. [171])

[Les Nazis] s'appuyaient dans ce domaine sur le penseur qui a découvert la vocation victimaire du christianisme, sur le plan anthropologique, Frédéric Nietzsche. (264–65)

([The Nazis] relied in this domain on the thinker who discovered the victimary vocation of Christianity as an anthropological phenomenon, Friedrich Nietzsche. [171])

Dans certains inédits de la dernière période, Nietzsche évite la double erreur positiviste et post-moderne et découvre la vérité que je ne fais que répéter après lui . . . dans la passion dionysiaque et dans la passion de Jésus c'est la même violence collective mais l'interprétation est différente. (265)

(In certain unpublished writings of his last period, Nietzsche avoids the double error, positivist and postmodern [of seeing either facts without interpretation or interpretation without facts], and discovers the truth that I am only repeating after him: . . . in the Dionysian passion and the passion of Jesus, the same collective violence is at work, but the interpretation is different. [171–72])

Pour discréditer le judéo-chrétien, Nietzsche s'efforce de montrer que sa prise de position en faveur des victimes s'enracine dans un ressentiment mesquin. . . . C'est la fameuse "morale des esclaves." (267)

(To discredit the Judeo-Christian, Nietzsche attempts to show that its stand on behalf of victims has its roots in petty resentment. . . . This is the famous "slave morality." [173])

And following the defeat and revelation of the horrors of Nazism, we have the victimary postmodern world of today, obsessed with victims to the point of suspecting even the most potentially creative modes of firstness:

> Loin d'étouffer le souci des victimes, [l'entreprise hitlérienne] a accéléré ses progrès mais l'a complètement démoralisé. L'hitlérisme se venge de son échec en désespérant le souci des victimes, en le rendant caricatural. (271)

> (Far from snuffing out concern for victims, [the Hitlerian enterprise] only accelerated its progress but has left it completely demoralized. Hitlerism has avenged its failure by making the concern for victims despairing and caricatural. [176])

Using Victimary Logic in a Partial Manner

The Judeo-Christian West, although it continues to play a predominant role, no longer simply dominates our "global" planet; its fundamental anthropology, which Girard has done so much to elucidate, is no longer without significant challenge. In particular, in addition to Iranian president Ahmadinejad's threats to ignore "no first use = don't cast the first stone" and use the Bomb, militant Islam has taken advantage of the victimary climate of the West both to terrorize it with the accusation of Islamophobia and to take an unapologetic stance in asserting its claim of unique religious validity. Aside from the most backward communist tyrannies, no non-Muslim country would dream of excluding churches of other religions and forbidding the possession of their religious materials, let alone executing converts to them. The contrast is obvious with the "oikophobic" West, which scarcely protests, let alone attempts to prevent such practices, which include the persecution of Christians in many countries (such as recently in Egypt). Part of the difficulty of the ongoing Syrian civil war is that religious minorities like Christians prefer the protection of the Alawite dictatorship with all its brutality to the Sunni Islamic forces that are likely to prevail if the former is overthrown.

What in this is of anthropological interest, both theoretical and practical, is that a world which has learned the lessons of World War II, that has become "Judeo-Christian" to an often caricatural extent, treating every Other as a potential victim and every act of the Other's violence as an occasion for forbearance—such a world is vulnerable to a strategy that rejects forbearance (since God is great and man exists only to serve him, man can, indeed, *must* exercise total violence on his behalf) and rejects concern for victims (since the supposed victims of God's true religion are apostates who deserve their fate), except insofar as the Iranian users of this strategy can manipulate their enemies into feeling that they have made *them* into victims.

The reason this logic is not more salient is simply that the West remains confident in its technological and military superiority. We have seen that this superiority is anything but an external contingency. It is the worldly confirmation of faith in the Judeo-Christian anthropology whose liberating force on the human front has permitted a qualitatively more massive transfer of initiative/firstness to the natural world of things, and ultimately to the constructed cultural subset of this world, the *laboratory*, from which have emerged the theoretical discoveries of natural science that in their turn have made possible our technological progress.

Were it not for this superiority in dealing with the natural world, which even after the end of total war continues to be tested on the field of battle, what we think of as the West's superior insight into the origin of humanity would not only lose influence through military defeat, but also its very value as anthropology would be called into question. In the long term, the capacity of an anthropology to serve as the foundation for the most successful society is the highest proof that it grasps the fundamental truth behind human social organization. Or to put it a bit differently, the anthropology, religious or other, that liberates humans to operate on natural reality with the most degrees of freedom is prima facie the most effective theorizer of the human itself.

No one can deny the West's historical status of firstness with respect to natural science and the weaponry that derives from it. Yet firstness is a mode of deferral, not of ontological differentiation; it cannot confer permanent superiority. And now that the techniques of war are approaching their ultimate limit, by dint of the anthropological superiority of its

Judeo-Christian heritage, the West may be said to have prepared the ultimate test of the eternal struggle between the irrational and the rational, *méconnaissance* and *connaissance*, or to put it in still more characteristically Girardian terms, the logos of violence and the logos of peace.

Iran's quest for atomic weapons may then be seen as a test of the relative anthropological truth of the Judeo-Christian and the Islamic traditions. What has empowered the Islamism of recent years is quite simply moral outrage at the kind of modernity that Christianity has made possible. Sayyid Qutb's focal position in this movement reflects his reaction to the "decadence" of American life in Colorado in the late 1940s; we need not imagine how he would react today, because we have plenty of evidence. Well, these traditional societies, brutally confining to women, whom they oblige to maintain high birth rates, limiting "knowledge" to the Koran, hostile to any form of self-expression, do have a point, even from the perspective of containing violence. For one thing, they don't defer enough violence to evolve the ideas of nuclear physics and generate atomic bombs. But now the paradox has come home to roost in the confrontation between the traditional and the modern made possible by penetration of the scientific, technological, and above all, military revelations of the West into an increasingly global marketplace. The originary paradox with which the human began cannot be transcended, not even by the Prince of Peace himself. If our fate is now "in our hands," we have only gone in a vast circle back to our beginnings.

Hiroshima mon amour

I have had more than one occasion to write about the 1959 Alan Resnais–Marguerite Duras film *Hiroshima mon amour* that opened the postmodern era. In this film, as you may recall, the Japanese and even the Germans are characterized not by massacres and militarism but by vulnerability. The war is no longer seen as it was by those who fought in it, as a struggle between good and evil, but as an unfortunate eruption of violence among brothers. It matters not who began the fight, nor who had "justice" on their side; the important thing is that it is over, and it is for the winners to offer sympathy and protection to the losers.

Hiroshima is the symbol of Japan's loss of the war, and the heroine's dead German soldier-lover is likewise a representative not of the Nazi occupation of France but of Germany's defeat. Love is accepting to see the losers in this light, as victims. This film sheds a positive light on the hypervictimary attitudes of the postmodern era.

But Resnais's film was made over fifty years ago, at a time when the winners could afford to be generous and the losers to be grateful for their generosity. Things are different today. Perhaps we may find a cautionary pendant to *Hiroshima mon amour* in Lars von Trier's remarkable *Melancholia* (2011). In striking contrast to Resnais's picture of love and rebirth, von Trier's film ends with the total destruction of the Earth. This destruction is presented as an astronomical event, and when I first heard of this, I imagined that *Melancholia* was just one more silly sci-fi disaster film. Not at all. A planet bearing the eponymous name Melancholia invades our solar system and destroys the Earth. It is a fantastic and daring objective correlative of the depression of the main character, played by Kirsten Dunst, who expresses in extreme terms the oikophobia that has infected the West. To quote her lines from the film: the Earth is evil, life on Earth is evil, *nobody will miss it.*

An apocalyptic fantasy. But René Girard has taught us to respect Apocalypse. And I fear there may be more realistic, more human objective correlatives to this sentiment than rogue planets afoot in the world today.

Notes

I would like to dedicate my participation in this joint conference [of the Generative Anthropology Society and Conference and the Colloquium on Violence and Religion] to the memory of my late colleague, Professor Herbert Plutschow. When Herb retired after thirty-two years teaching Japanese language and culture at UCLA and became dean at Josai University in Chiba, he looked forward to hosting a generative anthropology (GA) conference in Japan. He had begun working with the GA Society in planning this conference when he died unexpectedly in June 2010.

Herb was a dear friend and colleague who was adventurous enough to participate in my GA seminars that began in the late 1980s. He also published five articles in *Anthropoetics,* our online journal—three on China, two on

Japan—and served on its editorial board. Attending this conference in Japan but without Herb is a sad irony.

1. Perhaps the best argument for attracting Girardians to generative anthropology (GA) is to suggest that GA's minimalism offers the best because the least restricted chance of preserving Girard's core intuition that the human originates on a *scene* where, with the suspension of violence, the first noninstinctual attention can take place and be recalled as an *event*. It is the traditional province of religion to preserve the historical memory of this event. I think that Girard can be credited with the intuition that the "creation of man" is the moment at which the human community first expels—although I prefer to say, *defers*—the threat of self-destruction through mimetic violence.

2. Michael Rothberg, *Multidirectional Memory* (Stanford, CA: Stanford University Press, 2009).

3. Timothy Snyder, *Bloodlands: Europe between Hitler and Stalin* (New York: Basic Books, 2012).

4. René Girard, *Des choses cachées depuis la fondation du monde* (Paris: B. Grasset, 1978). Editor comment: All English translations are the author's. For the convenience of the reader, I have also added in square brackets, following his translations, the page numbers in the published English translation, *Things Hidden since the Foundation of the World*, trans. Stephen Bann and Michael Metteer (Stanford, CA: Stanford University Press, 1987).

5. René Girard, *Je vois Satan tomber comme l'éclair* (Paris: B. Grasset, 1999). Editor comment: Again, all English translations are the author's. I have added in square brackets the page numbers for the published English translation, *I See Satan Fall Like Lightning*, trans. James B. Williams (New York: Orbis Books, 2001).

CHAPTER 3

UNDIFFERENTIATION RECONSIDERED

ANTHONY D. TRAYLOR

Among the most important developments in the long course of Girard's career, the evolution of his position on undifferentiation stands out in particular in light of the implications it carries as well as the paradoxes it raises. Once, Girard's argument was that undifferentiation is not sought for its own sake but as a means toward re-differentiating the social body and thereby restoring order and peace to a community ravaged by mimetic upheaval. Subsequently, however, Girard adopted a fundamentally different stance on what he considers to be a possible outcome of the disintegration of cultural differences. Seeds of this change date back to *Things Hidden* (first published in French, 1978).[1] However, it is not until *Battling to the End* (first published in French, 2007) that Girard fully conceptualizes and articulates the idea that reconciliation between warring members of the community can be forged out of the melting away of differences independently of the scapegoat mechanism.[2] As such, this constitutes a substantial reversal of the former view, which holds that the slide toward undifferentiation inevitably entails either a sudden return to societal differentiation via the scapegoat mechanism or, if this fails, outright extinction of the community. Absent was precisely the scenario whereby the undifferentiation brought on by reciprocal violence bears within the potential for a radical transition into its diametric opposite. In the following, I attempt to spell out in some detail this innovation in Girard and end with a brief suggestion as to why it threatens to undermine his central thesis concerning the origin of sacrificial violence.

A convenient place to start is with the 1977–78 essay, "Differentiation and Reciprocity in Lévi-Strauss and Contemporary Theory,"[3] where Girard takes exception to the structuralist claim that ritual (unlike myth) embodies a "perverse nostalgia for the immediate." Rejecting a metaphysical dualism that pits a realm of "undifferentiation" (that which ritual strives to access in its quest for the "real") against a realm of "differentiation" (the stuff of myth and discursive thought), Girard underscores the fact that both ritual and myth exhibit traits of differentiation as well as undifferentiation (for instance, baptismal rites and flood myths). Girard is particularly frustrated by what he sees as structualism's failure to account for how the realm of undifferentiated immediacy gets "carved up" into the differences they so greatly prize. Wary as he is to embrace this so-called undifferentiation, Claude Lévi-Strauss is instinctively drawn in the opposite direction and becomes ensnarled in a metaphysical/linguistic antirealism, a philosophic position that, according to Girard, tends to degenerate into the kind of relativistic free-for-all plaguing the contemporary intellectual scene. Crucial for Girard, then, is that we abandon this antithesis altogether and concede that ritual is not invested in undifferentiation as an end in itself, but that undifferentiation constitutes an essential albeit "preliminary" moment subordinate to the goal of "(re)differentiation." In short, far from yielding to a desire for lost immediacy, ritual strategically orchestrates motifs of undifferentiation in order to replicate the conditions proven by past experience to be effective in generating communal harmony and renewal.

Needless to say, for Girard the kind of undifferentiation that gets reflexively reenacted in ritual is that of violent social upheaval (the mimetic crisis), whose sole antidote throughout human history has been its denouement in the "single victim mechanism." As argued throughout the Girardian corpus, cultural differentiation is responsible for channeling and therefore managing desire as it flares up in the context of human relations that have evolutionarily undergone an exponential increase in acquisitive mimesis, namely, the inclination to appropriate what the other desires (for instance, food, land, and sexual objects). As occasions for conflict and violence multiply, prohibitions are set up in order to place distance between the subject and the contested object as well as between the various contenders themselves in the form of neatly defined social divisions and hierarchies. Such prohibitions and hierarchical structures in archaic societies provide the necessary brakes and barriers against an outbreak of reciprocal violence. Societies tightly regulated by prohibition are thus pervaded by strategies of avoidance as a means of warding off potential conflict over the desired object. In *Deceit, Desire, and the Novel* (1965),[4] this is the arrangement that Girard refers to as "external mediation" (nonconflictual mimesis), and it is to an impressive degree successful in preventing the social fabric from unraveling. Eventually, however, the prohibitions wear thin, and there is the need to ritualistically reproduce the mechanism that originally brought them into existence, hence the cyclical and sacrificial character of archaic societies.

On closer examination, the proliferation of differences that reconstitute the cultural order can be thought of as restoring to the antagonists their former sense of being separate and autonomous. As such, the scapegoat mechanism merely postpones or deflects an immediate and decisive confrontation between autonomous selves, and this seems to be the principal reason why it provides only a "temporary crutch" for the community.[5] However, once the Judeo-Christian texts expose and derail this sacrificial cycle, a gradual yet irreversible deconstruction of the scapegoat mechanism is set into motion and the mimetic trajectory, especially in its final stages, can now be analyzed frame by frame, as it were, with modernity, in particular, presenting us with a kind of protracted mimetic crisis.[6] It is here that maximal light can be shed on the internal process of cultural disintegration as well as the possibility of envisioning for the first time an alternative to what hitherto appeared to be the only available options of re-differentiation or societal extinction.

Now, according to mimetic theory, the triangular character of desire all but guarantees an eventual clash between model and disciple as the distance separating the two slowly withers away. Consequently, the move from external to internal mediation (marked by the introduction of the rival or model/obstacle) ushers in a return of the violent reciprocity that the hierarchical stratifications of the cultural order temporarily held in check. Equality (undifferentiation) breeds conflict as the artificial barriers holding autonomous beings apart are systematically dismantled and the self's autonomy comes under assault by the threatening approach of the other.[7] With the onset of the mimetic crisis, the warring brothers (Girard calls them "doubles" to underscore their growing symmetry) react by desperately (violently) trying to restore lost differences with a view toward salvaging what little remains of their sense of autonomy. Despite (or rather because of) this frenetic attempt to restore autonomy, the lines separating rival parties become increasingly blurred as the social body perilously approaches a state of total undifferentiation. Formerly, there was always the scapegoat mechanism to fall back on to avert a complete collapse and resurrect social order. Absent this card in a de-sacralized world, we are forced to choose between what appears to be two diametrically opposed scenarios: mutual annihilation or mutual reconciliation.[8] There simply is no middle course for Girard, since all cultural institutions—whether religious, familial, juridical, economic, political, and even militaristic—have been (or are in the process of becoming) deprived of their legitimacy as a result of the historical de-sacralization brought on by the Judeo-Christian texts.

Now it is precisely the juxtaposition of these two extremes (annihilation and reconciliation) at the apocalyptic melting point of undifferentiation, coupled with what will reveal itself to be a remarkable passage from one kind of undifferentiation to another, that presents us with one of the most intriguing aspects of Girard's latest reflections on the vicissitudes of violence. With the anthropological turn in Girard's thought beginning with *Violence and the Sacred*, undifferentiation was invariably cast in a purely negative light as marking the paroxysms of the mimetic crisis immediately preceding the intervention of the scapegoat mechanism and the return to differentiation. The ground for this negative assessment was to a large degree already laid in *Deceit, Desire, and the Novel* by what appeared to be a sharp dichotomy drawn between the two main forms of mimesis, namely, external and internal mediation along with their respective corollaries, vertical and deviated transcendence. Not surprisingly, this gave some the impression that Girard was championing the one while condemning the other, since it is only with internal mediation that the rival (and hence all of the passions that give way to conflict and violence) comes on line. But with the discovery of the revelatory and demythologizing effect of the Judeo-Christian texts, which set the stage for an apocalyptic finale, the notion arises of another, decidedly positive kind of undifferentiation together with a deeply rooted suspicion regarding the possibility of ever turning the mimetic clock back to a world governed by ritual and strict prohibition. Even if this were feasible, such a return to external mediation could only occur through the immolation of further victims. For Girard, all cultural institutions (the family not exempted) are tainted with the blood of innocents and are thus predicated on "good" or "generative" violence.[9] On the other hand, Girard invests little faith in purely humanitarian remedies to violence, and it is not difficult to see why. Despite being unwitting heirs to the Judeo-Christian tradition and its concern for victims, these sorts of solutions never really get to the root of the problem inasmuch as they are incapable of renouncing the project of metaphysical autonomy. This is demonstrated in large part by the constant search for scapegoats who stand in the way of realizing their utopian dreams of unbridled freedom. We must ask then whether an absolute and final break with autonomy (in whatever shape or form) may be the only course available if humanity is to avoid self-destruction.

Does violence somehow hold the key again to its own overcoming? As early as *Things Hidden*, Girard begins to refer to "two forms of reciprocity which are at once very close and radically opposed."[10] The first form of reciprocity, what is variously described as negative, malevolent, or evil, is the violent reciprocity equivalent to the state of undifferentiation that marks the mimetic crisis escalating amid doubles. This is the community of antagonists who steadfastly cling to their autonomy, obstinately insist upon the "differences" that define and separate them, and from time immemorial search out victims who will securely (albeit temporarily) reincorporate them into a differentiated social order. Faced, however, with the specter of apocalyptic doom in the absence of the scapegoat mechanism, there arises now the counterpossibility of another kind of reciprocity, namely, one that is positive, beneficent, or benevolent.[11] This, according to Girard, is the message preached by the Gospel (the Kingdom of God), and it entails a radical simplification of human relations in the form of an unconditional or at minimum unilateral refusal to retaliate in favor of comportment grounded in reconciliatory compassion for others.[12] Now in order for the tide to turn in favor of universal reconciliation, it is necessary that all cultural differences be swept aside. This presupposes, however, a perilous yet inevitable descent into the night of violent undifferentiation where the dangers but also the chances of succeeding are at a maximum.[13] Essential here is the "loosening of cultural constraints" or the dissolving of "false differences" in order to prepare the ground for a possible breakthrough (or "conversion," as Girard calls it). Thus, it would seem that a certain threshold of violence must be collectively crossed before anything like genuine reconciliation can take root among rivals. Faced with a cultural climate that is no long capable of diffusing or deflecting confrontation, doubles reach a point where they can finally let go of false differences and own up to the truth of their fundamental identity and the "nothingness" that stands between them—something they are generally loath to do, given the deeply entrenched habit of clinging to their precious autonomy.[14] In short, what must be violently broken through in the name of lasting reconciliation are precisely the walls of separation culturally erected between selves who stubbornly invest in the project of metaphysical self-sufficiency. What love and violence thus share in common—what moves them closer despite the abyss separating them—is nothing other than this abolition of differences.[15]

Battling to the End picks up on these new trends introduced in *Things Hidden* and moves them into the rhetorical center. Attuned now to the strange analogy subsisting between negative and positive reciprocity, Girard resists smoothing over any of its paradoxical aspects. This, however, does not preclude further uncovering the structural similarities and differences. In the end, everything will hinge on the issue of autonomy, its potential dissolution, and what course that dissolution takes. A consideration of some key passages from this text will bear this out. Girard finds in Clausewitz's reflections on modern warfare intimations of his own mimetic theory, in particular, the notion of human relations governed by what the latter calls "the duel" or "reciprocal action," which if it goes unchecked devolves into an "escalation to extremes," in other words, the apocalyptic threat that so captivates Girard.[16] Thus, in Clausewitz, Girard discerns an embryonic version of his own more anthropologically worked out thesis of reciprocal violence, especially as it threatens to spiral out of control in a postsacrificial world. But aside from these considerations of Clausewitz as a forerunner of mimetic theory, we also run across a number of passages that shed light on Girard's vision of an alternative to mutual annihilation, once the prohibitive checks to violence and desire have been irreversibly lifted. Placing faith in neither progressive nor reactionary cures to human violence, Girard finds in "identity" (undifferentiation) not only the root of conflict, but also the nascent signs of Christian love, something he provocatively frames in terms of a "peaceful identity" located (as the "secret possibility") at the core of "violent identity."[17] As with *Things Hidden*, the analogical relationship linking negative (conflictual) with positive (peaceful) reciprocity is too conspicuous to ignore as "almost the same form of undifferentiation is involved in both cases."[18] In fact, to ponder one, for Girard, is "at the same time" to ponder the other, hence indicating a possible transition between the two. Girard further underscores the mysterious relation between the two forms of reciprocity when he suggests that "*reconciliation is the flip side of violence,* the possibility that violence does not [yet] want to see."[19]

The secret kinship uniting the two types of undifferentiation is without question considered now to be the hitherto unforeseen key to avoiding planetary catastrophe. Precisely why this should be the case brings us squarely back to the self's investment in autonomy, and it is here that the fundamental difference between both kinds of reciprocity (notwithstanding their common ground in undifferentiation) becomes most apparent. Girard's basic insight is something like the following. As warring rivals enter the crucible of undifferentiation and cultural differences dissolve away, the prospect of recognizing what "violence does not want to see" arises for the first time. What violence does not wish to see is precisely the nothingness which (strangely enough) under normal circumstances succeeds in dividing and distancing us from our fellow human beings, making others out to be implacable foes.[20] Yet if this masquerade of differences is recognized for what it is, identification with the other as essentially similar or equal to myself becomes more than just a theoretical abstraction.[21] This, for Girard, is none other than the Gospel message whereby we are enjoined to compassionately embrace our enemies. Now Girard strictly maintains that the precondition for passing from violent to peaceful identity is the elimination of "false differences," which in turn presupposes giving up any claims to metaphysical autonomy.[22] Thus, the divide separating violent from peaceful identity is marked by the presence or absence of autonomous self-assertion. It is significant, however, that the passage from one state to the other can only be made by means of a treacherous exposure to violence, a veritable "trial by fire."[23] Recourse to reason alone will not suffice to bring about the decisive breakthrough given its long-standing collusion with metaphysical desire.[24] On the contrary, what Girard has in mind is more a matter of an intuitive empathy for the other with regard to his or her existential vulnerability.[25] For if metaphysical desire only gains traction vis-à-vis our perceived models, once our models shed the aura of divinity and reveal themselves to be the ordinary souls they in truth are, guards can be let down as we refrain from scandalizing others by posing as rivals. The rule of the "Kingdom" is thus one of self-effacement and is governed not by the "negative contagion" of rivals but the "positive contagion" of imitating Christ.[26] Girard's reflections here may be summed up in the following: "I want to think about the *continuous*. This is why we have to leave behind the difference between war and peace, and try to understand the *mysterious kinship between violence and reconciliation*, negative and positive undifferentiation, the mimetic crisis and what Christians enigmatically call the 'mystical body.' It is impossible to go from one to the other except through a transformation internal to mimetism" (emphasis mine).[27]

Beyond the war of rivals, another face of violence is capable of revealing itself, one that brings in its wake the possibility of an unconditional effacement of the differences that are part and parcel of autonomous selves and hence for the first time of opening the door to a continuity that differs categorically from the conditional or "equivocal" sort of continuity characteristic of the unanimous crowd closing its ranks on scapegoats. For the unanimity purchased at the expense of the scapegoat is one that remains tightly wedded to the binary structure of doubles, not only in regard to facilitating the arbitrary substitution of one victim for all of the other possible victims within the community, but equally (if not more) important, with regard to the decisive shift that takes place among the members of the community itself, namely, from being "an individual feeling" to being "a communal force." Such a metamorphosis is intelligible only if the community collectively redefines itself vis-à-vis the victim. The community, in effect, has become the "double" of its victim, whose death now stabilizes and consolidates the play of vacillating and individual differences. It is precisely this "equivocal middle ground," where the moment of difference is projected onto the victim and that of unity onto the community, that allows the latter to suspend its internecine struggle. The burden of self-assertion, so to speak, has been lifted off each individual and placed squarely on the back of the community, which constitutes now a universal under which the particular can be subsumed instead of floundering about in a void of undifferentiation. With the departure of the god (the victim) and the quelling of the mimetic storm, transcendent meaning is restored as each member's identity is vouchsafed within a totality whose legitimacy is accepted without further ado. It is the equivocal nature of the resolution, then, which betrays the fact that metaphysical desire has not at all been renounced, but merely resituated on a higher plane under the guise of group solidarity. Otherwise, how could we explain the cathartic satisfaction everyone receives if the selfsame thirst for differentiation (autonomous self-assertion) were not on some level still active? So despite this shift in intentionality (in the phenomenological sense of the term), metaphysical desire remains alive and well, which explains why it is destined to revive time and again in its individuated, viral form.[28]

If the undifferentiation that sets in at the climax of the mimetic crisis is the necessary prelude to catching sight of an underlying continuity between rivals, violence (as it reaches a certain pitch and inflection) can be viewed as opening up channels of intimacy otherwise closed off in the tightly regulated network of cultural differences. Such openings would effectively clear the way for warring rivals to pass over to a state of Christian reconciliation. Counterintuitive as it may sound, it would seem that a turbulent collapse of the self's autonomy could, in fact, constitute a viable and even indispensable step toward lasting peace. Could this be the implicit lesson to be learned from *Battling to the End*?

And so it turns out that undifferentiation, contrary to what Girard had originally suspected, does indeed have a telos beyond that of setting into motion the scapegoat mechanism inasmuch as it can violently throw open the gates of the "Kingdom."[29] If there is any truth to the claim that violence in the end is groping toward continuity, the scapegoat mechanism could accordingly be viewed as a detour humankind has historically gone down in a dramatic yet abortive endeavor to permanently break down the barriers isolating one individual from another. Taking Girard's most recent reflections at their word, violence may oddly enough then contain the seeds of its own overcoming so long as it does not in a moment of Dionysian frenzy fail to catch sight of the peace mysteriously lying in the distant horizon. Perhaps the protracted character of our current mimetic crisis will for this very reason work to our advantage, affording us a reprieve, as it were, before we run headlong into the abyss, as may have been the fate of any number of prehistoric communities that, for having traversed the mimetic crisis too rapidly, were unable to resort to the scapegoat mechanism (let alone embrace Christ-like reconciliation).[30] Indeed, one is tempted to say that this slowing down effect may be a key ingredient in the providential plan. Lastly and most significantly, would not Girard's change of heart on undifferentiation force us to reconsider whether the scapegoat mechanism constitutes the innermost core of ritualistic sacrifice, that is, if violence has a telos above and beyond the one leading back to differentiation? Could not the violence perpetrated on the sacrificial victim be carried out with some vague and uncanny intuition of the continuity it momentarily unleashes? This seems to be an implication Girard has yet to consider.

Notes

1. René Girard, *Things Hidden since the Foundation of the World*, trans. Stephen Bann and Michael Metteer (Stanford, CA: Stanford University Press, 1987).

2. René Girard, *Battling to the End: Conversations with Benoît Chantre*, trans. Mary Baker (East Lansing: Michigan State University Press, 2010).

3. René Girard, "Differentiation and Reciprocity in Lévi-Strauss and Contemporary Theory," in *"To Double Business Bound": Essays on Literature, Mimesis, and Anthropology* (Baltimore: Johns Hopkins University Press, 1978), 155–77.

4. René Girard, *Deceit, Desire, and the Novel: Self and Other in Literary Structure*, trans. Yvonne Freccero (Baltimore: Johns Hopkins University Press, 1965).

5. Girard, *Things Hidden*, 444.

6. Ibid., 288. See also René Girard, *Violence and the Sacred*, trans. Patrick Gregory (Baltimore: Johns Hopkins University Press, 1977), 237–38.

7. Girard, *Deceit, Desire, and the Novel*, 14; Girard, *Violence and the Sacred*, 49–50.

8. Girard, *Violence and the Sacred*, 240; Girard, *Things Hidden*, 136, 201, 258.

9. Girard, *Things Hidden*, 208.

10. Ibid., 201.

11. Ibid., 202, 205, 217.

12. Ibid., 197, 200.

13. Ibid., 202, 207.

14. Ibid., 26.

15. Ibid., 270.

16. See chapter 1 of Girard, *Battling to the End*, 1–25.

17. Girard, *Battling to the End*, 46.

18. Ibid., 63.

19. Ibid., 72.

20. Girard, *Battling to the End*, 45, 48; Girard, *Things Hidden*, 26, 361.

21. Girard, *Battling to the End*, 48, 100, 131.

22. Ibid., 51, 72, 88, 131, 132. Contrary to what Girard insists, even more original than the sin of vengeance would have to be that of metaphysical autonomy. See ibid., 21.

23. Ibid., 97.

24. Ibid., 48.

25. Ibid., 100, 133. This newly won perspective on the vulnerability of our fellow human beings can be traced back to the second chapter of *Deceit, Desire, and the Novel*, where behind the mask of divinity the hero catches a fleeting glimpse of the existential void lurking in the depths of the other but lacks the courage to universalize this discovery.

26. Girard, *Battling to the End*, 109, 122, 133.

27. Ibid., 71.

28. See Girard, *Violence and the Sacred*, 79, 161, 247.

29. Ought we therefore accuse Girard of fetishizing violence, a vice he tends to denounce in his "nihilistic contemporaries"? I think it safe to say that what Girard has in mind in such cases mainly has to do with the conflict between doubles still tenaciously clinging to their autonomy and not the disintegration of this autonomy.

30. See Girard, *Things Hidden*, 27.

CHAPTER 4

A READING OF THE ATOMIC BOMBING OF NAGASAKI-URAKAMI WITH NAGAI AND GIRARD

YOKO IRIE FAYOLLE

René Girard insists that human beings are violent by nature due to their mimetic desire. For in Girard's account, the subject does not desire an object autonomously, but desires an object that is desired by another person, a person whom Girard calls the model or mediator. Especially in the event that the subject and model are either spatially or psychologically close to one another, their relation over the object becomes antagonistic. According to Girard, when this rivalry infects all other members of the society, they all face a crisis of mimetic violence. In his scapegoat theory, Girard explains that mythic or primitive societies end this crisis by choosing a scapegoat and transferring violence onto it. This process, analyzed through mimetic theory and the scapegoat theory, is called the "mimetic mechanism."[1] Through a closer examination, we find that the mimetic mechanism appears not only in primitive societies but also in today's postmodern societies.

Girard emphasizes that what reveals the scapegoat mechanism is none other than the Bible. According to Girard, Jesus was ultimately executed as a scapegoat in spite of his innocence. Jesus also encouraged people to become aware of their sin and to imitate him in order to liberate themselves from violence and save their souls. In this way, he informed them that the Kingdom of God, that is, a nonviolent society, which is not based on the sacrifice of the innocent, would come in the future under the condition of their conversion. Girard uses the Bible to illustrate a way of escaping from the mimetic mechanism, thus revealing the truth of Christianity.

But this revelation raises the following question: how are we to understand the scapegoat theory of Girard outside a Christian context, that is, in non-Christian, postindustrial societies like Japan?

In order to engage this question, we will focus on the Christian interpretation of the atomic bombing on Nagasaki of Takashi Nagai.[2] Nagai was a doctor specializing in radiology in Nagasaki Medical College Hospital. Though he had been an atheist in his younger days, he converted to Catholicism due to the impact of three major factors: the death of his mother; the reading of Blaise Pascal; and the influence of his future wife, Midori. After the conversion and his marriage to Midori, he was told he did not have much time to live because of his work as a radiologist. Hence, he intended to entrust the raising of their children to his wife. However, as a result of the atomic bombing of Nagasaki, it was not Nagai but Midori who died. Three months after the bombing, Nagai offered a funeral address for about 8,500 victims at a Catholic Mass at Urakami Cathedral. This address applied the words "providence of God" to the atomic bombing and considered its victims the sacrifices of nuclear "Holocaust," or scapegoats. Why did Nagai give this event such an interpretation?

In examining this question from Girard's viewpoint, we will surmount the difficult task of understanding both the truth of Christianity and Girard's theories in the secular context of Japan.

We begin this essay with a survey of the history of Christianity in Japan in order to clarify the historical and social background of Nagai's funeral address. Second, we will examine this address and different arguments surrounding it. Third, we will analyze Japanese social structure through the thought of two important figures, Alexandre Kojève and Girard. Finally, we will explore the significance of Nagai's funeral address in relation to Girard's scapegoat mechanism.

A Survey of the History of Christianity in Japan

Before Freedom of Religion

On August 9, 1945, in the final stage of World War II, the second atomic bomb was dropped on Nagasaki. Actually, another city, Kokura, had been nominated as the original target. Nagasaki was the second choice. When the B-29s of the US Air Force reached Kokura, with a population of around 170,000, low-hanging clouds prevented them from making a visual sighting of this city. Thus, they turned toward the secondary target. The sky of Nagasaki, with a population of about 240,000, had also been overcast at this time. However, they narrowly managed the drop because there was a break in the clouds over the northern area of the city. Fanned by a strong wind, the bomb exploded just over Urakami village in the north, about two miles from the center of the city.[3] Urakami was a Christian area. A Catholic church called Urakami Tenshudo was at the center of the explosion and was completely destroyed. About 8,500 of the 12,000 Catholics of Urakami died in an instant.[4]

Why were there so many Catholics in Urakami? Because the hidden Christians (*Kakure-Kirishitan*) had lived there in secret during the long period of Japan's prohibition of Christianity, roughly corresponding to the Edo period (1603–1868).

Thus, the introduction of Christianity to Urakami came centuries earlier. About twenty years after its first contact with Christianity in 1549, Nagasaki was flourishing as a city of Christians and a thriving international port. Catholic missionaries established sixteen churches and many Christian schools. However, Hideyoshi Toyotomi, who unified the political factions of Japan at that time, decreed expulsion orders for the foreign Catholic missionaries in 1587 because he thought that Christianity would have a dangerous influence, leading to social disorder. In this way, about three hundred years of oppression of Christians began. In 1597, twenty-four Christians were arrested in Kyoto and Osaka on the orders of Hideyoshi. Their left ears were cut off and they were forced to march a distance of some 620 miles to Nagasaki, a journey of about thirty days. On the way, two Christians who had taken care of foreign missionaries were also arrested. On February 5 of the same year, a total of twenty-six Christians—six foreign missionaries and twenty Japanese Christians—were crucified on the hill of Nishizaka in Nagasaki.[5] History records these twenty-six Christians as Japan's first martyrs.

After the end of reign of Hideyoshi, Tokugawa Ieyasu took power, marking the beginning of a new era in Japan—the Edo period. This government continued to issue edicts prohibiting Christianity in 1612 and 1613. It also instituted the closed country policy (*sakoku*) in order to completely shut out the influence of European countries.[6]

The Tokugawa government introduced a practice to ferret out hidden Christians called *efumi*, which involved stepping on a bronze plate with images of Mary or a crucifix.[7] Such an act amounted to a sacrilege for many Japanese Christians, and the government effectively exploited this. Those who would not step on a sacred image were exposed as Christians, tortured, and then executed. These executions were open to the public as a warning. Those who could prove themselves non-Christian by stepping on the image then went to the Shinto shrine for *yakubarai*,[8] a ritual to cleanse a person from the impurity called *kegare*. The concept of *kegare* is rooted in both Shintoism and Buddhism. Hiroyuki Okamoto explains *yakubarai*:

> Efumi was held as an annual function. Therefore, the way of thinking would be firmly established that something ominous lingered on the soles of their feet after stepping on Christian images and this impurity must be eliminated. . . . Generally speaking, *kegare* is not merely an idea, but something contagious in Japan. Considering this, *yakubarai* can be interpreted as a kind of repugnance against the contagion of *kegare*.[9]

Thus the prohibition of Christianity in this era implanted the notion of the impurity (*kegare*) of Christians into Japanese society.

After Freedom of Religion

In the early Edo period, *efumi* had been a very effective way to uncover Christians, and due to it many were executed. However, the further one gets into the Edo period, the more *efumi* became merely a formality.[10] The belief spread among the Christian survivors that God would pardon those who stepped on a sacred image so long as they believed in him in their hearts. Furthermore, they believed the prophecy of a Japanese missionary known only as Bastien who, according to legend, was arrested and executed circa 1660. Before the execution, he predicted that if the Christians endured their persecution for seven generations, then "confessors will come in a big black ship. You will be able to confess to him every week. . . . The good days will come. You will be able to walk while singing Christian songs."[11] Christians were able to keep on having hope for a long time because of these prophecies, even in the face of severe persecution. Villages of hidden Christians (*Kakure-Kirishitan*) dotted Japan, among them the village of Urakami.

Toward the end of Edo period, in 1853, Commodore Matthew Perry of the US naval fleet came to Uraga, located at the entrance of Edo bay, to urge Japan to open trade negotiations with the United States. In the following year, he visited again and signed the Kanagawa Treaty, which effectively ended the national isolation policy. While the treaty between the United States and the Edo government was unequal, it became a model for treaties that Japan subsequently concluded with other powerful Western countries. Japan learned later that these unequal treaties would ultimately obstruct the path to independence.[12]

In 1863 Bernard Petitjean, a priest of the Paris Foreign Mission Society, came to Nagasaki to assist in constructing a Catholic church for French residents. This church, called Oura Tenshudo, was completed in 1865. It immediately became popular among Japanese as "the French temple." Petitjean opened the church not only to French Catholics but also to Japanese visitors. On March 17, 1865, some visitors came from Urakami village. One of them whispered to Petitjean, "Our belief is the same as yours." Petitjean reported his experience, and the story quickly spread across European countries, who called it "the discovery of Christians." Petitjean held a mass for the hidden Christians of Urakami who came to the church as visitors and secretly guided them in the catechism.[13]

However, in 1867 certain members of the hidden Christians boldly declared their belief. In response, the Edo government had them arrested and tortured. In the next year, the Meiji government rose up, resulting in the downfall of the Edo government. Although this government aimed at modernization, it continued the policy of prohibiting Christianity, condemning those arrested to exile and torturing them cruelly to force them to abandon their beliefs. But most of them suffered bravely and kept their faith. All told, 562 of Urakami's 3,380 Christians died in exile.[14] This affair is called *Urakami Yonban Kuzure*, which means the fourth oppression of Urakami. This persecution provoked criticism from Western countries. Japan's reputation worsened day by day. The Meiji government realized that the policy of prohibiting Christianity was a barrier in negotiations to revise the unequal treaties. Accordingly, in 1873 the government abolished the prohibition of Christianity after nearly three hundred years of oppression. In the estimation of Mikio Naito, this abolition was "a great change in religious policy and also the event which indicated a turning point from early modern times (the feudal age) to modern times."[15] Although survivors coming back to Urakami saw that the whole village had become dilapidated, they began to reconstruct it with the joy of religious freedom. Then, in 1879 the Urakami Catholic Cathedral was constructed. This church became the epicenter of their beliefs.

After the granting of religious freedom, had Japan really changed as a modern state? Unfortunately, the answer is no. The Meiji government restored imperialism to Japan through what came to be known as state-Shinto, a combined political and religious force founded in Shintoism that essentially forced the people to worship the emperor. Soon after, Japan displayed its imperialistic tendencies in a quest for colonies.

Mokichi Saito (1882–1953), a famous Japanese poet, composed a short poem on this topic: "How miserable is Nishizaka; so tells the ground tainted by the Padres" (Nishizaka wo Baterenfujo no chi to ihite iitsuginikeri kanashikumoaruka).[16] The poem refers to the Hill of Nisizaka, where the twenty-six martyrs were executed in 1597 and which was still considered impure ground in the collective memory. Mokichi's poem reflects the presence of discrimination against Christians still thriving in Japan centuries after these first martyrs met their death.

Even though these twenty-six martyrs were canonized at the Cathedral of Saint Peter of Beauvais in 1862, they were still considered *kegare* by most of Japanese society, although the majority of the population was unaware of its own prejudice. Takashi Nagai refers to this fact in his book

Leaving My Beloved Children Behind (2008). "True to the adage that 'It is dark at the foot of a lighthouse' we in Japan were the only ones unaware of this."[17] In this short sentence, Nagai points out the *méconnaissance* (misrecognition) of Japanese society. We will later look into the function of this *méconnaissance*.

After the Japanese attack on Pearl Harbor in 1941, the Pacific war broke out. "The mimetic crisis," to borrow Girard's term, reached its peak in Japanese society. Within the framework of the imperialist ideology, Christians of Urakami were suspected of being spies for the United States.

And then the fateful day arrived: August 9, 1945. In the Urakami Cathedral, the sacrament of penance and reconciliation had been performed. A moment later, the atomic bomb exploded right above the cathedral. Every Christian there, including the priest, died.

At this time, a rumor spread among inhabitants of one city where the damage was relatively minor that the atomic bomb had been a punishment against Christians. Such a rumor was likely caused by the deep-rooted concept of *kegare* of the Christians in the Japanese society, and this eventually became known as the Urakami Punishment theory.

Hitoshi Motoshima 1922–2014, former mayor of Nagasaki and a descendant of the hidden Christians, testifies about the situation at that time:

> Since *Yonban Kuzure*, the Christians of Urakami have lived in extreme poverty and abuse, being called spies or traitorous foreigner (*hikokumin*), and yet worked for the war as hard as they could. Finally, they were exposed to radiation from the atomic bomb. What's worse, it was said that the atomic bombing had been their punishment for not going to worship at a shrine and for believing in a foreign religion. Their parents, brothers, and children died from exposure to radiation. They were utterly dejected both in mind and in body.[18]

Thus far, we have surveyed the historical context of Japanese society leading up to the atomic bombing. We have seen, first, that the oppression of Christianity implanted the idea of *kegare* and discriminatory feelings against Christians in Japanese society. Second, this discrimination led to the Urakami Punishment theory after the atomic bombing.

Nagai's "Urakami Holocaust Theory"

Nagai's funeral address must be read in the context described in the previous sections. Because of the atomic bombing, Nagai lost his beloved wife, who had guided him into the Christian faith. Her death left him feeling guilty because he had not been able to help her.

The Urakami Punishment theory also spread among the Christians of Urakami. For example, Ichitaro-san, who appears in a novel, *The Bells of Nagasaki* (1949), written by Nagai, asks this question: "Any Japanese could say what I am saying. The atomic bomb was a punishment from heaven. Those who died were evil people; those who survived received a special grace from God. But then . . . does that mean that my wife and children were evil people?"[19] Nagai answered this question thus: "The atomic bomb falling on Nagasaki was a great act of Divine Providence."[20] He reversed the Urakami Punishment theory by means of his new interpretation that the atomic bomb had been an act of providence. In this context, he read a funeral address at a joint mass for the 8,500 victims, which was held at Urakami Catholic Church in November 1945, three months after the bomb.

> An atomic bomb exploded over our district of Urakami in Nagasaki. In an instant, eight thousand Christians were called into the hands of God, while in a few hours the fierce flames reduced to ashes this sacred territory of the East. At midnight of that same night the cathedral suddenly burst into flames and was burned to the ground. And exactly at that time in the Imperial Place, His Majesty the Emperor made known his sacred decision to bring the war to an end.
>
> On August 15, the Imperial Rescript which put an end to the fighting was formally promulgated, and the whole world welcomed a day of peace. This day was also the great feast of the Assumption of the Virgin Mary. It is significant to reflect that Urakami Cathedral was dedicated to her.
>
> . . . The American pilots did not aim at Urakami. It was the providence of God that carried the bomb to that destination.
>
> Is there not a profound relationship between the destruction of Nagasaki and the end of the war? Nagasaki, the only holy place in all Japan— was it not chosen as a victim, *a pure lamb*, to be slaughtered and burned

on the altar of sacrifice to expiate the sins committed by humanity in the Second World War?

. . . Our church of Nagasaki kept the faith during four hundred years of persecution when religion was proscribed and the blood of martyrs flowed freely. During the war this same church never ceased to pray day and night for a lasting peace. Was it not, then, the one unblemished lamb that had to be offered on the altar of God? Thanks to *the sacrifice of this lamb* many millions who would otherwise have fallen victim to the ravages of war have been saved.

How noble, how splendid was that *holocaust of August 9*, when flames soared up from the cathedral, dispelling the darkness of war and bringing the light of peace! In the very depth of our grief we reverently saw here something beautiful, something pure, something sublime. Eight thousand people, together with their priests, burning with pure smoke, entered into eternal life. All without exception were good people whom we deeply mourn [emphasis mine].[21]

In these sentences, he did not interpret the victims as "evil people" or sinners, but as "good people." The fact that he described the victims as "sacrificial lambs" and the atomic bombing as "holocaust" deserves special mention. He then refers to the survivors, himself included:

Compared with them, how miserable is the fate of us who have survived! Japan is conquered. Urakami is totally destroyed. A waste of ash and rubble lies before our eyes. We have no houses, no food, no clothes. Our fields are devastated. Only a remnant has survived. In the midst of the ruins we stand in groups of two or three looking blankly at the sky.

Why did we not die with them on that day, at that time, in this house of God? Why must we alone continue this miserable existence?

It is because we are sinners. Ah! Now indeed we are forced to see the enormity of our sins! It is because I have not made expiation for my sins that I am left behind. Those are left who were so deeply rooted in sin that they were not worthy to be offered to God.

We Japanese, a vanquished people, must now walk along a path that is full of pain and suffering. The reparations imposed by the Potsdam Declaration are a heavy burden. But this painful path along which we walk carrying our burden is it not also the path of hope which gives to us sinners an opportunity to expiate our sins?

"Blessed are those that mourn for they shall be comforted."

We must walk this way of expiation faithfully and sincerely. And as we walk in hunger and thirst, ridiculed, penalized, scourged, pouring with sweat and covered with blood, let us remember how Jesus Christ carried His cross to the hill of Calvary. He will give us courage.[22]

We can derive the following three ideas from Nagai's funeral address. First, the atomic bombing on Urakami was an act of divine providence for an early settlement of the war. Second, the dead of Urakami were sacrificed by a nuclear Holocaust, so they must not be "evil people" but "pure lambs." Third, the survivors were left to atone for their sins. The atomic bombing was God's severe trial for the survivors. They were left with the responsibility of reconstructing the wasteland of Urakami.

Nagai's funeral address has encouraged the Christians of Urakami. However, it has been the subject of much controversy as well.

For example, Shinji Takahashi (1942–) calls Nagai's speech "the Urakami Holocaust theory."[23] From a political viewpoint, he critiques Nagai for exempting both Japan and the United States from responsibility for the war. Regarding US responsibility, Takahashi claims that "the Urakami Holocaust theory" justifies the atomic bombing of Nagasaki and opened a way for future approval of nuclear weaponry.[24]

Tetsuya Takahashi (1956–) criticizes Nagai for almost the same reason as Shinji Takahashi. In his book, *Kokka to Gisei* (State and Sacrifice) (2005), he reveals the "logic of sacrifice," a process by which the nation attempted to sidestep responsibility for the war by replacing the collective memory of guilt with distracting consecrations of the dead.[25] In this context, Tetsuya Takahashi insists that Nagai had taken part in this process by developing "the logic of sacrifice." According to Takahashi, Nagai's funeral address had "the effect of justifying the indiscriminate strategic bombing,"[26] by considering the atomic bombing an act of providence. Second, Takahashi remarks that Nagai avoided establishing Japan's responsibility, and particularly Emperor Showa's responsibility, for either the outbreak of the war or its propagation by designating the emperor's decision to end the war as "sacred." Actually, in Takahashi's account, this decision was "sacred [but] too late," because the emperor had rejected the proposition of then–prime minister Konoe that advocated an early realization of peace in February 1945. Takahashi concludes that "'the logic of sacrifice' is a process in which the death and cruelties were gradually deleted" from Nagai's funeral address.[27]

On the other hand, Chizuko Kataoka, president in 2016 of Nagasaki Junshin Catholic University, defends Nagai against these criticisms from a Christian perspective.[28] She emphasizes a fundamental thought of Catholicism: "By regarding our pains in the same light as this pain (the Passion), we can participate in Christ's work of salvation."[29] According to Kataoka, Nagai's funeral address, based on this understanding of faith, can be interpreted as inspiration for "a spiritual reconstruction of Catholics in the wasteland of Urakami." Through what she writes, we can understand that Nagai had suggested to the survivors of Urakami how they could live without anger and without a sense of vanity, and instead live while sharing the suffering of Christ. In other words, Nagai encouraged them to see that "the imitation of Christ" means a nonviolent way of life, praying for peace, and loving each other.

According to Hiroyuki Okamoto, we can find another meaning in Nagai's funeral address regarding the idea of *kegare*. Okamoto responds to a challenge issued by the *Nagasaki Shinbun* (Nagasaki Newspapers) on August 5, 2012 (the day before the anniversary of the bombing of Hiroshima), to reflect on Nagai's thoughts and engage in dialogue about them. Okamoto emphasizes that there had been a deep-rooted discrimination against the Catholics of Urakami, and he takes notice of Nagai's sense of determination. Nagai had become an unclean being by society's standards when he converted to Catholicism.[30] He was socially despised and humiliated. Nevertheless, he had a strong "determination for both showing the virtue of one who willingly allowed himself to be treated so unjustly and for trying to live with dignity" as with the people of Urakami.[31] According to Okamoto, Nagai had made his funeral address out of such a determination: "Considering the deaths from the atomic bombing as an irreplaceable foundation for bringing in a new age without the convention of *kegare*, Nagai interpreted this tragedy as providential. Therefore, he expressed in his funeral address the idea that the deaths from the atomic bombing had been "pure" and "sublime" (not *kegare*) and beautified it in pictures and *tankas* (Japanese short poetry structured in thirty-one syllables).[32] Thus, Okamoto finds that Nagai had tried to abolish the old convention of *kegare* by advocating the Urakami Holocaust theory.

As Tetsuya Takahashi points out, there may have been certain aspects of Nagai's discourse that were used politically to distract from the responsibility of the war. But if we analyze Nagai's address from a political viewpoint alone, we will not be able to understand what he intended. Nagai's address is not based on Girard's "rivalistic desire," but on nonviolence and the goal of freeing survivors from resentment and enmity. Before establishing responsibility for the war at the national level, Nagai attempted to address Catholic victims of the tragedy and to respond to them as individuals.

Thus far, we have found two positive aspects of Nagai's address. First, as Kataoka emphasizes, Nagai encouraged the survivors to live in imitation of Christ after the catastrophe. Second, as Okamoto argues, Nagai tried to abolish the deep-rooted idea of *kegare* for the democratic restoration of Japan. In addition to these points, we will suggest a third level of significance to Nagai's funeral address from the viewpoint of Girard, to be discussed in the last section.

But first, in the following section, in order to establish a context for our interpretation of Nagai, we will analyze the structure of Japanese society by referring to Alexandre Kojève and René Girard.

The Function of Japanese "Snobbery" as *Méconnaissance* (Misrecognition) in Japan

Alexandre Kojève (1902–1968) writes the following about Japanese society from his own point of view in a famous explanatory note 1 of his book, the revised edition of *Introduction à la lecture de Hegel* (1968) (*Introduction to the Reading of Hegel* [1969]).

> There I was able to observe a society that is one of a kind, because it alone has for almost three centuries experienced life at the "end of History"—that is, in the absence of all civil or external War (following the liquidation

of feudalism by Hideyoshi who was born into a lower-class family, and the artificial isolation of the country conceived and realized by his noble successor Ieyasu).

. . . No doubt, there were no longer in Japan any Religion, Morals, or Politics in the "European" or "historical" sense of these words. But *Snobbery* in its pure form created disciplines negating the "natural" or "animal" given which in effectiveness far surpassed those that arose, in Japan or elsewhere, from "historical" Action—that is, from walking and revolutionary Fights or from forced Work.[33]

Needless to say, "Religion, Morals, or Politics in the 'European' or 'historical' sense of these words" means Christianity. According to Kojève, it is "snobbery" that works as the basis of morality in Japanese society in lieu of Christian morals. He observes that all Japanese without exception are currently in a position to live according to totally formalized values—that is, values completely empty of all "human" content in the "historical" sense.[34]

Despite the shortness of his stay, it would appear Kojève has recognized a certain penetrating truth about Japanese society. Kojève observed that the behavior and the discourse of Japanese people were perfectly controlled by a certain ceremonial form without meaning. Those who followed the Japanese snobbery would never ask why they behave in this way, why they speak in this way, and whether they could ever do otherwise. Those who never asked these questions were completely robbed of any opportunity to change their ways. In the society where such peoples live, nothing ever happens. It appears to be very peaceful and calm in appearance. Kojève proposes that Japanese "snobbery" was one of the ways of posthistorical life meant to avoid the phenomenon he calls "animalization," in which society is violent, primitive, and uncontrolled.

It may be true that Japanese snobbery is one way to avoid chaos, considering that the Edo period persisted for almost three hundred years. But the "end of History" to which Kojève refers, the so-called Peace of Edo, corresponds to a period of prohibition against Christianity, as we have already seen. We have to remember that the process of Efumi by which the Edo government identified and executed Christians had become a matter of ceremony. Thus we can see that Japanese snobbery as a way of posthistorical life is not so much a way of avoiding violence as one of concealing it. In concealing violence, Japanese snobbery has the same function as *méconnaissance*, which Girard employs in his scapegoat theory.

To use Girard's vocabulary, we can consider the hierarchical society of the Edo period as "a functional society according to external mediation."[35] Girard explains "external mediation" thus: "We shall speak of external mediation when the distance is sufficient to eliminate any contact between the two spheres of possibilities of which the mediator and the subject occupy the respective centers."[36] According to Girard, mimetic desire means that the subject desires the object, which his model (mediator) desires. But when his model lives in another world, the subject can never possess the object desired by his model. Therefore, there is never any dispute between the two. This is "external mediation."

On the other hand, there is also "internal mediation." When the distance between the subject and his model is psychologically and physically small, Girard calls this relation "internal mediation." In this case, there is a possibility for the subject to take the object by force, and so "rivalry will eventually erupt."[37] When such a rivalry becomes widespread among members of the whole society, this society faces a mimetic crisis, an escalating of violence. It is the "scapegoat solution" that ultimately ends this crisis. The whole sequence, starting from the mimetic desire and ending with the scapegoat, is "the mimetic mechanism" described by Girard.[38]

Girard points out that "a functional society according to external mediation" is "one whose institutions work without being constantly disrupted by violence."[39] A society like this maintains "external mediation" by dividing the members of society into classes. That is, it is a hierarchal society that systematically separates the desiring subject from his model. However, Girard does not propose this kind of society as a posthistorical model. To give an example, he presents traditional Indian society "defined through the concept of *dharma*, which basically means the strict separation of castes, and as a result a society in which everybody does what they are ordained to do."[40] Japanese snobbery has performed functions similar to those performed by *dharma* in Indian society, even if they appear completely different on the surface. Japanese snobbery was a kind of form without meaning and persisted even after the social hierarchy appeared to have been abolished. In this way, external mediation was allowed to persist even in the absence of a strict social hierarchy. Thus, both societies *appear* to be without victims.

We have already seen that the society of Edo used Christians as one outlet for violence for the sake of social cohesion. Moreover, the ritualization of Efumi led to the concept of *kegare* and nationwide discrimination against Christians even in the period of modernization. The violence was concealed. Either nobody was aware that anybody had been victimized, or everybody lived under the delusion that the victims were absolutely guilty. After all, a society of this sort—"a functional society according to external mediation"—is never a posthistorical social model, but rather a sort of mythic society based on the scapegoat.

Girard explains the function of *méconnaissance* in the scapegoat mechanism as follows: "It [*méconnaissance*] allows one to have the illusion that one is justly accusing someone who is *really* guilty and, therefore, *deserves* to be punished. In order to have a scapegoat, one must fail to perceive the truth, and therefore one cannot represent the victim as a scapegoat, but rather as a righteous victim, which is what mythology does. . . . To scapegoat someone is to be unaware of what you are doing."[41] Girard emphasizes the paradox that if every member of society believes in the guilt of the object of persecution, they never recognize this object as a scapegoat, a pure lamb. Hence, as long as Japanese snobbery performs the same function for concealing violence, it can be interpreted as *méconnaissance* in the scapegoat mechanism.

For a long time, traditional Japanese society members never saw that they were using Christians as scapegoats. Their *méconnaissance* allowed them to keep the mythic order. Because of this social structure, those who spread the rumor that the atomic bombing on Urakami was a punishment against Christians must have been possessed by the delusion that the Catholics victims really were guilty.

The Significance of Nagai's Funeral Address from Girard's Perspective

Through the above considerations, we would suggest that Nagai reveals the *méconnaissance* of Japanese society by calling the victims of atomic bombs "pure lambs" and appealing to their innocence in public. The innocence of the scapegoat is revealed in the New Testament Book of Revelation. Girard elucidates this as follows: "Revelation is the reproduction of the victimary mechanism by showing the truth, knowing that the victim is innocent and that everything is based on mimeticism."[42] Thus, Girard asserts that "Christianity is precisely a way of saying, with maximum emphasis, that the victim is innocent."[43]

By defending the innocence of the Urakami victims, Nagai filled the role of the Paraclete. According to Girard, the "Paraclete is called on behalf of the prisoner, the victim, to speak in his place and in his name, to act in his defense."[44] In other words, the Paraclete is "the universal advocate, the chief defender of all innocent victims, *the destroyer of every representation of persecution.*"[45] In the precise meaning of the word, the Paraclete is Jesus Christ. This does not mean that Nagai had somehow alleged the second coming of Christ, but rather that he had asserted the victims' innocence by "putting them in Christ's place."[46] And thus Nagai performs the function of the Spirit working in the world. The Spirit is, according to Girard's definition, "another Paraclete,"[47] which reveals "what Jesus has already revealed, the mechanism of the scapegoat, the genesis of all mythology."[48]

At the opposite extreme, there is "Satan," who "is essentially the *accuser*, the one who deceives men by making them believe that innocent victims are guilty."[49] "Satan" is "no-being," who is unsubstantial. But he is a certain metaphor given to "the system of the bad mimesis."[50] Satan compels us to imitate him. But in enticing us to desire him, Satan himself becomes our rival, because he is also a desiring subject.[51] We can understand that, as far as he is unsubstantial, he is like a reflection in a mirror. Having fallen into a trap, the community can't help but face a crisis of mimetic violence. According to Girard, he is an obstacle, a "scandal."[52] Satan is "a powerful trope for describing the unanimity of the crowd when it accuses the victim of being guilty."[53] Therefore, in the circumstances just after the atomic bombing, those who propagated the Urakami Punishment theory can be likened to Satan.

Against Satan, there are martyrs. Following the legal context, this word means "witnesses." In an ethical context, it means "those who after his [Christ's] example have proved the strength and genuineness of their faith in Christ by undergoing a violent death."[54]

In Japanese society, many witnesses, that is, martyrs, appeared, but no one had ever come to their defense. It may have been Nagai who first played the role of the Paraclete, witnessing to their innocence and the truth of Christianity in a different way than martyrdom. He was close to the victims of Urakami who were being accused by Satan.

According to Girard, "Jesus saves all human beings because of his revelation of the scapegoat mechanism."[55] But how can we avoid a scandal leading to a crisis of mimetic violence without either reproducing sacrifices or artificially constructing "a functional society according to external mediation"? "Mimetic violence" is brought about when just one person succumbs to the temptation of Satan. Girard explains this: "Scandals between individuals are little streams that flow into the great rivers of collective violence. . . . The condensation of all the separated scandals into a single scandal is the paroxysm of a process that begins with mimetic desire and its rivalries. These rivalries, as they multiply, create a mimetic crisis, the war of *all against all*."[56] Nagai was also aware about the potential for a violent chain reaction. He argued the following in *We of Nagasaki* (1952).

> Don't say that even if only one thought of causing a war, he would not cause the war under conditions where a great number of people had a consensus to keep peace. Human beings love peace. However, they have Cain's bloodline. When this blood goes mad, they participate in a war while loving peace. It is just like the Uranium-235 fission process. If at least one of the nuclei broke up, a chain reaction is sustained. Finally, it makes a nuclear explosion. The war breaks out also; with the result that a murderous design conceived in one person's mind sets off a chain reaction in the others.
>
> I pray our voice of the nuclear wasteland carries to every nook and corner of the world and every last human being takes an oath that they will never cause a war.[57]

Girard suggests that the only way to realize Nagai's prayer and avoid a scandal is "the imitation of Christ": "In order to free oneself from sacrifice, someone has to set the example, and renounce all mimetic retaliations: 'turn the other cheek,' as Jesus says."[58]

Why did Nagai say to the survivors that the atomic bombing was an act of God's providence? Nagai was trying to persuade the survivors to abandon all plans of mimetic retaliations. Choosing the way of prayer, not of anger or of hatred, he encouraged them to imitate Christ, because neither anger nor hatred produce anything. In this way, he prayed that post–World War II Japanese society would be reborn as a society independent of sacrificial protection. He wrote the following sentence in the last chapter of *The Bells of Nagasaki*: "Grant that Nagasaki may be the last atomic wilderness in the history of the world."[59]

Considering the circumstances described above, we can derive the following significance of Nagai's funeral address from Girard's perspective. First, Nagai revealed the *méconnaissance* in traditional Japanese society by acting as the Paraclete and witnessing to the innocence of victims, thus revealing the truth of Christianity that the scapegoat is innocent. Second, by encouraging the imitation of Christ based on neighborly love, he established the foundation for the reconstruction of Japanese society without sacrifices. Third, by appealing to the innocence of victims in Japan, he has opened the possibility of understanding Girard's theory in a non-Christian context.

However, in spite of Nagai's prayer, the two atomic bombs dropped on Japan ironically inaugurated what turned out to be the atomic age. Nuclear technologies might begin to develop with the intent for "world peace," but we should not forget that "pride goes before destruction, and a haughty spirit before a fall" (Proverbs 16:18). Once nuclear power is out of control, it is difficult to avoid risks of falling into ruin. Unfortunately, the Fukushima nuclear accident happened in 2011.

How can we really avoid mimetic violence? Is a society without sacrifices possible in the future? Now, seventy years after Nagai's prayer, we are asking these questions in a new nuclear wasteland.

Notes

1. René Girard, with Pierpaolo Antonello and João Cezar de Castro Rocha, *Evolution and Conversion: Dialogues on the Origins of Culture* (New York: Continuum International, 2007), 56.

2. Nagai lived from 1908 to 1951.

3. Nagasaki City, ed., *Nagasaki wa Kataritsugu: Nagasaki Genbaku sensaishi* (Nagasaki Hands Down: Records of the Nagasaki Atomic Bombing and Wartime Damage) (Tokyo: Iwanami Shoten, 1991), 91.

4. See Anan Sigeyuki, "Nagasaki no Hisabetsuburaku" (The Discriminated Community of Nagasaki), in *Nagasaki kara Heiwagaku suru!* (Doing Peace Studies from Nagasaki), ed. Shinji Takahasi and Funakoe Kōichi, pt. 4 (Kyoto: Hōritsu Bunkasha, 2009), 165.

5. See Eijiro Nagatomi, *Nihon Nijuroku Seijin Junkyōki* (A History of the 26 Martyrs of Japan) (Tokyo: St Paul Publications, 1997).

6. Fumihiko Gomi, Toshihiko Takano, and Yasushi Toriumi eds., *Shōsetsu Nishonshi enkyū* (Detailed Study of Japanese History) (Tokyo: Yamakawa Shuppansha, 2006), 234–56.

7. See Yakichi Kataoka, *Fumie* (a plate with a crucifix) (Tokyo: Nihon Hōso Shuppan Kyōkai, 1961).

8. Ibid., 107–8.

9. Hiroyuki Okamoto, "Nagai Takashi wa Naze Genbakushi ga Kami no Setsuri dato Kyōchōshitanoka? *Kegare* kara kangaeru kokoromi" (Why Did Dr. Nagai Takashi Bless the Catholic Victims of Nagasaki? Dying Beautifully on the Atomic Field), *Kyōiku kagaku seminarī* (Education Science Seminary) 42 (2011): 5 (my translation).

10. See Rumiko Kataoka, "Gōmon to Junkyō no chi" (The Torture and the Blood of the Martyrs), in *Zusetsu Nagasaki no Rekishi* (An Illustrated History of Nagasaki), ed. Mikio Yotoyama (Tokyo: Kawade Shobō Shinsha, 1996), 128.

11. Yakichi Kataoka, *Nihon Kirishitan Junkyōshi* (A History of Japanese Christians' Martydom), vol. 1 of *Kataoka Yakichi Zenshū* (Yakichi Kataoka's Complete Works (Tokyo: Tomo Shobō, 2010), 389 (my translation).

12. See Gomi, Takano, and Toriumi eds., *Shōsetsu Nihonshi Kenkyū*, 309.

13. See Kataoka, *Nihon Kirishitan Junkyōshi*}, 393–99.

14. Ibid., 399–482; Yakichi Kataoka, *Urakami Yonban Kuzure* (The Fourth Oppression of Urakami) (Tokyo: Chikuma Shobo, 1991).

15. Mikio Naito, "Meijiseifu no Shukyōseisaku to Kirishitan Shūraku" (The Changes of the Kirishitan Settlement Inside around the Removal of the Official Notice Board of the Ban on Christianity), *Taishō Daigakudaigakuin Kenkyū Ronshū* (Journal of the Graduate School of Taisho University) 36 (2012): 109 (my translation).

16. Mokichi Saito, *Tsuyujimo* (Tokyo: Iwanami Shoten, 1946), 37 (my translation).

17. Takashi Nagai, *Leaving My Beloved Children Behind* (1948), trans. Maurice Tatsuoka and Tsuneyoshi Takai (Tokyo: St Paul's Publications, 2008), 135.

18. Hitoshi Motoshima, "Urakami Kirishitan no Junan: Kinkyōrei, Yonbankuzure, Genbaku" (Passion of Urakami Christians: Edicts Prohibiting Christianity, the Fourth Oppression, the Atomic Bomb), *Seibo no Kishi Catholic Monthly* (Catholic Monthly of the Militia of the Immaculata) 753 (October 2000): 7 (my translation).

19. Takashi Nagai, *The Bells of Nagasaki* (1949), trans. William Johnston (Tokyo : Kodansha International, 1984), 106.

20. Ibid.

21. Ibid., 107–8.

22. Ibid., 108–9.

23. Shinji Takahashi, *Nagasaki ni atte tetsugakusuru: Kakujidai no Shi to Sei* (Philosophizing at Nagasaki: Death and Life in the Atomic Age) (Tokyo: Hokuju, 1994), 193.

24. Ibid.

25. Tetsuya Takahashi, *Kokka to Gisei* (The State and the Sacrifice) (Tokyo: Nihon Hōso Shuppan Kyōkai, 2005), 52–76.

26. Ibid., 69.

27. Ibid., 75–76.

28. For a more developed analysis of the religious interpretations of the atomic bombing, especially for the comparative viewpoints of Christian and Buddhist discourse, see Yuki Miyamoto "Rebirth in the Pure Land or God's Sacrificial Lambs? Religious Interpretations of the Atomic Bombings in Hiroshima and Nagasaki," *Japanese Journal of Religious Studies* 32 no.1 (2005): 131–59. In this article, the author analyzes Nagai's funeral address as a Christian discourse. She also published *Beyond the Mushroom Cloud: Commemoration, Religion, and Responsibility after Hiroshima* (New York: Fordham University Press, 2011).

29. Chizuko Kataoka, "Nagai Takashi to Nagasaki no Kane" (Nagai Takashi and the *Bells of Nagasaki*), in *Hibakuchi Nagasaki no Saiken* (*Reconstruction of the Bombed Areas of Nagasaki*), ed. Chizuko Kataoka and Rumiko Kataoka (Nagasaki: Nagasaki Junshin Daigaku Hakubutsukan, 1996), 74 (my translation).

30. Okamoto, "Nagai Takashi," 8.

31. Ibid. (my translation).

32. Ibid. (my translation).

33. Alexandre Kojève, *Introduction à la lecture de Hegel: Leçons sur la Phénoménologie de l'Esprit professées de 1933 à 1939 à l'École des Hautes Étude*, ed. Raymond Queneau (1947; rev. ed, Paris: Gallimard, 1968; pbk. 1980), 437 (*Introduction to the Reading of Hegel: Lectures on the Phenomenology of Spirit*, trans. James H. Nichols Jr., ed. Allan Bloom [1947; rev. ed., New York: Cornell University Press, 1969], 161, translation partly modified by author).

34. *Introduction to the Reading of Hegel*, 164.
35. Girard, *Evolution and Conversion*, 240.
36. René Girard, *Deceit, Desire, and the Novel*, trans. Yvonne Freccero (1961; 3rd ed., Baltimore: Johns Hopkins University Press, 1984), 9.
37. Girard, *Evolution and Conversion*, 57.
38. Ibid., 56.
39. Ibid., 240.
40. Ibid.
41. Ibid., 85.
42. Ibid., 205.
43. Ibid., 84–85.
44. René Girard, *The Scapegoat*, trans. Yvonne Freccero (Baltimore: Johns Hopkins University Press, 1986), 205.
45. Ibid.
46. Ibid., 202.
47. Ibid., 206.
48. Ibid., 207.
49. Ibid.
50. Girard, *Evolution and Conversion*, 225.
51. René Girard, *I See Satan Fall Like Lightning*, trans James G. Williams (New York: Orbis Books, 2001), 32–33.
52. Ibid., chapter 2, "The Cycle of Mimetic Violence."
53. Girard, *Evolution and Conversion*, 225.
54. Ibid., 226.
55. Ibid., 206.
56. Girard, *I See Satan Fall Like Lightning*, 24.
57. Takashi Nagai, "Ishi mo Sakebu" (Stone Also Cries"), in *Watashitachi wa Nagasaki ni Ita* (We of Nagasaki), ed. Takashi Nagai (1952; repr., Tokyo: St Paul Press, 1997), 253–54 (my translation).
58. Girard, *Evolution and Conversion*, 203.
59. Nagai, *Bells of Nagasaki*, 118.

PART 2

MIMETIC THEORY AND JAPANESE CULTURE

CHAPTER 5

GIRARDIAN STRUCTURE AND DIONYSIAN COMPONENTS

SHOICHIRO IWAKIRI

> It was all like a strange dream.
> —*The Tale of Genji*

About one thousand years ago in the early eleventh century, when the culture of aristocracy blossomed in Japan, a woman named Murasaki Shikibu authored *The Tale of Genji*, a story that is by no means inferior to modern Western novels. If only René Girard had had an opportunity to become familiar with Japanese classics, this story would have been an ideal model to use in his *Deceit, Desire, and the Novel* (1961) to support his theory concerning the mimetism of desire and violence.

At the beginning of this story there lies a void, a void that determines the series of love affairs in which the main character will engage. This void is created by none other than a kind of victimizing mob violence of the court. The victim, being of modest background, triggers a mass jealousy when she is favored almost exclusively by the emperor, surpassing the other ladies-in-waiting. Naturally, she is harassed and bullied. Grudges build up; she falls ill and eventually dies.

This lady, Kiritsubo, had not sinned in any way. Yet she had indeed brought unease and abnormality to the courtly order of love by monopolizing the emperor's favor.

The harassment against Kiritsubo, who is the mother of Hikaru, the hero of *The Tale of Genji*, cannot be looked upon as some irrelevant violence executed to restore the order of court that is somehow otherwise endangered. Thus, some may not consider Kiritsubo a scapegoat in the Girardian sense of the word. She herself has caused turmoil, so she is the one who has to be expelled. It is clear, however, that here we see a stereotype of collective violence, because Kiritsubo bore the "sign" of the victim by being favored, which created a situation in which other ladies of court became undifferentiated from one another.

Hikaru was too young to remember his mother's situation when she died. Years later, he learns from an emperor's servant, Naishinosuke, that a woman named Fujitsubo looks a lot like his mother. He instantly falls in love with her and begins an affair. On a different occasion, he is attracted by a young girl, Murasaki, who turns out to be related to Fujitsubo and hence resembles her. He raises the girl to his liking and then betroths himself to her. This is an example of the influence of mimetic desire originating in a model.

In the famous episode in *The Tale of Genji* known as "Appraisal of Women on a Rainy Night," we can also see mediation operative in Hikaru's interest in Yugao, another woman whom Hiraku loves.[1] Hikaru thinks it would be wonderful to find the most beautiful woman, the kind Samanokami, a colleague of Hiraku, would fancy, in a place that would be despised by his rival, Tono Chujo, as the dwelling of lowly woman. And when he fell in love with Yugao, she was the woman in whom was realized the idealized image of Samanokami, and this allowed Hikaru to best Tono Chujo because Hikaru found a charming woman where Tono Chujo had declared it impossible to find that kind of lady.

Not only does this kind of desire, conveyed by internal mediation, occur frequently in this drama of the court. It can also be seen with other characters besides Hikaru.

As a whole, we can trace the moments of "conversion" from the episodes of love and politics surrounding Hikaru, through the theme of detaching oneself from the empty world as seen in "Ukifune," the last chapter of the *Genji*. Girard has marked out the very same moments in such novels as *Don Quixote*.

Hikaru, who does, in this tale, live a life of the kind of mediated desire that fits well with the theories of Girard, remains a strange character when viewed from the standpoint of Girard's theory of collective violence. A physiognomist from Korea foretold that his assuming the position of emperor would cause a nationwide disaster; but the physiognomist also said that he is destined not to serve the emperor as his subject. So Hikaru could be the source of a social crisis, in which case he conforms to the stereotype of those who become the victim of collective violence. In the light of Girardian theory, he is "too beautiful," and thus he becomes liable to be persecuted. However, the plot is cunningly constructed so that the victimary mechanism will not touch Hikaru. He is granted the last name Minamoto, and by the end of his story, in the chapter "Fujino Uraba," he prospers as he holds the position of *jun daijo tenno*, which is equal to that of a retired emperor.

We can now see why *The Tale of Genji* would have appeared attractive to Girard. It seems equally plausible that this tale, with its theme of the protagonist's desire toward women who look like his mother, is compatible with an interpretation based on the Freudian Oedipus complex (a theory against which Girard has argued). Moreover, Hikaru is a kind of personified Dionysus, a deity that Girard despises. Much like Semele, the mother of Dionysus who died because of a vicious plot designed by Hera, the jealous wife of Zeus, Kiritsubo also dies after she was harassed by the jealous women of the court. Of course, Hikaru is only a mortal, and he is even jilted from time to time. But basically he is very popular among women, thus resembling Dionysus, who often caused a frenzy among them. Also, they both have androgynous qualities.[2]

Semele, who gives birth to Dionysus, is a daughter of Cadmus, king of Thebes. As is well-known, this city provides the stage for the tragedy of Oedipus. We can see that this Dionysus-Oedipus quality exists in *The Tale of Genji*, with the difference that here the mechanism of tragedy is thwarted.

With these reflections as a kind of introduction, we can see that novels are determined in a way that is multilayered, both in their structure and their dialectics. It is impossible for a single theory to totally account for a novel. In this article, I would like to discuss the "space" of novels as a Girardian structure in relation to Oedipus. This structure also includes a Dionysian component, although this quality is deemed satanic by Girard. Also, although it may seem like a bit of a stretch, I want to tie this in with current affairs of Japan, where we are faced with nuclear disaster.

Richard Seaford, a classics scholar, points out that the tyrant, who appears in the title of Sophocles' *Oedipus tyrannus*, sees the most value in the power of money. This idea sheds new light on Oedipus, a light that is both different from and more symbolic than that shed by either Freud or Girard. According to Seaford, a tyrant is "isolated from the gods and even from his own kin, obsessed with money," and is "a transgressor against the ancient moral codes of reciprocity, the sacred, and kinship."[3] Money enhances individual autonomy and pulls its possessor out of the old moral codes. For the sake of money, the king would gladly violate these codes at any moment. The protagonist of Sophocles' *Oedipus tyrannus* is such a king, a tyrant.

With this idea in mind, let us take a closer look at King Oedipus and his obsession with money and power. Thebes, Oedipus's realm, is devastated. The situation of the city is so similar to Japan today that it is almost frightening. The priest says the following:

> The city, as you can see for yourself,
> Is like a ship caught in a storm at sea, unable
> To keep afloat and escape the deadly waves.
> She's wasting away—in the husks her soil produces,
> Wasting away in the pasturing herds, and in the children
> Stillborn to our women. The fiery god has struck
> And is driving our city—a plague hated by all.
> He is emptying the house of Cadmus; and with our groans
> And lamentations, black Hades is growing rich.[4]

The country is devastated because of "the pollution we've been nursing in this land" and thus must be cleansed. Creon tells the king that according to the direction of Phoebus Apollo, "someone must be exiled, or a death must pay for a death." The death, or the blood once spilt, was that of his predecessor, Laius, whom Oedipus unknowingly killed. Laius went off to a journey, saying he would "consult the oracle," and never returned.

To the explanation of Creon that "a group of robbers" have "killed him," Oedipus answers this: "What could have made a robber so daring—unless he was hired to do the job by someone here?"

So he believes that the one who slew Laius was seeking money. Even after he is told by Tiresias, the blind prophet, that it was in fact Oedipus himself that killed the former king and went on to indulge in an abominable relationship with his mother, he is infuriated, believing that all of these are false charges maneuvered by Creon. As Oedipus says, "Who invented all this? Was it Creon?"

> Wealth, royal power, and skill surpassing skill—
> In life with all its heavy load of envy,
> What resentment you have stored up in you, if
> For the sake of this power, which the city placed
> In my hands as a gift—I did not ask for it—
> For this, Creon—who was from the first my trusted friend—
> Steals up on me and wants to overthrow me.
> He's got this swindling sorcerer in his pay,
> A money-grubbing trickster, with a good eye
> For gain, but blind when it comes to prophecy.

It seems that Oedipus's thinking runs along the lines of the Girardian mechanism of desire. His position on the throne, which he gained without wanting it, has now, according to Oedipus, become Creon's object of desire, or to put it in Girardian terms, the object of mimetic desire.

That is to say, the riches and the power for which Oedipus never wished have become the source of his rivalry and struggle with Creon once Oedipus possesses them. At this point, he judges others using two standards: jealousy and profit. In other words, he guesses that his enemies are "motivated by money."[5]

Seaford's interpretation highlights the fact that Oedipus had gained his wealth and sovereignty through "self-sufficient intelligence alone,"[6] not by any god's help. Oedipus claims that "[Sphinx's] riddle was not for any passer-by to solve; it requires a seer." When Tiresias failed to solve the riddle, Oedipus "came along, I, ignorant Oedipus, and I stopped her. I used my wits; I didn't rely on birds."

Seaford also points out that the relationship between Oedipus and his mother is a form of endogamy, and this signifies, in Athens and elsewhere, the accumulation of wealth within the family. And in the context of tragedy, endogamy is often linked with blindness, darkness, and male imprisonment (sometimes underground) of the female. This is also how precious metals and money are treated. They are usually hidden underground. Both money and women have a symbolic trading value by which they are transmitted from one person to another. Moreover, money "reproduces" interest, as in sexual reproduction.[7]

In this view, Oedipus puts human intelligence above divine powers. As well, he places domination by the symbolic power of money at the center of human relationships.

Seaford believes that the contemporary audience of this play, the people of Athens in fifth century BCE, protected both the solitude of their independent souls and the social order against the disruptiveness of monetization through this play in which Oedipus is punished.

As is well known, Oedipus, the one who values money most highly and is a tyrant, gouges out his eyes as if to unite himself with the blind Tiresias whom he once mocked, after everything becomes clear. He is guilty of being a tyrant.

This same character, however, holds a quite different and even opposite position in the interpretation by Girard. In this interpretation he is a victim, nothing but a sacrificial goat, who is deemed a "stranger" and a "cripple." To borrow from Koichi Namiki's summary, he has fallen from the object of "devotion" to that of "hatred" and becomes the target of violence that is "sanctified as the general will of the social group." Oedipus, unlike Job in the Old Testament, hears the song of the "manhunt, aimed for the man who is to be sacrificed" and "finally succumbs to the judgment of the people, to which he spontaneously confesses his own filth."[8]

Girard points out that *Oedipus tyrannus* contains all the stereotypes of persecution: the obliteration of difference, crime, the mark or sign of the victim, and violence. Indeed, according to Tiresias, the prophet,

Oedipus is the one who is obliterating the difference because as "Father and brother at once to his own children he'll be revealed; and also son and husband to the woman who bore him; sowing the same furrow as his father, and his father's murderer." And although he was born in Thebes, he is said to have come from "a foreign land" and is a man with a "swollen foot."

Now, let us take a look at the Thebes in *Oedipus tyrannus*.

> She's wasting away—in the husks her soil produces,
> Wasting away in the pasturing herds, and in the children
> Stillborn to our women. The fiery god has struck
> And is driving our city—a plague hated by all.
> He is emptying the house of Cadmus; and with our groans
> And lamentations, black Hades is growing rich.

Such a situation would be, in Girardian terms, "the crisis of society or culture where obliteration of difference is generalized,"[9] but is it correct to simply categorize it as such? Of course, such conceptualization is not impossible. But the situation is not merely a condition for persecution; it is also a reality in which human beings live.

At this point, I would like to make a detour and focus for a moment on Japan today. We may identify the situation in Thebes with that of the devastation caused by the tsunami of the Great Eastern Japan Earthquake and its attendant nuclear accident. And in doing so, the questions that derive from the myth must change their forms. Thus, in the situation of Japan, we are led to ask, whom should we treat as King Oedipus?

If we look at this in Girardian way, one innocent person would be chosen as the sacrificial victim. This person would be forced to be the culprit of the disaster. A politician, perhaps? Or could it be the technicians who certified nuclear power plants to be safe? (In today's Japan, a slip of the tongue, a love affair, or even a good position in the society—anything that could be the target of envy and gossip or be seen as scandalous can be used as a "sign to choose the victim" when social tensions must be dissolved.)[10] On the other hand, looked at from Seaford's point of view, the culprit will be someone who was proud of his or her "self-sufficient intelligence."

Both of these views are plausible in their own way, but I believe that of Seaford is more helpful if we are to understand the reality Japan is facing. This is because the state of our knowledge is questioned today, at the very moment when we are confronted with unforeseen natural and nuclear disasters.

In particular, when we focus on the nuclear power plant, we see that there is something in it similar to monetary currency. The best example would be a plutonium-thermal project. Plutonium, on the one hand, is something hidden underground as nuclear waste, but on the other hand, it is something that is to be "bred" after chemical reprocessing. In both cases, the process will go on for thousands of years, and to us humans, this implies everlasting "power."

However, it is now more obvious than ever that plutonium is only valuable when used to construct nuclear weapons. Unlike the symbolic value of the currency, plutonium threatens us with its warped materiality. It was the endless desire for convenience and wealth that fueled the research. In short, we are responsible. It is ourselves, or our minds, or the intelligence of modern civilization that claims to be able to solve all the enigmas (of the universe, life, materialism, and so on) around it, and thus deserves to be called King Oedipus.

Thebes, where the play is set, was erected by Cadmus. Dionysus was born as the offspring of Semele, Cadmus's daughter, and Zeus. The values of Oedipus go against those of Dionysus. To make this clearer, let us put King Midas in the place of Oedipus, as a person who, carelessly enough, placed money/gold above all things. By doing so, we can see two worlds that are mutually exclusive to one another.

The first world is the moneyless world of Dionysus, which is also related to the world of Silenus. Here we see the world of immediate pleasure and nature-oriented cultures, featuring wine and musical instruments. In the other world there resides the powerful man of money, who is able to capture the former world.[11]

The two men, both having acquired money and power, go separate ways. While King Oedipus was blinded and fell from grace, King Midas—it must be noted that Midas used to own a rose garden (his connection with nature) and once welcomed Silenus—was able to cleanse himself in the river Pactolus. He has recognized his mistakes and greed.

After this he "came to hate men, and strolling in the mountains with a cane in his hand, admired Pan, the god of the wild." He enjoyed "boasting his technique with reed flute to the nymphs."[12] In other words, he returns to the Dionysian world. Although they were both "exiled" from their own people, one is miserable and the other is happy.

In the Girardian view, Dionysus is understood to be satanic. Girard says that through the tragic actions of the Bacchantes, gods including Dionysus wander through the cities, spreading violence wherever they go and causing crimes using satanic techniques to seduce.[13] Further, he declares that it is impossible to spot such revolting things if we are under the influence of Nietzsche or Rudolf Otto. For Girard, one must rely on Christian faith to enter into real life.

Indeed, Dionysus is a frightening figure, one who would say "I was born a god, and now you mock me" to a despairing mother who realized that she has killed her son Pentheus for the sake of Dionysus.[14] The faith in Dionysus was the largest counterforce against Christianity in ancient Rome, and one of the things Jesus did was to sever the brutal chain of revenge that gods forced upon human beings in order to sever that same chain that existed among human beings. Because Christianity is similar to Dionysian faith in many ways, this difference is important.

Nevertheless, we should not ever underestimate the gravity of Dionysian qualities abundantly present in people's cultures. It now seems necessary to walk away from the misery of King Oedipus and "convert" ourselves towards the direction of Midas, who (although once mocked for his donkey ears given by Apollo) lives in harmony with nature.

While it is clear that Girardian anthropology opposes Dionysian, undifferentiated desire, symbolized by wine and dance, it is also widely recognized that the Christian dogma of death and rebirth and the symbolic values of wine have many things in common with the Dionysian mystery cult.

If Seaford's statement about the meaning of King Midas's story is true—that is, if the "absorption in happiness in the abstract (money) is incapacity for happiness in the concrete" is true—then the embodiment and directness of Dionysus should be denied for the sake of Christian happiness.[15] What is being sought in Christianity is not money, of course, but still it is a happiness in the abstract, or happiness as a *différance*.

Should we, then, identify Dionysian, or concrete happiness, with satanic desire as Girard would? Indeed, Dionysus brings about the obliteration of difference (for example, in the nation of Pentheus, the differences between male/female and man/animal/god/human no longer exist) as well as the butchery of Pentheus, but that obliteration and butchery is, at the same time, the liberation of women and lowly people. Girard does not mention this aspect of liberation; rather he stresses the destructive aspect, saying that the Dionysian eruption is the ruining of institutions and also the corruption of cultural order, which is clearly shown at the peak of the action when the royal palace is demolished.[16]

In the Homeric epic, Dionysus is not treated so nobly. Seaford points out that Homer makes light of Dionysus for political reasons,[17] because aristocratic clans, whose ideal consists in heroism and glory, exclude ideas concerning mystery cults, farming, communal festivals, and even city-states from their narrative sphere. Although the aristocrats had a relation with this god of wine, as we can see from the scene where Dionysus supplies wine at the wedding of Peleus and Thetis, they despised the inclusiveness of Dionysus and the celebration of the whole community that is implied by him. The cold treatment toward Dionysus and Demeter proves the inferior status of agriculture, and the same treatment towards Hephaestus proves the inferior status of the craftsmen.[18]

Modern Japanese society holds this attitude toward farmers and craftsmen in common with the Homeric aristocracy. We value heroism and glory. Perhaps our custom of holding celebrations with *sake* under the cherry blossoms in spring to revive the occasional community, one without difference, serves as a safety valve.[19] We, the individuals, who are part of an aristocratic society, strive to become heroes. We avoid any situation that would make us a faceless figure among a certain, ardent group (an exception here might be a soccer game or other sport events where we cheer). (Lately, in Japan such excitement is mythologized as nostalgia toward the period of high economic growth in the 1950s and 1960s.) We exclude all the things Dionysian with a certain coquetry by which one keeps on desiring oneself, who is at the same time to be desired by others.

Are there any Dionysian values concealed in the stories with the Girardian structure of desire and dialectics? By Dionysian, I mean the components of unmediated pleasure and by Girardian structure I mean stories that he himself has analyzed.

Let us take an example from Stendhal's *The Red and the Black*, a work praised by Girard for possessing the "novelistic truth." As is widely known, the protagonist Julien Sorel is an avid admirer of Napoleon, and it is in taking his and Rousseau's books as models that Julien navigates through life. Thus, his actions, as well as his desires, are mimetic. According to Girard, he will be awakened from such illusions at the end of the story, when he converts by looking back at his life and renouncing it. There he finally reaches the truth.

Indeed, his admiration for Napoleon and his head-over-heels love towards Mathilde, a lady whose desire is so mediated that it almost seems like a caricature, both fade away. But one thing goes on until the end, something the novel cannot proceed without: the love for Madame de Rênal. In the distinction between "love in the heart" and "love in the brain," this is the former.

Stendhal, in his *De l'amour*, writes that "even the wisest of men could become a fanatic when music is concerned, because one cannot understand the *why* of one's sentiments" (C'est parce qu'on ne peut se rendre compte du *pourquoi* de ses sentiments, que l'homme le plus sage est fanatique en musique). The moment where "one cannot understand the *why* of one's sentiments" comes to Julien when he first meets Madame de Rênal: "'What is your name, monsieur?' She asked him, with a tone and a grace of which Julien felt all the charm, *though he could not have explained why* [*sans pouvoir s'en rendre compte*].'I am called Julien Sorel, madame'" (trans. Roger Gard, emphasis mine).

Madame de Rênal, when asked about Julien by her husband, betrays her true feelings without noticing: "'What d'you make of this new acquisition?' M. de Rênal asked his wife. With an almost instinctive impulse, of which she was certainly not aware in herself [Par un mouvement presque instinctif, et dont certainement elle ne se rendit pas compte], Mme de Rênal disguised the truth from her husband. 'I am not nearly so enchanted as you with this little peasant.'"

Julien finds Madame's speech and gestures charming. However, because he is a commoner and does not possess the sociocultural code to decipher his social superiors, his reason cannot function as a proper receptor. Therefore, he cannot consciously understand her charms. On the other hand, although Mme de Rênal was "enchanted by Julien" (the word *enchantée*, of course, is used casually on a daily basis; it is important to notice how she uses this word in a superficial manner toward her husband, not being aware of its stronger, potential meaning), she, without noticing her mind's own deceptiveness, tries to hide her feelings from her husband. Or, to be more precise, Madame de Rênal is not aware of her own truth, and it is not a lie, because to lie means to tell something untrue when one is aware of the truth. The only ones who are aware of the truth, at this point, are the narrator and the reader.

In both of these scenes, Stendhal uses the expression *"se rendre compte de"* (in its negative form), and in each scene we find a word that derives from "song," which concerns magical charm: one is *charme* (from Latin *carmen*, "magical song") and the other is *enchanter* (from *incantare*, "casting a spell"). Stendhal most likely used such similar expressions on purpose, to point out that Julien and Madame de Rênal are experiencing emotions of the same nature.

The reception of an object beyond reason is recorded here. The couple were deeply enchanted with one another as soon as they were introduced, but neither of the two is able to consciously understand what is happening. And from there onwards, regardless of the fact that it is their "truth" that is urging them, Julien thinks it is his "duty" to engage in the love affair (naturally, there is something in him that builds such a sense of duty), while Madame de Rênal is unable to name her tender feelings towards him "love." It is only after the process of "gaining consciousness" that mediated desire starts to operate, in forms such as jealousy and doubt.

Julien is disillusioned with Napoleon as a result of self-reflection in jail, and deems actions of Napoleon at St. Helena as phony. On the other hand, he nourishes deep affection with Madame while he waits for death.

The charm that grasps one's mind, and eventually opens up a new horizon within one's individuality, can be deemed Dionysian in the sense that it is a magical song. Novels not only throw light on the mechanism of mimetic desire, but also on the force of unmediated charm.

What about the case of *Don Quixote*, another novel highly praised by Girard? Presumably, it constituted some sort of a crevasse out of which his desire originated when he was devouring chivalric romances. A giant leap into a vision follows, made possible through the imagination: a life that one ought to live (this vision, in turn, implies the boredom of the present). And this leap must take place in reality. To make this happen calls for insanity, another exemplary form of Girardian, mediated desire. However, confronting reality, he applies various metaphoric approaches, for example, the famous episode of him seeing Mambrino's helmet in the place of a barber's basin. That is to say, he wears a "mask," and this mask is nothing but a creation of the Dionysian space of festivity.

As Girard points out, parallel to Julien freeing himself from mimetic desire, Don Quixote undergoes a conversion before his death by denying the values embedded in chivalric romances. Still, it should be noted that others already recognize the function of his insanity.

In the novel, Bachelor Sansón Carrasco poses as The Knight of the Mirrors and The Knight of the White Moon to bring Don Quixote out of his insanity. This, however, is the reaction of Don Antonio: "Oh! Sir, reply'd Don Antonio, what have you to answer for, in robbing the World of the most diverting Folly, that ever was expos'd among Mankind? Consider, Sir, that his Cure can never benefit the Publik half so much as his Distemper (trans. Peter Motteux, rev. Ozell).

Don Antonio also takes his story to the Viceroy: "[The Viceroy] was vex'd to think that so much pleasant Diversion was like to be lost to all those that were acquainted with the Don's Follies."

If we are to arrange the story such that one character is against all the others, then we can see everybody is "enjoying" Don Quixote's insanity. Is this a new form, or perhaps a variation, of stoning?

Don Quixote returns to his village in the end, and at that point, it seems that a change has occurred in the model of action, a change that implies the shift from chivalric romances to baroque novels. Because here, Don Quixote thinks he should "immediately commence [being a] Shepherd, and entertain his amorous Passion solitarily in Fields and Woods" and give suitable names to his friends. Hearing this, the people around him "were struck with Amazement at this new Strain of Folly."

Let us take a look at the final scene, right after he aborted his adventure based on his new insanity. "My Judgment is return'd clear and undisturb'd. . . . Now I perceive their Nonsense and Impertinence [of those damnable Books]. . . . I find, Niece, my End approaches; but I wou'd have it such, that though my Life has got me the Character of a Mad-man, I may deserve a better at my Death."

Girard stresses that Don Quixote has returned to sanity. But isn't he leaving out, purposefully, Quixote's obsession with his self-image as seen by others that is still operating inside him?

At the beginning of the novel, when he began to devour chivalric romances and "started to get absorbed into most awkward fabrications that he believed to be true," he had decided to do something "so outrageous that no madman has ever imagined," which was to "become a knight himself, sporting an armor, mounting a horse, with plans to wander all around the world in seek of adventures, ready to execute all he has learned through his readings." The reason for his resolution was that, once he is successful with his adventure, his "fame will forever go down the history, which was the perfect thing both in *certifying his honor* and *serving his country*."

Both in the state of insanity (or while he is acting insane, as Nobuaki Ushijima, a scholar of Spanish literature, indicates) and of sanity, Don Quixote never seems to stop desiring attention from others by conveying his inner truth to the outside world. If this is the case, Girard's critique on *The Stranger*'s Meursault, which states "[t]he romantic does not want to be alone, but *to be seen alone*,"[20] seems a fitting way to describe the *sanity* of Don Quixote as well.

Why is Don Quixote loved by so many? We must take into consideration another "truth" that is different from Girard's, which also exists within the novel: "For indeed, either as Alonso Quixano, or as Don Quixote de la Mancha, as it has been observ'd, the sick Gentleman had always shew'd himself such a good natur'd Man, and of so agreeable a Behaviour, that he was not only belov'd by his Family, but by every one that knew him."

So this other truth is the truth of communality, which is flexible enough to contain insanity. Communality can be defined as "the sum of the feelings and actions of several individuals that promote and express their simultaneous belonging to the same group."[21]

But I am not trying to prove that Girard has missed the point. Let us listen to the "author" of the novel, Cide Hame: "The two Sallies that he has made already (which are the subject of these two Volumes, and have met with such universal Applause in this and other Kingdoms) are sufficient to ridicule the pretended Adventures of Knights-Errant." And he thus concludes, "As for me, I must esteem myself happy, to have been the first that render'd those fabulous, nonsensical Stories of Knight-Errantry, the Object of the publick Aversion. They are already going down, and I do not doubt but they will drop and fall altogether in good Earnest, never to rise again." To defeat the enemy, the process starts with imitation, and ends with the target's total malfunction. That is the tactic of Cervantes, which is analogous to the relationship between myth and the Gospels in the Girardian sense of the murder by group, and it also operates equally with the method of Christianity that embraced the Dionysian cult while nullifying its mechanism.

In fact, we enjoy one quality as a result of the malfunctioning process of chivalric romances. It is not a quality of the chivalric romance per se, but a quality that inhabits the dimension of insanity. A new type of story and a pleasure is born that, nevertheless, may "make people despise the phony, nonsense stories in the books on chivalry."

Paradoxically, chivalric romances were saved from oblivion thanks to the "drop and fall" of the genre caused by Don Quixote. Now, can we say the same when Girard claims that "the Gospels aim to destruct the whole religion of mankind and cultures built on it"? Christianity has already succeeded in destroying the Dionysian cult. If we look back at the history of Christianity, what Girard claims about the Gospels should also be applied on the present state of Christianity as well. For example, anything Dionysian, such as songs, incense, and art, should be discarded altogether. But in such a world could any culture or literature be nurtured upon the Girardian Gospels?

For someone like me, who studies [French] literature in a country where an eleventh-century woman writer could instantiate Girardian theory under the influence of Buddhism but not the Gospels, one cannot help but see a certain dogmatic limitation in Girard's thinking.

We have already seen that King Oedipus set the highest value on money and power through his self-sufficient intelligence and that this leads to his miserable downfall. Let's return to the *Tale of Genji*. What was, then, the ideal for Hikaru, who avoided tragedy? He erects Rokujo-in, a palace that symbolized the harmony of four seasons, and lets his favorite women occupy it. It was his utopia of love, which harmonizes deeply with nature. After his death, the story soon loses its bright character and shifts toward dark eternity while it gives an account of Ukifune. Ukifune, loved by two young aristocrats, is the target of a typical rivalry of mediated desire. She gets so fatigued by her situation that she tries to drown herself but fails to die. Then she says the following: "I am trying to remember, but nothing will come back, and I cannot make out what it was that I dreamed" (translation by Royall Tyler).

When I listen to her grave words, I hear the vibrations of deep and absolute literary truth. This truth is at the same level as that of Julien and Don Quixote, and the religious conscience plays a principal role there. But when this kind of truth is repeated throughout literature, it appears not only under Christianity but also under other religions (in the case of *Genji*, Buddhism). The love of literature does not permit me to enter into a polemic on the origin of culture, nor to consider Christianity as the only key to realize the dysfunction of an infernal mimetism deeply rooted in our human mind.

Notes

1. Yugao died suddenly after the first night of love. His love toward her is mediated by Umanokami's opinion on love affairs and motivated by his rivalry against Tono Chujo.

2. Hikaru has a feminine charm ("As he sat in the lamplight leaning against an armrest, his companions almost wished that he were a woman," "Hahaki" [The Broom Tree]).

3. Richard Seaford, *Dionysos* (London: Routledge, 2006), 148.

4. Sophocles, *Oedipus Tyrannus*, trans. Ian McAuslan and Judith Affleck (Cambridge: Cambridge University Press, 2003), vv. 22–30. Subsequent quotations are from this translation.

5. Richard Seaford, *Money and the Early Greek Mind* (Cambridge: Cambridge University Press, 2004), 312.

6. Ibid.

7. Ibid., 313.

8. Koichi Namiki, *Collected Essays on The Book of Job* (in Japanese) (Tokyo: Kyobunkan, 2007), 91–92. Translation mine.

9. René Girard, *Le bouc émissaire* (Paris: B. Grasset, 1982), chapter 2, "Les stéreotypes de la persécution."

10. For example, a spokesman of the Nuclear and Industrial Safety Agency was replaced due to his "improper behavior," a scandal exposed in a magazine.

11. Seaford, *Money and the Early Greek Mind*, 307.

12. Shigeichi Kure, *The Greek Myths* (in Japanese) (Tokyo: Shincho-sha, 1979), "Shincho-bunko," 1:314. Translation mine.

13. René Girard, *La Violence et le sacré* (orig. pub. 1972), in *De la violence à la divinité* (Paris: B. Grasset, 2007), 458. ("Tout au long de l'action tragique [des *Bacchantes*] le dieu erre à travers la cité, semant la violence sur son passage, provoquant le crime avec l'art d'un séducteur diabolique.")

14. Kure, *Greek Myths*, 291.

15. Seaford, *Money and the Early Greek Mind*, 305.

16. Girard, *La Violence et le sacré*, 451. ("L'éruption dionysiaque, c'est la ruine des institutions, c'est l'effondrement de l'ordre culturel qui nous est nettement signifié, au paroxysme de l'action, par la destruction du palais royal.")

17. Seaford, *Dionysos*, 27.

18. Ibid., 30.

19. Traditional Japanese craftsmanship is praised when we intend to emphasize our potential power in technological industries.

20. René Girard, "Camus's Stranger Retried," *PMLA*, The Modern Language Association of America, vol. 79, no. 3 (December 1964): 527.

21. Seaford, *Dionysos*, 26.

CHAPTER 6

THE SACRIFICE OF THE MEDIATOR

A Murder on Gifu's Sugou Plateau and Folk Performing Art

MIZUHO KAWASAKI

The Murder Motif in *Sugou-shishi*

In Sugou, a region in Hida city in Gifu prefecture, there is a unique old *Shishi-mai*, or ritual dance, by a performer/performers wearing a lion's mask, called *Sugou-shishi* (sometimes called *Koma-jishi*). *Sugou-shishi* is said to have been written by a Buddhist priest named Ryūkan during the Taihou Era (701–704 CE) in what is now Korea. He was inspired to write this play by a scene he witnessed in a place called Meotoiwa, where several lions in their natural habitat were behaving in a wildly playful manner.

The performance of *Sugou-shishi* is held at two shrines in Japan, the Hakusan and the Matsuo-Hakusan shrines, both of which are located in the same region. The performances take place on September 5, when they hold their annual festivals. In these performances, each *shishi* or lion is played by two performers inside a costume. The one in front plays its head (*shishi-gashira*) and its forelegs, and the other plays the two hind legs. The giant head of the lion or the *shishi-gashira* reminds us of the Daikagura style (a kind of acrobatic lion's dance). Various acrobatic stunts are performed like the ones we see in *Gigaku* (an ancient Japanese masked dance that originated in China).

The first act, "Kyoku-shishi," portrays the scene where male and female lions dance madly in their natural state, without reserve.[1] In the second act, "Tengu-shishi," the Shishi, or lion, is joined on stage by a Tengu (a well-known Japanese long-nosed goblin), a monkey, and a bear. One by one they appear and begin to dance. However, when the Shishi starts to behave badly and wildly, the Tengu gets angry and defeats the Shishi.[2]

The third act, "Kinzou-shishi," depicts the moment when the peasants become happy because they have captured the violent lion. The peasants' faces are represented by masks: Okame, a flat-faced woman, for the females, and Hyottoko, a clownish face with protruding lips and squinting eyes, for the males.[3]

In Japanese folk art, we often encounter the motif of murdering the mediator. In my opinion, more research on this subject is necessary. *Sugou-shishi* provides us with a good example for this kind of research because we can clearly see the murder of a mediator in the second act, in which the Tengu is killed. As René Girard has emphasized, sacrifice is a "commemoration of generative violence." The results of my own fieldwork indicate it is highly possible that some of the actions that depict the sacrifice in the second act have strong connections with the generative violence of territory disputes that occurred in the Edo period (1603–1868). Girard also claims that violence, "founded on an act of generative violence, [is] maintained by ritual."[4] It is my intention to present *Sugou-shishi* as a Japanese example of the Girardian model by studying this scene in detail.

The Murder of Tengu as a Sacrifice

Let us examine the second act, "Tengu-shishi," more closely. First, the Shishi appears on the stage and dances, and then the Tengu makes an appearance followed by the monkey and the bear. They all start to dance around the Shishi in various kinds of performances (*shosa*). We note in particular that the Tengu is killed by the Shishi but later revives and defeats the Shishi. This concludes the second act.

What does this act with its murder of the Tengu signify? One of the key elements for finding the answer to this question is to examine the character of the Tengu. Based on previous research, I maintain that the Tengu, one of the most famous characters among Japanese gods or spirits, is a clownish mediator, a "trickster" in mythological terms.[5]

I also maintain that the most noteworthy thing about the Tengu is his role as a "mediator." In the rural communities of premodern times, Tengu was regarded as a mediator between the community and the outside world and he was imagined to look like a mixture of a human and a beast. Although I cannot go into great detail here, one can summarize a Tengu's qualities as follows: living in the forest in the mountains, having a plasticity to his figure, being ambivalent about his divinity, having ambivalence about his being right or wrong, having supernatural power, and being the cause of mysterious phenomena. These qualities have similarities with those of the tricksters of Western mythology, like Hermes in the Greek myths. In his book *Folklore of the Clown* (1985), the Japanese anthropologist Masao Yamaguchi states Hermes's characteristics as follows:[6]

1. Causing disturbance in the order by theft or trickery.
2. Being ubiquitous: appearing anywhere at any time.
3. Being able to create new things by innovative combinations (e.g., the invention of Lyra by combining a tortoiseshell and a cattle gut).
4. Communicating between different worlds by becoming a traveler, a messenger, or a guide.

These qualities apply to a Tengu as well: First, we often find in our folklore that a Tengu is the cause of a disturbance. Second, although a Tengu lives in the forest, he often appears in human habitats. Third, we find this quality of creating new things, especially connected to music, in the folklore. For example, "in the village in Aichi prefecture where 'Hanamatsuri' (a kind of performing arts) has been handed down for generations, the Tengu is said to be an authority in music; he loves music and dancing and it is believed that he kidnaps people if he or she whistles, sings songs, or plays music in the mountain."[7] Fourth, we find a similarity with the Saenokami (gate god) of Sarutahikonokami, whom the people often regarded as the same being as a Tengu. Yamaguchi also points the similarities between Hermes and Saenokami: "The original form of Hermes emerged perhaps as herma (hermai) in Attika, some islands in the archipelago, Imbros island, Samothrace, and so on. Herma is a stone pillar which has a human's head in the upper part and a penis in the middle part. These were usually put by the roadside or to mark a boundary of a field or a pasture. It originally was a spirit which had the property of being a gate god and who symbolized fertility and productiveness."[8] The stone pillar he mentions here corresponds to the *dousojin* or stone pillar of Sarutahikonokami that we often encounter on the roadside of almost any rural area in Japan. In addition, the quality of Hermes as a guide seems to correspond to the fact that Tengu and Sarutahikonokami often play the roles of guides in the festivals held in various regions in Japan. In conclusion, it is quite clear that Hermes as a trickster has many characteristics in common with those of Tengu.

An Interpretation of "Murdering Goroubei" as Generative Violence

Given that we can view the Tengu as a mediator, I propose interpreting his death in the second act of *Sugou-shishi* as a sacrifice in Girardian terms. When one interprets defeating a mediator as murdering a mediator, then one can say that this act is a sacrifice. Girard writes that "from every point of view the fool is eminently 'sacrificeable'":[9]

> He [the surrogate victim] is seen as a "monstrous double." He partakes of all possible differences within the community, particularly the difference between within and without; for he passes freely from the interior to the exterior and back again. Thus, the surrogate victim constitutes both a link and a barrier between the community and the sacred. To even so much as represent this extraordinary victim the ritual victim must belong both to the community and to the sacred.[10]

As Girard points out, a sacrificial victim should be both in the community and outside of it. The Tengu belongs exactly in such a marginal area in folklore. This helps to explain why the Tengu has to be sacrificed. Yet there are still unanswered questions, such as, What sort of a crisis brings about the death of Tengu? And what does the Shishi symbolize as the one who kills the mediator, Tengu? To solve the mystery of sacrifice, Girard presents the idea of "generative violence." According to his theory, generative violence always precedes the violence we see in the rituals of a community. "The extraordinary number of commemorative rites that have to do with killing leads us to imagine that the original event must have been a murder. . . . And the remarkable similarities among the sacrificial rites of various localities suggest that the murder was always of the same general type."[11] According to Girard, the crisis that precedes the ritual of sacrifice in the community is called "generative violence," and the ritual is a mimesis of it. "Although generative violence is invisible, it can logically be deduced from myths and rituals once their real structures have been perceived."[12]

If there was such generative violence in the Sugou plateau, then there is the real possibility that the performance of *Sugou-shishi* might be the mimesis of it, designed to commemorate that generative violence. In fact, there really is a genuine and very suggestive historical site, the tombstone of Goroubei, and a story about it that has been handed down orally for generations.

In the Meiwa era (1764–72) of the Edo period, a territorial dispute occurred that concerned mountainous areas in the Sugou district. This dispute came to an end and the peace was restored when one of the peasants involved, named Goroubei, was killed. Today, we can see a tree, a stupa, or a tall narrow wooden tablet set up behind a grave for the repose of the dead, a stone Buddhist image, and a *jizou*, a small stone statue of the guardian deity, at the alleged murder site. As for the oral tradition concerning this incident, it has been kept alive by a group of people associated with the late Satobei Yamamura, a respected figure in the Sugou area, and goes as follows:

> Once upon a time, I heard it happened in the Meiwa era, that Nishi village and Sugou village had been constantly fighting over their border in the Iriai mountains. One day, a man of Sugou village cut down a tree in the Sofugahara area, one of the disputed spots. The people in Nishi village,

who heard that a Sugou man was cutting down the trees in a disputed area, got very angry and came down to Sugou in great numbers carrying fire hooks and sickles. "You cut down the trees in our mountain, you will pay dearly for it!" shouted a Nishi village man. "Oh, no. The mountain is ours. We can cut down any trees there," a Sugou man shouted back.

After thus quarrelling back and forth, one Nishi village man began attacking them with a fire hook and hit Goroubei, a Sugou man, on the head. He died instantly. Both parties were shocked by the death, and the dispute ended there.

A fire hook made a hole in Goroubei's head and, it is said, in that hole, a person from Nishi village placed some flowers he had picked in the field. And all the Nishi village people, throwing away their fire hooks and sickles, scurried back to their village.

Although the long dispute had finally come to an end, thanks to the sacrifice of Goroubei, this incident left an uneasy feeling among the villages. Thus, they decided to plant a yew tree as a mark of Goroubei's grave. . . . It is said that before something unusual happens in the village you will see fire-balls around this yew tree as an omen. The dispute concerning the Iriai mountains ended in favor of Sugou village people thanks to Goroubei's death. . . .

It was a small dispute that happened a long time ago when the people concerned were poor peasants; and yet we still hold a memorial service for Goroubei's death every year at Goroubei's grave site.[13]

Yūjirou Nakamura, a Japanese philosopher, states in his book *The Compilation of Terminology* that "Girard considers cultural order to be a system constructed by systematized differences and the loss of these differences causes the prevalence of naked/defiled violence."[14] Girard also states, "It is not these distinctions but the loss of them that gives birth to fierce rivalries and sets members of the same family or social group at one another's throats."[15] Let's look again at the recorded Sugou oral tradition. The cause of the violence is both parties' desire for the same territory; they lost their distinction by desiring the same thing. Girard also states, "All the rancors scattered at random among the divergent individuals, all the differing antagonisms, now converge on an isolated and unique figure, the *surrogate victim*."[16] Goroubei is exactly the surrogate victim, or the scapegoat, Girard mentioned here; his death transforms *la violence* into *le sacré*. "The beneficial character of the generative unanimity tends to be projected onto the past, affecting the initial impression of crisis and making it seem other than it was. The violent dismissal of distinctions now acquires a favorable connotation, which will eventually manifest itself as a festive display."[17]

When it is recorded that "we still hold a memorial service for Goroubei's death every year at the Goroubei's grave site," this indicates that the tombstone of Goroubei is now a place of worship. As Girard has written, "The various bad incidents caused by the generative violence will gradually be transformed into something beautiful." Furthermore, the story relates that "in that hole, a person from Nishi village placed some flowers he picked in the field." The scene shows that Goroubei, a Sugou man who should be the target of hatred, was transformed into Hotoke, which means both "the dead" and "Buddha" and was consecrated by the flowers. The transformation into something sacred is clearly confirmed by the record: "It is said that before something unusual happens in the village you will see fire-balls around this yew tree as an omen."

Generative Violence and Ritual of Sacrifice

Let us review "Tengu-shishi," the second act of *Sugou-shishi*, adopting Girard's model. First, the mediator, Tengu, is killed by the Shishi, and the scene resonates with Goroubei's death. As I mentioned in the first section of this essay, this act introduces the Shishi, the Tengu, a monkey, and a bear onto the stage. They all dance, but gradually the Shishi begins to show his beastly nature and starts to behave wildly. This angers the Tengu, and he makes Shishi quiet in the end of the second act. This sequence corresponds exactly to that of Girard's: the killing of the mediator (the Tengu) by the beast (the Shishi), the revival of the Tengu and his anger and suppression of Shishi, and the restoration of peace. The killing of the mediator by the violence of nature restores cultural order: the disappearance of the figure by disorder causes the appearance of order, relatively speaking: "The decisive act of violence is directed against this awesome vision of evil."[18]

It is clear from what has been mentioned here so far that the monkey and the bear who appear in the second act deserve special attention. They might represent the villagers of both villages, Nishi and Sugou. Some may question this interpretation, but the roles of the animals are played in the second act by the same actors who play the peasants in the third act, "Kinzou-shishi" (see the first section above). This means that the animal roles and the peasant roles are interchangeable.[19] According to Kouichi Tanaka, who is one of the performers of *Sugou-shishi*, the monkey and the bear try to help the Tengu. The monkey tries to hunt the lion with a rod that is baited with a rice dumpling on a hook. After the Tengu is struck down, the monkey and the bear perform various acrobatics as in the first act, "Kyoku-shi." According to Tanaka, they try to attract the attention of the Shishi to prevent the coup de grâce to the Tengu.[20]

In the plot, however, they fail to attract the lion's attention, and so the Shishi murders Tengu in the end. Thus, although they tried to help, the Tengu was murdered by the Shishi. This explanation is analogous to one of the oral traditions of Goroubei's murder. Both sides seem steadfastly to insist that the murder was accidental. These two cases perhaps hint that the murder was necessary for the restoration of order with unanimous consent.

From what has been discussed above, it is possible for us to establish a hypothesis that the relation between Goroubei's murder and *Sugou-shishi* is identical to the relation between generative violence and ritual as sacrifice in Girard's usage. The discontinuity between Goroubei's murder and *Sugou-shishi* gives authenticity to this hypothesis. According to Girard, in the ritual as sacrifice, the generative violence is forgotten, and it is mimicked because it is forgotten: "In order to retain its structuring influence the generative violence must remain hidden."[21]

In conclusion, it is the violence that has been mimicked in this place. Furthermore, in light of the relation between the Tengu and Goroubei, a very interesting structure appears. I interviewed Kyūtarou Shimoda, who knows the oral tradition on Goroubei, about the kind of person Goroubei was. According to Shimoda, Goroubei was a representative of Sugou village, and he had sat down at the negotiating table with the Nishi village in this capacity. Therefore, I assumed that Goroubei was Murakata-sanyaku (a kind of managerial post at village in Edo period), and I asked

Shimoda if this was correct. But he answered that Goroubei was not a public servant but a common peasant.[22]

Thus, Goroubei was not clearly distinctive from the other peasants, but nevertheless he did have the particular and mediatory existence as a delegate. Perhaps this way of thinking about Goroubei was created in the narrative about him after he was murdered. For this reason, to borrow Girard's phrase, it suggests "the metamorphosis of reciprocal violence into generative violence by means of the murder of *somebody, no matter whom*—a figure chosen, as it were, at random,"[23] so that as a result, anyone can be selected as a scapegoat. A victim of sacrifice, however, must not only be a different person from the community but also have a characteristic of a mediator. Girard writes, "All sacrificial rites are based on two substitutions. The first is provided by generative violence, which substitutes a single victim for all the members of the community. The second, the only strictly ritualistic substitution, is that of a victim for the surrogate victim. As we know, it is essential that the victim be drawn from outside the community. The surrogate victim, by contrast, is a member of the community. Ritual sacrifice is defined as an inexact imitation of the generative act."[24]

Thus, it can be inferred that the reason why Goroubei was given a special position in the story, like the "representative of the village," is that he had to be someone special, a mediator, who "deserved to be killed." In other words, the violence accidentally made him "sacred" after the fact, not vice versa.

The above inference can be proven by the fact that Goroubei had no official position—he was just one of the peasants. Although Goroubei, a common peasant, is made to be a mediator by violence, the Tengu, on the other hand, was chosen to be a sacrifice because he is the mediator. (See figure 1.)

It could be safely said that in the Sugou area, the incident of killing Goroubei has been mimicked up to today by people who have no conscious knowledge of the incident they are mimicking. It can also be said that we will understand the sacrificial aspects of *Sugou-shishi* properly only by interpreting them as the reflection of the past generative violence (murdering Goroubei).

The Sacrifice of the Mediator

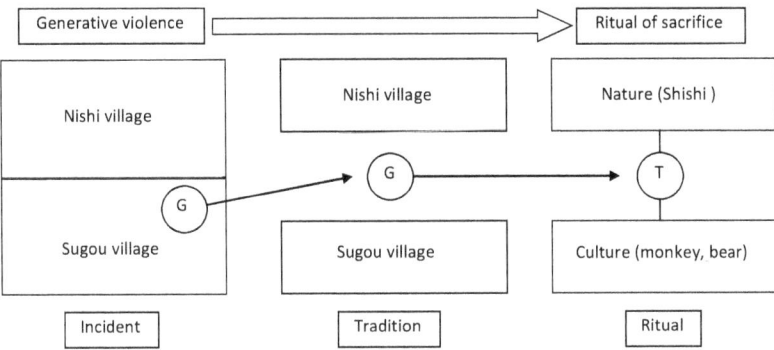

Figure 1. The Murder of Goroubei as Generative Violence, and *Sugou-shishi* as a Ritual of Sacrifice (G = Goroubei, T = Tengu)

Yet it is possible to argue against this theory, especially for those who are well versed in Japanese folk performing arts, by pointing out the fact that one can find the same kind of performing arts all over Japan. It is not my intention to prove that the performing art, *Sugou-shishi*, was "created" in order to mimic the generative violence, the murder of Goroubei, that took place in this area. Although it is true that the original form of this performing art was created in some other area and then brought to Sugou in the past, it does not affect my argument. Consider what Girard has to say about the matter:

> Between this instance of complete originality and the mechanical repetition of rites at the other end of the scale, we can assume the existence of an infinite number of intermediary forms. The fact that certain religious and cultural themes pervade a vast area does not exclude the possibility that truly spontaneous collective violence, working through one of the intermediary forms and endowed with real (if limited) creative powers on the mythic and religious level, might occur in many places. This would explain the many variants of the same myth, the same cults, from locality to locality, and also the claim made by various places to be birth place of the same god.[25]

In other words, if the generative violence could happen in the Sugou district, it could also happen in any other districts as well, and if any folk performing arts that were suitable for mimicking were available at those times and in those districts, they could have served the purpose. It can also be said that the existence of the generative violence created the space into which those folk performing arts could enter.

This study makes it clear that, to understand the structures of the Japanese folk performing arts, adopting the Girard model can be very useful. By using Girard's method, it is quite possible to study many of the mysteries in our folk performing arts from a new point of view.

Notes

I would like to thank informants in the Sugou area: Kyūtarou Shimoda, a performer of *Sugou-shishi*; Kouichi Tanaka, a performer of *Sugou-shishi*; the personnel of an eating house, Sugou; Takayuki Furuta, a deputy head of Sugou ward; and Miyoshi Seichou, a member of the board of education in Hida city. I deeply appreciate their cooperation. Furthermore, Keiko Shindou and Kunio Nakahata helped me with my translation; for them, I have no words to express my gratitude.

1. Koujirou Masahiro Nishitsunoi and Haruo Misumi, eds., *The Glossary of Folkloric Performing Arts* (Tokyo: Tokyodou Press, 1981), 244.

2. Ibid.

3. Ibid.

4. René Girard, *La Violence et le sacré* (Paris: B. Gasset, 1972); English translation, René Girard, *Violence and the Sacred*, trans. Patrick Gregory (Baltimore: Johns Hopkins University Press, 1977), 163.

5. Mizuho Kawasaki, "*Sanrin-otogami-kou*: A Study of *Tengu* in Folk Performing Arts from the Perspective of Structural Anthropology," The Society for Research in Asiatic Music (Tôyô Ongaku Gakkai, TOG), East Japan Branch, 56th regular meeting, April 23, 2011.

6. Masao Yamaguchi, *Folklore of the Clown* (Tokyo: Chikuma, 1985), 77–78.

7. Makoto Ueno, "Hana Matsuri to Tengu Densho: Manekarezaru Seireitachi no za" (The "Flower Festival" and Tengu: Positions of the Uninvited Spirits), *Minzoku Geino Kenkyu* (Studies on Folkloric Performing Arts) 9 (Tokyo: Minzoku Geino Gakkai, 1989), 12–25, quotation at 23.

8. Yamaguchi, *Folklore of the Clown*, 78.

9. Girard, *Violence and the Sacred*, 12.

10. Ibid., 271.

11. Ibid., 92.
12. Ibid., 310.
13. Satobei Yamamura, *Sugou in Hida* (Gifu, Japan: Satobei, 1979), 102–3.
14. Yūjirou Nakamura, *The Compilation of Terminology: Disturbing Terms* (Tokyo: Iwanami, 1984), 178.
15. Girard, *Violence and the Sacred*, 49.
16. Ibid., 79.
17. Ibid., 120.
18. Ibid., 161.
19. In the third act, "Kinzou-shishi," there are four roles: Shishi, Kinzou, Hyottoko, and Okame, which correspond to four roles in the second act, "Tengu-shishi": Shishi, Tengu, a monkey, and a bear. This correspondence is unquestionable because of the identity of the performers. Thus, the relation between the two acts is a variation on the theme. The fact that the roles that used monkey and bear masks in "Tengu-shishi" are performed by human masks (Hyottoko and Okame) proves clearly that the monkey and bear can be replaced with humans.
20. Kouichi Tanaka, interview with author, September 5, 2012.
21. Girard, *Violence and the Sacred*, 310.
22. Kyūtarou Shimoda, interview with author, May 20, 2012.
23. Ibid., 218.
24. Ibid., 269.
25. Ibid., 113–14.

CHAPTER 7

DECADENCE AND CONVERSION

On the Thought of Ango Sakaguchi

KUNIO NAKAHATA

To Be Ethical

When ye see a cloud rise out of the west, straightway ye say, There cometh a shower; and so it is. And when ye see the south wind blow, ye say, There will be heat; and it cometh to pass.
—*Luke 12:54–55*

This essay introduces the work of a Japanese novelist and essayist, Ango Sakaguchi (1906–1955), in particular, "Darakuron" ("Discourse on Decadence") and "Zoku darakuron" ("Discourse on Decadence Part II"). But allow me to explain why it is of value to write about him at all.[1]

I read Girard's works as dealing with a radical principle of ethics. If humans could not refuse positions or roles given in the system of sacrifice, that is, could not choose whether to persecute or to be persecuted, it is meaningless to talk about ethics. How, then, is it possible for us to reject these positions or roles? This is a difficult problem because, as Girard shows us, we cannot innocently trust our subjectivity. I think the possibility is implicit in the experience of conversion in its general meaning. By "general meaning," I signify that I use the word "conversion" not in the sense of formally becoming a Christian, but in a more general sense, where our old values are destroyed and new ones constructed. I will use the word "conversion" in this secularized sense for the present, although in the conclusion it will be considered in the biblical or Christian context. The concept of conversion as I intend it became a theme in the study of the psychology of religion with William James,[2] and Bernard Lonergan also categorizes a certain type of it as ethical.[3] The paradox is that while an experience of conversion cannot be sought subjectively, it is still up to the subject who has the experience to decide whether to give that experience the profound significance of a conversion or not. So there is an ethical sense in this decision. I think that Ango talks about conversion in this sense in many of his works, though he does not use the term itself. In "Darakuron," which was published the year following the end of the Pacific War, he described the defeat as an opportunity given to the Japanese people to convert and wrote about his own experience of conversion as well.

In "Darakuron," Ango expressed his thoughts on the paradox of what he calls "*karakuri*." Simply put, *karakuri* are systems in a broad sense that include not only visible systems but also invisible systems, or a second nature, internalized by the mind of the Japanese, for example, which they transform into the outer realities surrounding them. Hegel's notion of "objective mind" might help us to understand what Ango means here. Hegel wrote that "what is rational is actual and what is actual is rational."[4] The mind or reason peculiar to the Japanese brings forth a reality peculiar to them, and whether it is visible or invisible, the reality has a more or less political sense.[5] The relationship between the visible and the invisible is paradoxical in that the former is based on the latter, but in the former, the latter is lost sight of. This is a typical state of alienation.

I would like to emphasize here that though a *karakuri* is constructed, it is still a firm reality for those who live in it. In fact, it is the totality of reality for them. Reality is not just one alternative. Usually, those who live in it will never come to know that it is constructed and will never find another reality or *karakuri* that is completely unrelated to their own. Even after some dialectical process to overcome alienation, the old reality that is to be overcome is sublated into the new one; it is not that the old reality is dismissed and a completely new reality begins, unrelated to the old one.

As we shall see in detail later, Ango thinks that the emperor system is a *karakuri* that is quintessentially Japanese. He wrote the following about the emperor system: "A scheming race like the Japanese needs the emperor, both to work their manipulations and to order their world. Individual political players may not have consciously felt the need for an emperor, but that didn't matter: the instincts that history had bred into them precluded their questioning the political reality they had inherited."[6]

It was not that the emperor system was selected as necessary for the Japanese. For the Japanese, it was reality itself without any alternatives, and without any doubt they believed that they were in it. Ango said, "The same is true of the emperor system: there is no innate truth in it, nor is it at all natural. Still, the emperor system represents a long history of innovations based on keen observations, and in this it has a profound significance that we cannot easily dismiss. Analyzing it through self-evident truths and the laws of nature just doesn't get to the heart of the matter."[7]

Although the *karakuri* of the emperor system was "not an innate truth and not natural at all," in other words, even though it was only a construct, the mere fact that people lived in it could never be rationally explained or denied.

First, we should have a look at the process in which *karakuri* is constructed.

To Make a Person a God

> And Pilate asked him, Art thou the King of the Jews? And he answering said unto him, Thou sayest it.
>
> —*Mark 15:2*

Ango wrote that the motivation for constructing *karakuri* is the universal desire to have things of beauty forever frozen in that state. *Karakuri* is justified because submitting to it is supposed to be a beautiful way to live. It is not simply forced on citizens unilaterally by politicians or military leaders. Rather it is accepted on the side of citizens and becomes a virtue. *Bushido*, which orders soldiers to die rather than suffer the shame of being taken as prisoner, is also an instance of *karakuri*.

Of course, such a *karakuri* was not virtuous but a deception and could be supported only during wartime. In fact, survivors of the kamikaze brigades later became *yamiya*, or black marketeers, forgetting such virtues. But such a *karakuri* was not constructed independently of the mentality of the Japanese. Rather, politicians or military leaders knew the weakness of the mentality of the Japanese very well. They knew very well that "of all the races, the Japanese are at heart among the least inclined to hatred" and that "without percepts like these it would have been impossible to spur the Japanese on to war."[8] Ango declares, "The code of the samurai is a list of prohibitions controlling our natural and instinctual urges and, as such, it is grounded in a keen observation of human emotions and instincts, there is something altogether human about it as well."[9]

Who, then, invented *karakuri*, or what was the origin of *karakuri*? According to Ango,

> There have been a handful of geniuses who brought a real creativity to the acts of organization and supervision. Their accomplishments have taken on a life of their own, serving as models for the mediocre politicians and being handed down through the ages as the backbone of a long string of political systems. History is not a chain of autonomous eras distinguished by distinct political systems. It is, rather, itself a massive, independent living organism. History absorbs all the particular political phenomena that have merged up to that point and is tremendously influenced by them.[10]

Given that Ango wrote "a handful of geniuses," it might seem that he supposes some subject constructed *karakuri*. But rather, we should interpret it to mean that it is useless to suppose such a subject as the origin of *karakuri*. If we dare to point to the subject that constructed *karakuri*, it is history itself, and we can't but express it metaphorically as "a massive, independent living organism." History itself constructs *karakuri*, the social or political mechanism, so it is useless to ask about its origin.

Ango thinks the emperor system is one such *karakuri*, "one that is both quintessentially Japanese and quite original."[11] Moreover, "It certainly didn't come into being because of the emperors themselves, who have, as a rule, done nothing. Though there have been occasions when the emperor himself instigated a play for power, there isn't a single example that ended successfully, and the emperor would inevitably be exiled to some distant island or escape deep into the mountains—at least until his political utility was recognized once again."[12]

Politicians have always found a position for the emperors in their political systems. "The political utility of the imperial house was something sniffed out" by politicians; they "had observed the idiosyncracies of the Japanese people and discovered within them the possibilities for an emperor system."[13] In the political system of Japan, a person occupying an absolute position was needed, and the emperors were such persons. The important thing is that the person who occupies the absolute position exists, not who he or she is. Ango wrote that Japanese people "could very well have gone for the descendants of Confucius, Gautama Buddha, or even Lenin."[14] "It's just pure coincidence that others than the imperial house didn't go that route."[15]

I would like to emphasize that at least in "Darakuron" and in "Zoku darakuron," Ango criticizes the emperor system as *karakuri*, not the emperors themselves. Those familiar with Girard's theory will well understand that it is nonsensical to criticize the emperors in a system like this. Moreover, Ango mainly criticizes not the politicians or military leaders, but rather the Japanese people who were not aware of their being in the system. Ango wrote that the Japanese are "a scheming race," and they "need the emperor, both to work their manipulation and to order their world."[16] "Political scheming may be the work of the devil but that doesn't mean that these devils themselves don't worship like children at the feet of gods they themselves have conjured up."[17]

To Be Alive without Knowing Self-Deception

> Father, forgive them; for they know not what they do.
> —*Luke 23:34*

Ango explains that at the top of the hierarchy were the leaders of the times and that the emperor himself was not part of this hierarchy. This was because, for the leaders, "worshiping the emperor was a means of both indicating their own prestige and reveling in it."[18]

Rather than issue decrees they themselves realized, they could have the emperor proclaim them instead. Then, by being the very first to submit to the decree—and by making a good show of it—the Fujiwara regents or the shoguns could be sure that the new orders would be followed near and far. These imperial proclamations, of course, did not reflect the emperor's will, but rather that of the shoguns or the Fujiwara regents. By acting on their desires in the name of the emperor, they were able to demonstrate compliance with the decree. This compliance then became a model of submission to the imperial will that could be foisted upon the masses, and through this process the Fujiwara regents and shoguns were able to force their will upon the populace.[19]

An emperor was positioned outside this hierarchy as a god.

Seeking infinite respect from the masses by presenting oneself as a deity of some sort is a pursuit doomed to failure. It is, however, possible to elevate the emperor to divine status by prostrating oneself before him, and to then impose that behavior on the masses. The Fujiwara regents and the shoguns did just this, propping up the emperor as it suited them, and forcefully impressing his magnificence upon the masses by themselves bowing down before him. They then used the aura they had manufactured to issue their decrees.[20]

For Ango, "The leaders elevate the emperor to divine status by prostrating oneself before him, and then impose that behavior on the masses."[21] And the people imitate this behavior. Those who are at the top of the hierarchy are models for the members who belong to it. The people became rivals with each other over how much allegiance to the emperor they could show. "We were left speechless by the absurdity of being forced to bow our heads each time the streetcars took the turn below Yasukun Shrine but, for certain types of people, performing such acts is the only way they are able to confirm their own worth."[22] But this rivalry among the people was, commonly, not over some advantage, but to escape some disadvantage. For example, those who would not show respect to the emperor were prosecuted as unpatriotic.

Whether it is the emperor system or *bushido*, such *karakuri* in principle ultimately forces the people to die. And the more dignity one wants to feel in comparison to one's rivals, the closer one goes toward death. In fact, many soldiers and civilians died in the name of the emperor. Nevertheless, people persisted in such *karakuri*, or, to be more precise, they could not help persisting in it. As we shall see in detail below, Ango, who experienced conversion in a general sense during and after the war and then watched *karakuri* being reconstructed after the war, discovered that such persistence was self-deception. The following passage, which clearly shows Ango's hatred for such self-deception, is worth quoting in full despite its length. It was written in 1946.

> Last year, on August 15, the war was ended in the emperor's name. People claim that it was he who saved us. The historical evidence, in fact, supports this claim: history has always turned to the emperor as a creative solution in such times of crisis, the military intuitively understood his usefulness as a trump card, and we citizens instinctively waited for them to play it. So, the catastrophic final scene that was August 15 was really a collaborative effort between the military and the masses.
>
> We were called upon to obey His Majesty's order, told "to bear the unendurable, to bear the unbearable." The standard narration then tells us that the masses wept but, because it was at the command of none other than his Imperial Majesty himself, they bore the unbearable and conceded defeat. It's all lies! Lies, lies!
>
> Wasn't it the case that we civilians ourselves wanted nothing more than to end the war? Wasn't it true that we couldn't stand the idea of falling dead, like one wooden soldier after another, as we tried to repel tanks with the thrusts of our bamboo spears? We desired an end to the war, and we desired it desperately. And yet we cannot bring ourselves to admit it. Instead, propelled by some misplaced sense of what constitutes proper comportment, people claim we surrendered because the emperor ordered it. People speak about "bearing the unbearable." It is all part of the mechanism [*karakuri*] by which we delude ourselves. Is it not just one big, pitiful, disgraceful historical illusion that we are to perpetuate? And yet we do not recognize it as such. And the fact is that if it had not been for the emperor's command to end the war, we would have thrown ourselves against the tanks, disgusted with it all but still dying bravely, toppling over one after the other like so many wooden soldiers. The military

actually betrays the emperor while outwardly worshipping him. While we civilians are not as fervent in our worship of him, in much the same way we put him to good use, too. As we bask in the glory of his imperial dignity, we realize neither how cunning we are nor how sneaky is our use of conventional properties. The whole psychology is contrived and deceitful beyond all words. We were possessed by that hoax [*karakuri*] that history has produced, and because of it we have lost sight of what it means to be truly, authentically human.[23]

On the one hand, the emperor was always and already positioned outside of the whole *karakuri* and was utilized as a god or potential sacrificial victim. In fact, and this has long been the subject of a dispute since the war, there seems to have been a possibility that the emperor would be tried on account of his responsibility for the war by the International Military Tribunal for the Far East from 1946 to 1948. On the other hand, in order to preserve the whole *karakuri*, the people were, in fact, the victims. And by deceiving themselves, or rather without realizing such self-deception, the people existed in a *karakuri*.

How can we avoid such self-deception? Describing his own experiences in wartime, Ango indicates a possibility. It is the possibility of finding a root of humanity, and it means to fall outside of the *karakuri* at the same time. This possibility can also be that of the beginning of a conversion.

To Seek "Signs of Life"

> . . . the life was the light of men. And the light shineth in darkness.
> —*John 1:4–5*

During the Pacific War, Ango dared to stay in Tokyo. In a situation where he could be killed at any moment, or in a "colossal destruction" as he called it, he became conscious of life, whether it was his own or others.

> I imagined myself lying low in that shelter as the U.S. troops swept over Japan, spraying heavy artillery in all directions. I was resigned to that fate, readied myself for it. Still, as much as I realized I could very well die there,

I must also have been convinced that I would somehow make it through. It's not as if I had hopes and dreams for life as a survivor in the ruins. All I could think about was making it through alive. The curiosity I felt towards the coming miraculous rebirth in an unimaginable new world was by far the most striking emotion I've ever experienced.[24]

In contrast, many people were surprisingly indifferent to death: "Over on Dōgenzaka, itself now nothing more than a plain of whirling ash, lay a corpse covered with a sheet of corrugated steel, a casualty not of the bombing, it seemed, but a traffic accident. Over the corpse stood a soldier, his bayonet at the ready, while in both directions long, meandering lines of casualties stumbled by in a trance. Hardly a soul noticed the pool of blood on the road; the few who did paid it no more attention than they would a scrap of trash."[25]

There was a strict distinction between life and death, between the living and the dead. And it was only those who were alive that gave meaning to the world around them. The dead part of the world, including the dead, the heaps of rubble, and the ruins, whether they were from war damage or not, were given meaning as such by those who were alive. "People who had scrambled to safety through the raging fires would huddle together near a home that was starting to burn so as to warm themselves in the cold. They would be only a few feet away from others struggling to douse the flames, but these people would be in a different world entirely."[26] In Girard's theory, the victims of war are considered to be sacrifices of the system, but what is important here is that Ango himself, who experienced the war damage as described above, was a potential victim who might enter the dead part of the world at any moment, and the same was true for all those who survived the bombing. "Darakuron" can be read as the testimony of one of the potential victims.

This distinction between being part of the living or one of the dead has a radical function for us, and we can call this function "intentionality" in the sense that Husserl used it. Ango was strongly conscious of the distinction between "being alive and being dead" or of "life itself" as a root of the *karakuri*, or the reality in which we humans exist. This consciousness is radical in the sense that it is prior to the constructed *karakuri* or reality, and we can call this consciousness "a radical intentionality toward life." In the colossal destruction, Ango found both his own and the people's radical intentionality toward life:

> The Americans described the Japanese in the days after the defeat as relieved and psychologically exhausted, but the emotional state of the casualties marching through town in the wake of a bombing was something altogether different. They exhibited a settled, contented resignation that was startling; they were like children who unquestioningly accept their fate.[27]

"Suffer the little children to come unto me, and forbid them not: for of such is the kingdom of God. Verily I say unto you, Whosoever shall not receive the kingdom of God as a little child, he shall not enter therein" (Mark 10:14–15). In Girard's theory, the condition "as a little child" is interpreted as a condition uncontaminated by mimetic desire, outside the systems of sacrifice. "Massive destruction side-by-side with startling camaraderie. Grand destinies alongside surprising tenderness."[28] Through the destruction and destinies, the fact was discovered that humans could survive and would continue to live on, even outside the *karakuri*. Ango wrote of the destruction and destinies coexisting with camaraderie and tenderness because they took the people outside the *karakuri* or left them in the condition of "a little child."

The following text shows well both the people's and Ango's intentionality toward life.

> When you heard laughter, it was always the teenage girls, and their smiles were a real delight. You would see them sifting through the ruins, carrying in a charred bucket whatever dishes and cups they could salvage, or sunning themselves by the side of the road as they stood watch over a few measly pieces of luggage. What motivated these girls, all on the brink of womanhood? Maybe the misery of the moment faded in the face of their dreams for the future; maybe they were driven by a sense of pride. Either way, the one thing I looked forward to was discovering their smiles in the burnt-out ruins of the city.[29]

We will inevitably go against the *karakuri*, or *fall*, as long as we live as human beings. As described above, to find "signs of life" can be delightful. Ango discovered this fact during the war. But after the war, Ango came to think that he and those he found around him were far from authentically human. He described himself as being like "a little child" at times during the war.

> I quaked in fear, but I was enthralled by the beauty of the war raging around me. There was no need for me to think because I was surrounded by beauty, with everything human removed from the landscape. . . . Wartime Japan was an unbelievable idyllic utopia—the only problem is that the beauty that bloomed there was empty, false. It was not a truly human beauty. But as long as we didn't stop to think, wartime Japan offered a pleasing, grand spectacle that was hard to beat. Though the next bombing was a constant threat, if we could only push this from our minds, we were free to just sit back and lose ourselves in the drama of it all. I was a fool through the war, naively making a game of it.[30]

In one of his essays, titled "Bungaku no Furusato" (The Birthplace of Literature), he had written that "the birthplace is our cradle, but the mission of us adults is never to go back there." To get out of the condition of being "a little child" and to realize our mission as adults, in other words, not only "to be merely alive" but also to live "as humans," the people must reconstruct a new *karakuri*. And after the war, in "Darakuron" and "Zoku darakuron," Ango also explained what the relationship between the human condition and the *karakuri* should be. His intention is summarized in the words "to live, and to fall into decadence."[31] It was not until he experienced the conversion during the war that he could write these words, and the fact that he wrote these words itself indicates that his conversion had deepened after the war.

To Live, and to Fall into Decadence

> And the publican, standing afar off, would not lift up so much as his eyes unto heaven, but smote upon his breast, saying, God be merciful to me a sinner. I tell you, this man went down to his house justified.
> —*Luke 18:13–14*

"Darakuron" begins as follows:

> Six months pass and nothing seems the same. "We, the humble shields of our Sovereign Lord, march forth." "We are resigned to die at His Majesty's side and never look back." These young men, the *kamikaze*, did die, scattering like the cherry blossoms. Those who escaped with their lives, though, now hawk goods on the black market.
>
> "We dare not hope for long lives together. And yet we pledge ourselves to you who will one day sally forth as His Majesty's humble shields." It was with admirable commitment that these young women sent their men off to war. Six months later, though, they're only going through the motions as they kneel before their husband's mortuary tablets—and it won't be long before they've got their eye on somebody new. It's not people that have changed; they've been like this from the very start. What has changed is just the surface of things, the world's outer skin.[32]

As we saw in the last section, as long as we are alive, and true to the radical intentionality toward life, we humans will inevitably go against the *karakuri*. We humans have "been like this from the very start." But after the war, while "nothing seems the same," and while the new *karakuri* was being groped for, the condition of the ordinary people, even though it never changed essentially, was considered to have "fallen into decadence." Ango could not overlook this situation.

> People say that the morals of our countrymen have declined since Japan lost the war. That may indeed be the case. However, if the implication is that the "wholesome" morals of prewar Japan should be revived, or that we should deem those morals felicitous, then I would have to strenuously object.[33]

> Though I call for Japan's fall into decadence, I mean precisely the opposite. Today Japan and its modes of thought have sunk deep into a great decadence, and we must twist free of the so-called "wholesome morals," shaped as they are by the idiosyncratic cerebral machinations [*karakuri*] left over from the feudal era. We must stand naked on the vast plains of truth. It is by falling away from the "wholesome morals" that we must recover our true humanity.[34]

We should interpret the phrase "fall into decadence" as meaning to be true to the radical intentionality toward life, or to stand outside the *karakuri*. But in this sense, "humans cannot fall forever."[35]

> We've been granted all sorts of liberties since the end of the war but these have just called our attention to the unfathomable limitations and restraints of the human condition. Humans can never attain true freedom. The reason? We live, we're destined to die, and we think. Sure, political reforms can be enacted in a single day, but changing humankind isn't so easy.[36]

We cannot stand nihilism, and more than "being merely alive," we will always and already give meanings to the world around us. "Humans are pathetic, they're frail, they're laughable. All the same, they're simply too weak to fall to the very bottom."[37] Founded on such a human condition, a new history will begin, and it is the history which will be made by the Japanese or "real humans" who "have been born from the womb of all truth: decadence."[38]

This new history is that of humans' self-actualization, contrary to the old history, in which humans unconsciously actualize the *karakuri* by accepting the roles or positions they are given in it. Therefore, Ango was critical of discussions that insisted on redeeming the people only by reconstructing the *karakuri* as political or social systems.

> Politics and social systems cast only the coarsest of nets over the world, and humans are the type of fish that will forever slip through the holes. Even should we demolish that contrivance [*karakuri*] that is the emperor system and institute some new structure [*karakuri*] in its place; that, too, would be nothing more than a more highly evolved contrivance [*karakuri*]. While it is our fate to be forever trapped within this cycle, humans will always slip through the cracks. They will be decadent, and the systems will thereby get their comeuppance.[39]

For example, after the war, Shiga Naoya, who was called "a god of the novel," put forward a "re-education for returned soldiers," and Ozaki Gakudō, who was called "a god of politics," called for a "World Federation." Whether reactionary or progressive, Ango hated ideas that prioritized values systems over the human condition. Since the new *karakuri* that was given to the Japanese was even further from the human condition of the Japanese, the emperor system might have been better because, in a paradoxical way, at least it had its root in the mind of the Japanese, as we saw above. The new history will improve, repeating the pattern of decadence and construction. Every time apocalypse returns, opportunities to convert will also. "The most we can hope for are slow, incremental improvements."[40] As the *karakuri* becomes more suitable for the human condition of the Japanese, the human condition of the Japanese will become better. And in the course of time, the *karakuri* will be based not only on the human condition of the Japanese, but more radically on the human condition itself. To start such a new history, the Japanese "first must follow the path of decadence, falling properly and to the very bottom."[41] "Only by falling to the very depths" do we humans "discover ourselves" and thereby "attain salvation," or, in other words, become able to convert.[42]

"To live, and to fall into decadence"—in writing this famous phrase in the dark time soon after the war, Ango imagined such a new history for Japan.

To Be Catholic

> Go home to thy friends, and tell them how great things the Lord hath done for thee, and hath had compassion on thee.
> —*Mark 5:19*

In this section, I will examine Ango's thought, as I have introduced it so far, by comparing it with Girard's thought. There are two important points or problems. The first is whether or not Ango was what Girard calls a "romanticist" and his conversion also just a "romantic conversion," and the second is whether or not we should consider many kinds of conversions experienced outside the Christian context as Christian.

As to the first problem, Girard criticizes Heidegger's "romantic" attitude.[43] His attitude was based on an inauthentic and mimetic desire, and he excluded himself from the mimetic mechanism he discovered, though he was actually in it. Girard says, "Martin Heidegger believes that he stands apart from any mimetic influence from his social surrounding, with *Das Man*, that is the tagging along of all these people who believe and desire everything which is believed and desired around them. Therefore, in the moment in which everybody became Nazi around him, Heidegger became Nazi too."[44]

Furthermore, Girard also defines "an authentic conversion" as "a conversion in which you accept that you are part of the mimetic mechanism which rules human relationships, in which the observer acknowledges the fact that he himself is implicated in his observation."[45] In addition, about "a real individual" who experienced an authentic conversion, he wrote as follows: "Undoubtedly, from the perspective of the mimetic mechanism, which is also a Christian perspective, there is a real individual. This is one who goes against the crowd for reasons that aren't rooted in the negative aspects of mimetic desire. . . . The Christian individual contradicts the crowd; he or she doesn't join the multitude in the scapegoat resolution of the mimetic crisis."[46]

About "being an individual" or "being alone," Ango wrote,

> Decadence is, in and of itself, always a trifling, undesirable thing, but it does exhibit in an irrefutable manner a great truth about the human condition: each of us is alone. In other words, to be decadent is, always, to stand alone, to be abandoned by others, to be forsaken by parents. To be decadent is to accept a destiny where we have no choice but to stand on our own two feet. Being good puts us in a comfortable position, one that allows us to rest easy in the empty values and conventions shared by our families and the human race. It allows us to surrender ourselves, body and soul, to the social system and go to our graves peacefully. But he who pursues decadence is inevitably cast out of this circle to walk the desolate plains alone. Evil is a pretty pursuit, but the solitude it brings is a path to God. The following lines express precisely the same idea: "The good person attains birth in the Pure Land; how much more so the evil one." We see it again in Jesus as he prostrated himself at the feet of prostitutes. This act of respect was surely an acknowledgement of the fact that these women, too, travelled the desolate plains alone . . . it is this road alone that may lead to salvation.[47]

As a Christian, the real individual that Girard defines could imitate Christ. Ango himself was not a Christian, and we can hardly suppose that he appreciated the significance of such mimesis. Nevertheless, as seen in the passage above, it is clear that he had some sympathy with Christianity.[48] Furthermore, in "Darakuron" and "Zoku darakuron," what was at the center of Ango's concern was not to criticize what the Japanese were during the war; rather, he admitted that he himself was among them, as we saw above. Moreover, as we saw in the last section, if Ango criticized the idea of the reeducation of returning soldiers, it was because he could not overlook the fact that the returning soldiers were being positioned to be "in the wrong" or "evil" in a new *karakuri* or reality, and so he refused to side with those who persecuted them. In these aspects, Ango's conversion seems to have had much in common with the conversion Girard defines. And this is related to the answer to the second problem.

Simone Weil, to whom Girard often refers, wrote, "We have to be catholic" ("Il faut être catholic").[49] I think that we researchers on Girard's thought should take the catholicity of Christianity as indicating a conversion in the sense that Girard defines and seek it even in non-Christian periods or areas. Weil also tried to do so, motivated perhaps by this idea of catholicity. In the Gospel, the man possessed by demons was not allowed to be a disciple of Christ, but he was entrusted with the task of telling the others what happened to him (Mark 5:18–19). I myself, in a country far from Nazareth, based on notions of secularized conversions, study a conversion of a Japanese novelist and now, in return, am trying to reveal Christian or catholic principles at work in it. Indeed, as Girard says, it may be "much easier to recover biblical principles if one doesn't know they are biblical."[50]

Notes

All biblical quotations are taken from *The Holy Bible Containing the Old and New Testaments: King James Version* (Philadelphia: National Publishing Company, 1978).

1. I would like to make some comments on terminology employed in this essay. I considered using the term "depravity" instead of "decadence" to translate "daraku" in Japanese into English, because the former has a theological connotation, in particular, that of original sin. However, in the study of Ango, it is better to use "decadence" because Ango himself uses that term, for example, in the title of one of his essays, "Dekadan Bungakuron" (On Decadent Literature).

However, the difference in connotations of the term "decadence" between the West and Japan is problematic. I cannot comment in detail on the difference here, but I point out that the connotation of the term "decadence" in Japanese, at least in the way Ango used it—though in a paradoxical way, as shown later in this essay—is not so far from that of "depravity."

2. William James, *The Varieties of Religious Experience* (New York: Modern Library, 1936), 187–253.

3. Bernard Lonergan, *Method in Theology* (Toronto: University of Toronto Press, 1994), 237–44.

4. Georg Wilhelm Friedrich Hegel, *Grundlinien der Philosophie des Rechts* (Frankfurt am Main: Suhrkamp, 1965), 24. My translation.

5. Ango pointed out that the mind or reason of the Japanese worked as some kind of convention in a distorted way. In many of his works, he criticized Japanese culture from this point of view. Regarding this point, see Karatani Kōjin, "The Irrational Will to Reason: The Praxis of Sakaguchi Ango," in *Literary Mischief: Sakaguchi Ango, Culture, and the War*, ed. James Dorsey and Doug Slaymaker, trans. James Dorsey (Lanham, MD: Lexington Books, 2010), 23–33.

6. Ango Sakaguchi, "Discourse on Decadence" (Darakuron, 1946), trans. James Dorsey, in *Literary Mischief*, 178. Subsequent English quotations and citations of both "Discourse on Decadence" (Darakuron, 1946) and "Discourse on Decadence Part II" (Zoku darakuron, 1946) are from the translations in *Literary Mischief*, with some amendments and adaptation.

7. Ango, "Discourse on Decadence," 178.
8. Ibid., 176.
9. Ibid., 177.
10. Ibid., 176–77.
11. Ibid., 177.
12. Ibid.
13. Ibid.
14. Ibid.
15. Ibid.
16. Ibid., 178.
17. Ibid.
18. Ibid.
19. Ango, "Discourse on Decadence Part II," 190.
20. Ibid.
21. Ibid., 191.
22. Ango, "Discourse on Decadence," 178.
23. Ango, "Discourse on Decadence Part II," 191. The bracketed terms ([*karakuri*]) in quotations are my interpolation.

24. Ango, "Discourse on Decadence," 179.
25. Ibid., 180.
26. Ibid., 181.
27. Ibid., 180.
28. Ibid., 181.
29. Ibid., 180–81.
30. Ibid., 182.
31. Ibid., 181.
32. Ibid., 175.
33. Ango, "Discourse on Decadence Part II," 187.
34. Ibid., 192.
35. Ango, "Discourse on Decadence," 182.
36. Ibid.
37. Ibid.
38. Ibid., 181.
39. Ibid., 194.
40. Ibid., 195.
41. Ibid., 182.
42. Ibid., 182–83.
43. René Girard, with Pierpaolo Antonello and João Cezar de Castro Rocha, *Evolution and Conversion: Dialogues on the Origins of Culture* (London: T & T Clark, 2007), 45–46.
44. Ibid.
45. Ibid., 45.
46. Ibid., 239.
47. Ango, "Discourse on Decadence Part II," 192–93.
48. Ango studied the history of Christians in Japan (*kirishitan*) and wrote an essay titled "Inochigake" (Life on the Line). In it he wrote about the fact that those who executed martyrs themselves converted to Christianity because they were moved or impressed deeply watching martyrs killed without any resistance from them. Therefore, it seems that Ango at least had some ideas about what it is like to imitate Christ.
49. Simone Weil, *Waiting on God*, trans. Emma Craufurd (London: Fontana Books, 1959), 61; *Attente de Dieu* (Paris: Fayard, 1977), 104.
50. Girard, *Evolution and Conversion*, 257.

CHAPTER 8

LIVING IN A STATE OF ABANDONMENT

The Anime Vexille's *Supplementary Apocalypse*

ANDREAS OBERPRANTACHER

> Die Katastrophe ist nicht kritisierbar (The catastrophe cannot be criticized).
>
> —*Bertolt Brecht,* Kleines Organon für das Theater

The Surplus of Humanity

In an essay titled "Abandoned Being" that was first published in 1981, Jean-Luc Nancy explores the ontological implications of the notion of "abandonment" by asserting that "abandoned being has already begun to constitute an inevitable condition for our thought, perhaps its only condition,"[1] and, a few pages later, that "our time—our epoch—is more than ever the time of time, the time of the temporal ontology of abandonment."[2] What he is possibly referring to when stressing that abandonment is not just a general predicament of being among others, but "the sole predicament of being,"[3] and, indeed, the very condition of our being in these times, gains in plausibility when considering that according to

Nancy, the authority of transcendentals has come to an end. This is to say that the onto-theological regime of the *unum, verum,* and *bonum* (unity, truth, and goodness) has lost its binding force as well as its persuasive charm. And in the course of this loss, being finds itself exposed at the limits of what was once called History. Not least in this sense, the syntagma "apocalyptic loneliness" is a matching proposition for what may have driven Nancy's thoughts at the time of writing: a philosophically nuanced sensation of living at the limits of historical time—a sensation for which Friedrich Nietzsche once had reserved the term "nihilism."

Of particular importance, yet, for what will follow next—as an illustrated effort to chart what it may mean to be abandoned—is Nancy's subsequent remark that there is no abandonment, if not (also) in legal terms. Or, as he prefers to put it, "One always abandons to a law."[4] This is to say that according to Nancy, abandonment is a state, a state of being that does not just occur, but that remains obliged to what is capable of putting being at *bandon*. Inasmuch as the word "*bandon*" reminds the abandoned of a power that continues to strike and to banish (*bandits*)[5] at the limits of law, according to Nancy being abandoned means to be "turned over to the absolute of the law . . . [and] thereby [to be] abandoned completely outside its jurisdiction."[6] In Nancy's words that rank prominently in contemporary political theory, "Abandoned being finds itself deserted to the degree that it finds itself remitted, entrusted, or thrown to this law that constitutes the law, this other and same, to this other side of all law that borders and upholds a legal universe: an absolute, solemn order, which prescribes nothing but abandonment. Being is not entrusted to a cause, to a motor, to a principle; it is not left to its own substance, or even to its own subsistence. It is—in abandonment."[7] One is left to wonder if it is a mere coincidence or what one may rather call a *constellation* with Walter Benjamin, but considering Mike Davis's arguments in *Planet of Slums*—a book that was first published in 2006 and a fine example of how sociological expertise can be combined with a pronounced political sensibility—Nancy's essay from 1981 may also be read as a philosophical, more precisely, as a left-Heideggerian figuration of what is, in political-economic terms, the consequence of the "brutal tectonics of neoliberal globalization since 1978."[8] Along the lines of Davis's book, it becomes quite possible to argue, in fact, that Nancy's essay, dedicated to exploring abandoned being, is proposing itself as if it was a cautious, early consideration of the growing slumification (and progressive desertification) of the world too, of what living in a slum and thus being abandoned at the cognitive outskirts of political modernity might amount to in philosophical terms—being at the mercy of economic laws that do not constitute any kind of jurisdiction and thus do not guarantee democratic accountability.

Furthermore, it is crucial to be aware that slums are no marginal phenomenon, as Davis contends in the context of a wide mass of empirical data. On the contrary, "Since 1970, slum growth everywhere in the South has outpaced urbanization *per se*,"[9] that is, slums have become a space sui generis, a space where, as Davis puts it in his epilogue, a "surplus humanity" is managed.[10] Whereas Hernando de Soto Polar, a Peruvian economist in favor of radically liberal models, has argued—by inverting Marx's dictum—that those living in slums are practically "oppressed extralegal small *entrepreneurs*,"[11] and Michael Mutter, a senior advisor for the UN Habitat Program, has further suggested in downright absurd terms that slums should be conceived as Strategic Low-Income Urban Management Systems,"[12] Davis maintains to the contrary and in quite apocalyptic terms that

> the cities of the future, rather than being made out of glass and steel as envisioned by earlier generations of urbanists, are instead largely constructed out of crude brick, straw, recycled plastic, cement blocks, and scrap wood. Instead of cities of light soaring toward heaven, much of the twenty-first-century urban world squats in squalor, surrounded by pollution, excrement, and decay. Indeed, the one billion city dwellers who inhabit postmodern slums might well look back with envy at the ruins of the sturdy mud homes of Çatal Hüyük in Anatolia, erected at the very dawn of city life nine thousand years ago.[13]

Otherwise stated, it is as if the city and, with it, the promise of a good life in the city, is exposed to and haunted by not only the human-made devastation of war, of nuclear attacks, and of radioactive fallout, and by visible events of extremely aggressive rivalry; but also, as these events' sinister supplement, perhaps, by the (contagious) agony of lives lived in sheer misery and deprivation—daily catastrophes in slow motion, which for many too many result in a precarious life consumed in a state of abandonment.

A Japanese anime that has recently presented images of slums by condensing them into a tremendous biopolitical sci-fi epos is *Vexille*. In this essay, I will pose and propose the following questions: whether or in what sense this anime gives an account of a bloodless apocalypse that is unfolding at the margins of humanity and at the limits of the audience's attention; how it could be related to contemporary configurations and analyses of biopolitical governance; and what its potential use-value for a critical reevaluation of Girard's warning of the risk of a lasting sacrificial crisis may be.

Vexille as a Biopolitical Paradigm

In *Vexille*—a 2007 Japanese anime written and directed by Fumihiko Sori,[14] with Haruka Handa as the co-author[15]—the audience is fast-forwarded to a future approximately seventy years distant from the movie's release date. We are in the year 2077, and Japan presents itself as a country in "splendid isolation." After the United Nations had declared a unilateral ban on all further robotic research in 2067, following a growing concern about the possibly adverse impacts of cybernetics, Japan, which was at the forefront of robotics and home of the mighty conglomerate Daiwa Heavy Industry,[16] decided to opt out from the United Nations, to withdraw from international politics, to deport all foreigners, to prohibit immigration, and to establish the network R.A.C.E.—an energy grid comprising almost three hundred ocean-based antennas capable of neutralizing all communication with the outside, thus making electronic surveillance impossible. Otherwise stated, the anime suggests that in the near future Japan will decide once again to practice *sakoku*,[17] to exist just for itself, to be its own law.

The story unfolds about ten years after the beginning of Japan's effective isolationism, when the special military unit SWORD of the United Nations Navy is ordered to capture Saito, a Japanese informant working for Daiwa, following a mysterious tip-off by an anonymous source. Despite SWORD's surprise incursion, Saito manages to avoid being captured by means of a spectacular escape, in the course of which he is forced to cut off one of his legs. As subsequent analyses of the limb reveal, Saito consists, at least in part, of biometal, which makes him a technologically enhanced posthuman android and, according to a United Nations officer's evaluation, a "threat rivaling nuclear technology."

As a matter of fact, SWORD was suspecting all along that Japan had silently continued its research on and development of banned biotechnology. In order to gather more reliable information on what is actually happening in Japan, an officially unauthorized mission to infiltrate the secluded country is launched with the goal "to expose the true face of Japan" by transmitting a special signal from the inside capable of disrupting the protective energy grid so that the United Nations may eventually monitor the situation. Even though the SWORD agents manage successfully to get beyond the R.A.C.E. grid, they are soon discovered by security forces and thus blocked from completely transmitting the disruptive signal. While the female agent Vexille, the leading character of the anime, manages to get away by jumping into the open sea, the rest of her team is killed in a massive shootout, apart from Leon, Vexille's lover, who is arrested and brought to Daiwa's headquarters as a prisoner.

What follows next brings us right into the heart of the story and back to the main concern of this essay. After being saved by Japanese locals, Vexille awakens in what turns out to be the "true face" of Tokyo in the year 2077. She awakens not in a prosperous, avant-garde megacity, but in a colossal slum that is surrounded by massive walls and whose inhabitants are all ruled by Daiwa—with the exception of a small resistance movement headed by a female partisan called Maria. It is Maria, then, who successfully uses Vexille's backup transmitter to broadcast the distortion frequency and shares the details of what has happened in the last ten years, while the surveying United Nations officers are shocked to learn that Japan had become a dystopic wasteland, or, as one might put it with Davis, a future Kinshasa (in the Congo), that is, "a vast city where the formal economy and state institutions apart from the repressive apparatus, have utterly collapsed."[18]

As the audience is told, Japan started becoming a wasteland after an unknown disease that was secretly engineered and spread by Daiwa had struck the population. Even though the initial interest of Daiwa was not that of harming the Japanese population, the engineered disease was nevertheless meant to provoke a situation in which it became practically possible for the corporation to introduce a vaccine that was a nanotechnological experiment in disguise. Instead of offering a cure from the disease, the vaccine began turning one Japanese citizen after the other into a consenting synthetic life-form. Yet the nanotechnological experiment was still in a beta stage, thus creating unforeseen side effects: in place of a smooth conversion from organic to synthetic life, the infected humans slowly started to mutate into lifelike machines and run amok, eventually generating the Jags, monstrous accumulations of semi-sentient biometal that roam through the open wastelands and devour everything that has not yet mutated. The only secure space left on the islands of Japan in 2077 is Tokyo, a slum sheltered by an inedible wall made of ceramic, that is, an ultramodern Thebes in a permanent state of exception.

In the final part of *Vexille*, the resistance movement around Maria devises a plan to lure the Jags over a service bridge into the middle of Tokyo Bay where the corporate headquarters of Daiwa are located. But the plan fails, and both the partisan Maria and the agent Vexille are captured and taken to the corporation's criminal mastermind, Kisaragi. As it happens, Kisaragi, who devised the biotechnological experiment, is already planning to repeat it in America in order to make Daiwa the new global hegemon. Following a surprise knife attack with which Vexille wounds Kisaragi, it becomes evident that his blood is still human and that he therefore had not undergone the very biotechnological process designed to enhance all other people's lives. In the grand finale, the town council of Tokyo decides to open its ceramic gates in order to let the Jags devour their way through the city and right into Daiwa's headquarters. Kisaragi, who manages to survive an attack of the infuriated Saito, tries to escape, but eventually Maria stops and immobilizes him until a Jag destroys them both. Just as the Daiwa headquarters begin collapsing into Tokyo Bay and Japan is finally turned into an absolutely lifeless space, Vexille and Leon are rescued by a SWORD helicopter. The anime ends with the somewhat conciliatory (and concealing) comment that in spite of all the destruction witnessed, humanity may still gain eternal existence as long as hope is passed on to the next generation.

Lives That "May Be Killed and Yet Not Sacrificed"?
Crossing Girard with Agamben

What makes *Vexille* an anime that is worth being discussed, in the context of a conference dedicated to revisit and thus to carefully commemorate narratives of the apocalypse, is perhaps less its all-too-obvious apocalyptic configuration—a configuration that is characteristic for a wide variety of Japanese anime and manga, and certainly not for *Vexille* alone.[19] Rather, it is the anime's preference to visualize a catastrophic situation that presents some features that exceed the more prevalent scenarios of a future nuclear cataclysm—insofar as the catastrophic situation in the anime *Vexille* is not just screened as a violent explosion (or an explosion of violence), but also as a biopolitical experiment that unfolds its devastating effects in slow-motion, as a violent contagion. This is to say that apart from the scenes and episodes of extreme violence that are very much structuring the storyline of *Vexille* from the beginning to the (oneiric) end, and apart from the overtly collective violence that is directed first against the limping informant Saito and later against the evil mastermind Kisaragi (in a certain sense Saito's alter ego), the movie confronts us with violence also in a further, that is, in a supplementary sense. In other words, quite evidently *Vexille* reproduces the "typical" mimetic scenario where overlapping rivalries (Japan/the United Nations; Tokyo/Daiwa; human Kisaragi/android Saito, etc.) are subsequently intensified, condensed in a generalized crisis, and finally "resolved" by a double sacrificial gesture: by the sacrifice of the evil scapegoat Kisaragi and by that of the brave Maria, who has to give her life in order to veil the truth or, better, to re-mystify the scapegoat mechanism. But besides that, the anime *Vexille* also visualizes Tokyo as a colossal slum and its inhabitants as deprived dwellers subsisting without promise in a state of dire abandonment at the threshold of life and death. Certainly, in the midst of the mimetic rivalries that are unfolding their blind(ing) force in *Vexille*, Tokyo is bound to succumb. But does this mean that all the nameless slum dwellers are being sacrificed (violently)? Is the violence directed against the slum dwellers sacrificial in nature, or is it rather the by-product of a generalized sacrificial crisis?

In order to discuss this question within a more discrete theoretical framework, let me return to the beginning of my essay and quote again Nancy's remark that being abandoned to a law means to be "abandoned completely outside law's jurisdiction." In fact, it is precisely this remark that builds one of the, if not *the*, cornerstone of Giorgio Agamben's treatise *Homo Sacer*—a treatise that is serious about the assumption that what may be referred to as "bare life" in the history of political thought[20] is a life that "*may be killed and yet not sacrificed*,"[21] that is, a life that is both unworthy of being saved *and* unworthy of being sacrificed. Because, as Agamben puts it, the "relation of exception [by which 'bare life' is included in the political realm] is a relation of ban. He who has been banned is not, in fact, simply set outside the law and made indifferent to it but rather *abandoned* by it, that is, exposed and threatened on the threshold in which life and law, outside and inside, become indistinguishable. It is literally not possible to say whether the one who has been banned is outside or inside the juridical order."[22] Put otherwise, it is as if life is at the mercy of a violence that is both devastating and unaccountable, once it has been separated from its (civil) form and set aside from a political community by operations of exception, that is, once it presents itself as bare and abandoned. According to Agamben, the "limit sphere of human action" that is created by such relations of exception—for which a variety of contemporary examples can be given[23]—may be understood "as an excrescence of the profane in the religious and of the religious in the profane, which takes the form of a zone of indistinction between sacrifice and homicide. *The sovereign sphere is the sphere in which it is permitted to kill without committing homicide and without celebrating a sacrifice, and sacred life—that is, life that may be killed but not sacrificed—is the life that has been captured in this sphere.*"[24] Or, to express it in a slightly more tangible sense, not least with regard to the anime *Vexille*: slumlike conditions do not just conjure mimetic crises in the sense of making such crises more likely due to the social distress that such conditions of deprivation create. Rather, it is slums that may be understood as "biopolitical zones of indistinction" into which people that are of no evident use for the postindustrial knowledge industries are relegated, that is, left aside.

In this respect, it is quite revealing, for example, that Paul Romer, professor of economics at New York University and a likely Nobel Prize candidate in economics, has devised the idea that so-called developing countries should pass laws with which a tract of land for new Charter

Cities can be set aside so that these cities may eventually be managed by a powerful third-party guarantor.[25] What Romer envisions (along with others) amounts basically to a new political topography of aggregated, heteronomous zones, a topography that comes quite close to Agamben's analyses of contemporary biopolitics insofar as such Charter Cities are projected as extraterritorial spaces governed by means of sovereign and almost unaccountable decisions.[26] Moreover, this visionary topography also comes close to Davis's critique of how the subcontracted networks of major corporations (that are usually aligned with third-party guarantor states) "extend deep into the misery of the *colonias* and *chawls*."[27] Put differently, what *Vexille* visualizes as a dystopic future, as an apocalypse to-come, is already be-coming, even though it is hardly noticed because it does not present itself as an explosive event.

Where does this leave *us*, in the context of this illustrated discussion of the anime *Vexille*? What I would like to suggest in the form of a tentative hypothesis is that René Girard's concept of the "sacrificial crisis" might be linked to Agamben's theorem of a life that "may be killed and yet not sacrificed," that is, of a multitude of lives abandoned in a "zone of indistinction," insofar as it is precisely the "sacrificial crisis [that] can be defined," according to Girard, "as a crisis of distinctions—that is, a crisis affecting the cultural order."[28] More precisely, as Girard argues in *Violence and the Sacred*, the sacrificial crisis "coincides with the disappearance of the difference between impure violence and purifying violence. When this difference has been effaced, purification is no longer possible and impure, contagious, reciprocal violence spreads throughout the community."[29] If one further concedes, as does Girard, that there is no guarantee that "the unanimous violence directed against the surrogate victim" will eventually "succeed" and solve the sacrificial crisis,[30] it becomes quite possible to maintain, with Agamben, that we have become used to arranging our lives in a lasting crisis,[31] and that

> the birth of the camp in our time appears as an event that decisively signals the political space of modernity itself. It is produced at the point at which the political system of the modern nation-state, which was founded on the functional nexus between a determinate localization (land) and a determinate order (the State) and mediated by automatic rules for the

inscription of life (birth or the nation), enters into a lasting crisis, and the
State decides to assume directly the care of the nation's biological life as one
of its proper tasks. . . . The camp as dislocating localization is the hidden
matrix of the politics in which we are still living, and it is this structure of
the camp that we must learn to recognize in all its metamorphoses into the
zones d'attentes of our airports and certain outskirts of our cities [as well as
in slums or in Charter Cities].[32]

Insofar as we may indeed speak of a lasting (sacrificial) crisis that is still redefining the violence in the political space of modernity and, even more so, of these days, when the state progressively cedes its powers to non-state actors, it becomes indeed imperative to question and perhaps also to reassess the prevalent focus on typical scapegoat mechanisms. Couldn't it be the case that the preference for the scapegoat—not just in terms of a historical mechanism to overcome sacrificial crises—but also in terms of a genuine epistemological preference, of a mimetic desire prevalent among scholars, may distort one's critical attention and sensibility to the extent that one hardly notices all the excessive violence that is not bound and structured by mimetic rivalry? And is not also the anime *Vexille* perhaps to be viewed and understood as a paradigmatic example of how the main storyline of the anime is not only concealing the truth of the scapegoat mechanism, but even more so, that of the bloodless, nonsacrificial biopolitical violence invested in the very slumification of Tokyo—which is nothing but a euphemistic image of the actual desertification of the contemporary world?

In this sense, then, I would like to express my worries that what is called (and sometimes revered as) "apocalypse" is not necessarily an *event* that might or will unfold in the future, but more likely another name for an undifferentiated violence that perhaps has always been unfolding at the limits of history—and also at the limits of *our* attention, which is usually focused on mimetic rivalries. If the scapegoat is truly the "work" of mimetic rivalry, that is, the *ergon* of mimetic theory, it might be of help to consider what Jacques Derrida has said about the *parergon*,[33] the supplement or after-work: "A parergon comes against, beside, and in addition to the *ergon*, the work done [*fait*], the fact [*le fait*], the work, but it does not fall to one side, it touches and cooperates within the operation, from a certain outside. Neither simply outside nor simply inside. Like an accessory that one is obliged to welcome on the border, on board [*au bord, à bord*]. It is first of all the on (the) bo(a)rd(er) [*Il est d'abord l'à-bord*]."³⁴ In similar terms, we should be aware that there is a surplus violence, which is not the immediate result of mimetic desire, but rather the devastating by-product of states of undifferentiation that cannot be contained by sacrificial mechanisms (anymore). Very much like Derrida's explication of the *parergon*, such violence is neither simply outside nor is it simply inside mimetic rivalry. Rather, it is the tremendous excrescence of a lasting sacrificial crisis that is redefining the contemporary state of affairs—an excrescence that does not fall aside but that should provoke our sensibility.

Notes

1. Jean-Luc Nancy, "Abandoned Being," in *The Birth to Presence*, trans. Brian Holmes (Stanford, CA: Stanford University Press, 1993), 36.
2. Ibid., 41–42.
3. Ibid., 36.
4. Ibid., 44.
5. As Giorgio Agamben remarks in *Homo Sacer*, the "life of the bandit, like that of the sacred man, is not a piece of animal nature without any relation to law and the city. It is, rather, a threshold of indistinction and of passage between animal and man, *physis* and *nomos*, exclusion and inclusion: the life of the bandit is the life of the *loup garou*, the werewolf, who is precisely neither man nor beast and who dwells paradoxically within both while belonging to neither." Giorgio Agamben, *Homo Sacer: Sovereign Power and Bare Life*, trans. Daniel Heller-Roazen (Stanford, CA: Stanford University Press, 1998), 104–5.
6. Nancy, "Abandoned Being," 44.
7. Ibid., 44.
8. Mike Davis, *Planet of Slums* (London: Verso, 2006), 174.
9. Ibid., 17.
10. Ibid., 201. And let us not forget Zygmunt Bauman's book, *Wasted Lives: Modernity and Its Outcasts* (Cambridge: Polity Press, 2004).
11. Davis, *Planet of Slums*, 179.
12. Ibid.
13. Ibid., 19.

14. To anime aficionados, Sori is well-known for having produced *Appleseed* (2004), an anime based on the manga of the same title created by Masamune Shirow.

15. Before co-scripting *Vexille*, Handa had written the screenplay of the aforementioned anime *Appleseed*.

16. Daiwa means "Great Harmony" or "Great Japan."

17. For a better understanding of Japan's *sakoku* politics in the sixteenth century, see Michael S. Laver, *The Sakoku Edicts and the Politics of Tokugawa Hegemony* (Amherst, MA: Cambria Press, 2011).

18. Davis, *Planet of Slums*, 19.

19. Apocalyptic scenarios are extremely frequent in Japanese manga and anime. See, for example, *Future Boy Conan* (1978), based on Alexander Key's novel *The Incredible Tide* (1970); *Hokuto no Ken* (Fist of the North Star, 1983–1988); or *Neon Genesis Evangelion* (1994–2013).

20. See Hannah Arendt, *The Origins of Totalitarianism* (New York: Harcourt, 1951), 54; Walter Benjamin, "Critique of Violence," in *Walter Benjamin: Selected Writings*, ed. Marcus Bullock and Michael W. Jennings, vol. 1, *1913–1926* (Cambridge, MA: Harvard University Press, 2002), 250.

21. Agamben, *Homo Sacer*, 8.

22. Ibid., 28–29.

23. For example, Judith Butler, "Indefinite Detention," in her *Precarious Life: The Powers of Mourning and Violence* (London: Verso, 2006), 50–100.

24. Agamben, *Homo Sacer*, 83.

25. What some thought would remain an idea has only recently been turned into practical politics: Honduras decided to adopt Romer's vision and to create four Charter Cities. See Annie Bird, "Privately Owned 'Charter Cities' in Honduras: Entire Urban Areas Handed over to Corporations: From Neo-Liberalism to Neo-Colonialism," *GlobalResearch*, September 15, 2012, http://www.globalresearch.ca/privately-owned-charter-cities-in-honduras-entire-urban-areas-handed-over-to-corporations/5304672 (accessed November 4, 2012).

26. The concept for Charter Cities outlined by Paul Romer consistently avoids the term "law" and instead prefers to speak of "rules" and "norms" by which such cities shall be governed. Also, it suggests that instead of having elections to select local leaders, a charter city "could allow for the type of governance used at the central bank; the central government could appoint a leader and specify a clear mandate. It could hold the executive leader accountable through the threat of removal or refusal of reappointment. The executive would have wide discretion in the day-to-day decision making that is necessary to fulfill the mandate. If the central government created cities of both types, it would be

interesting to see which type of city attracted more residents." See "Charter Cities," http://chartercities.org/home (accessed November 4, 2012).

27. Davis, *Planet of Slums*, 178.

28. René Girard, *Violence and the Sacred* (London: Continuum Books, 2005), 51–52.

29. Ibid., 51.

30. Ibid., 98.

31. Girard seems to support a historical reading of the risk that the sacrificial crisis may become lasting when he explicitly refers to the "increasingly aggravated state of undifferentiation that marks our present situation." René Girard, *Things Hidden Since the Foundation of the World*, trans. Stephen Bann and Michael Metteer (London: Continuum Books, 2003), 359.

32. Agamben, *Homo Sacer*, 174–75.

33. Interestingly, Agamben defines "paradigm" in quite analogous terms: "The paradigm is neither universal nor particular, neither general nor individual, it is a singularity which, showing itself as such, produces a new ontological context. This is the etymological meaning of the word "paradigm" in Greek, paradigme is literally 'what shows itself beside.' Something is shown beside, 'para.'" Giorgio Agamben, "What Is a Paradigm?" Lecture at European Graduate School, Saas-Fee, Switzerland, August 2002, http://www.egs.edu/faculty/giorgio-agamben/articles/what-is-a-paradigm (accessed November 4, 2012).

34. Jacques Derrida, "Parergon," in *Truth in Painting*, trans. Geoffrey Bennington and Ian McLeod (Chicago: University of Chicago Press, 1987), 54.

CHAPTER 9

SUBCULTURE, CONFORMITY, AND SACRIFICE

Kamikaze Girls *through a Mimetic Lens*

MATTHEW TAYLOR

Kamikaze Girls is the rather inapt English title for the 2004 youth movie *Shimotsuma Monogatari* (Shimotsuma Story), directed by Tetsuya Nakashima and based on the offbeat novel by Novala Takemoto.[1] Though the novel is fairly insubstantial, Nakashima transforms the material into a film of unexpected textural and thematic depth. It is an outrageously inventive film—a hilarious yet affectionate social satire, a poignant depiction of youthful angst and Japanese subcultures, and an interesting chronicle of postbubble Japan at the turn of the millennium. The film jumps wildly through various social strata, frenetically mixing numerous film and TV genres, blurring fantasy and reality, and constantly intruding on itself with jarring sight gags, lowbrow sound effects, and blatant self-references. Yet surprisingly, the audience does not suspend belief in the overall narrative arch of the film and develops a great deal of sympathy for the two main characters Momoko (Kyoko Fukada) and Ichigo (Anna Tsuchiya), who are highly unique film characterizations in their own right.

The future of *Kamikaze Girls* seems assured as a cult classic, both in Japan and among Japanophiles abroad. For that reason, however, the film is unlikely to garner broader attention outside of Japan, which is unfortunate. While the film's fans have valorized it as a paean to nonconformity and missed some of its key insights, most of the global film audience will simply never see *Kamikaze Girls* because it sits in an obscure youth movie bracket. In addition, many of the film's contemporary references are fading from cultural memory, even in Japan, while Lolita fashion (the raison d'être of Momoko's existence), already a tiny subculture when the movie was released, has an even more reduced presence today. Yet *Kamikaze Girls* is a significant film. Before it fades further into critical oblivion, it would be worthwhile to take stock of it from a mimetic perspective. For all its comic exaggeration, *Kamikaze Girls* is a frank and perceptive exploration of imitation and subcultural identities. Surprising for an oddball comedy, the film also evolves into a substantive treatment of scapegoating, myth, and sacrifice.

Momoko and Ichigo adopt their respective Lolita and *yanki* (delinquent) identities through a series of mediating influences. Ironically, if unsurprisingly, their defiant antisocial incarnations entail scrupulous conformity in language, manners, clothing, musical preferences, and the like. However, Momoko's Lolita fashion is escapist and sets her off as utterly different from her mundane peers. Ichigo's *yanki* identity, by contrast, is not for the sake of escapism but truly a means of escape. Ichigo was saved from merciless bullying in school through her association with a biker girl gang.

The anthropological insights of the film intensify toward the end. Ichigo is marked for scapegoating again, this time by the biker gang itself. Her victimization is intended to forge unity between two biker gangs. A dubious urban legend of Himiko is invoked by the gang leader, and the scene is sacralized by an enormous Buddha (a local landmark) placidly standing in the background. The sacred artifact clearly evokes the opening scenes of Stanley Kubrick's *2001: A Space Odyssey* (1968), connecting the power politics of the biker gang with human and cultural origins.[2] In a dangerous act of self-sacrifice, Momoko intervenes, brazenly writing herself into the Himiko legend in an attempt to rescue her friend. *Kamikaze Girls* builds an unmistakably sacrificial momentum but develops an overall vision that is strongly anti-sacrificial.

Clothing and Ubiquitous Subcultures

The omnipresence of subcultures is observed from the very first scenes of *Kamikaze Girls*, and the observation never lets up. Virtually every character in the film is a caricature, and hardly any character appears who does not clearly belong to some distinct subculture. Through Momoko's clothing-obsessed eyes, it becomes equally clear that each subculture has its own self-enforced dress code.

The film's cryptic opening shows a feral girl biker gang in an animated clip, soon followed (in Momoko's dreamy fantasy of the life she should have lived) by scenes of ornately dressed, hedonistic denizens of eighteenth-century Versailles, which Momoko claims as inspiration for her "rococo" philosophy. The next scene shows Shimotsuma, source of the story's Japanese title, the dull, nondescript rural town where Momoko is fated to live. Locals dress themselves in modest, inexpensive clothes from the huge retail chain and stop mid-dialogue to strike modeling poses, the prices flashed beside them as in newspaper ads. The "normal" residents of Shimotsuma thus comprise their own peculiar subculture. In a continuing series of jarring transitions and jump cuts, Momoko proceeds to review her life (appearing suddenly as a mini-documentary on a train station TV). Momoko was born not in Shimotsuma but far away in Amagasaki, a city in the Kansai area stereotyped as a den of gangsters, low-life delinquents, and counterfeiters. Momoko describes it as Tracksuit Country, where everyone is born and dies in a tracksuit.

Thus, in the first minutes of the film at least four distinct subcultures have been presented, each with its own uniform, and a number of finer subcategories are implied even in Momoko's old neighborhood: *yanki*, ex-*yanki*, pushy mobs of housewives converging on counterfeiters' stalls, gangsters, aspiring gangsters transitioning from *yanki* to gangster (like Momoko's father), and gaudily overdressed bar hostesses (like Momoko's mother). Even students, with their mandated uniforms, self-organize into distinct sub-subcultures (not infrequently by modifying the uniform), like the hearty athletic girls and intimidating *yanki*s, both of whom Momoko disdains.

In middle school, Momoko joins an embroidery circle, another subculture; it is Momoko's first step in escaping into a world of daintiness and away from her raucous milieu. Later, Momoko's favorite boutique is also depicted as comprising its own subculture of flowery, soft-spoken employees dressed in the shop's Lolita outfits. Another subculture is Ichigo's favorite haunt, the ubiquitous pachinko parlors (arcades for a kind of Japanese pinball) full of slovenly compulsive gamblers.

Momoko's Lolita identity is born out of a desire to transcend the dreary conformity of the world in general and her disreputable background in particular. The longing for transcendence is presented literally: several times Momoko is shown floating up into the sky in a dreamy reverie. Her mother is an overwrought coquette who abandons her family to run off with the gynecologist who brought Momoko to birth. Her father is a failed gangster, too softhearted to be a hit man but wildly and unexpectedly successful as a counterfeiter. By slapping the Versach (Versace) label on a number of garish goods, he inadvertently creates his own brand appeal; the fake Versach items become the genuine article, highly sought after by *yanki*. He combines clashing counterfeit labels (Versach and Universal Stadium) into even more popular products, until he is threatened with legal action by the offended brands and the ire of the gangsters who have been sponsoring his fakes.

Momoko and her father go into hiding and end up living in the home of Momoko's grandmother in Shimotsuma. Momoko's father is thus a social reject rejected by social rejects. Nevertheless, his failure as a hit man indicates relative success as a human being. Though Momoko continually calls him *dame oyaji* (useless father), she chooses to live with him rather than her mother. She inherits important traits from him: a knack for design, an untapped reserve of empathy, and a dormant capacity for fierceness when in dire need.

Her father's leftover Versach goods remain in the story, having become highly valued collector's items. The gaudy counterfeits establish a dialectic concerning imitation and authenticity that extends to Momoko's much more artful embrace of Lolita fashion (and Tokyo's highly influential street fashion in general). At a certain level of brazen audacity, the derivative becomes original; the dazzling fake becomes the real thing. Proof of this in real life can be seen with the aesthetic of Lolita fashion itself. Though reverently modeled on eighteenth-century Versailles, it has been embraced with wild enthusiasm outside Japan on its own merits, probably nowhere more enthusiastically than among French youth.[3] The "true" original is thus not Versailles but Harajuku, the center of Tokyo street fashion where Lolita fashion emerged.

Momoko and the Lolita Identity

Kamikaze Girls is framed on both ends by Momoko's biological birth and near death. Her character is likewise developed through a series of metaphorical deaths and rebirths, the shedding of successive identities to adopt new ones. Momoko pursues Lolita fashion with the extravagant zeal and perfectionism that have made Japanese subcultures globally famous, but it too emerges in Momoko in distinct stages. Though she discovers Lolita fashion after she enters high school, she does not wholeheartedly commit to it until she encounters a stunning rococo dress by designer Akinori Isobe in a display window. The death-rebirth metaphor is presented here literally; the dress raises its arm and shoots Momoko in the heart (with an elegant miniature pistol), and she falls down dead, overwhelmed by its beauty. "The old 'me' died," she says. "The new 'me' was born."

From this point on, Momoko's life is thoroughly consumed by Lolita fashion. Isobe, a pompous and effeminate caricature in the movie (but a top designer of Lolita fashion in real life) is her god. Momoko is maniacally driven to purchase as much of Isobe's clothing as she can, and she stoops to telling her father preposterous lies of friends in distress to get money for clothes. In addition to Momoko's wardrobe and accessories, her reading material and musical preferences (Strauss waltzes), including her cell phone ringtone, reinforce her extravagantly selfish "rococo" lifestyle. Needless to say, though Momoko presents herself as a devoted student of the rococo period, this patchwork of accoutrements is mismatched (rococo Strauss waltzes?). However, like her father's clashing counterfeit logos (Versach and Universal Stadium), the combination works; it is a *real fake* that creates its own consistency.

Some explanation is in order, since in Japan the term "Lolita" (at least in relation to Lolita fashion) does not at all have the connotations it does in the West. Far from suggesting Nabokov's prematurely sexualized child, "Lolita fashion" represents the reverse: the infantilized and to a large extent *desexualized* female teen or young adult. In fact, no fashion trend in Japan does more to cover up the female body. Lolita outfits aggressively discourage sexual attention, a point that Momoko emphasizes in the novel:

> Lolita is defined as a type of street fashion known only in Japan. But to me, Lolita goes far beyond fashion and serves as my unwavering, absolute personal policy. Wearing a frilly blouse, a skirt over a huge ruffly petticoat with my waist squeezed into a corset, and a totally outlandish headdress, is my way of pledging that I have totally devoted myself to Rococo. If I didn't dress in this totally conspicuous and bizarre way, I'd make friends and be popular with boys . . . is what people tell me, and the more they say that, the more it fans the flames of my Lolita passion and stiffens my resolve to be a Lolita through and through.[4]

Later Momoko further expounds: "I cannot speak on the phone with an unfamiliar male. I even have trouble being friendly with familiar males. I think I have a slight case of androphobia. Or perhaps it's male aversion? I mean, guys are so dirty. And smelly. And crude. And just plain yucky."[5]

Lolita fashion, both in the film and in real life, tends to be a solo act. Lolitas do not as a rule seek to congregate with other Lolitas. They stand out very conspicuously in a crowd, adorned in layers of strikingly ornate clothing like a French or Victorian doll, their ensemble complete from head to toe, and (as observed above) largely desexualized. Though mediating influences are undeniable, as we have seen in Momoko's case, the identity is played out as a form of conspicuous individualism. A Lolita projects a persona that is childish, virginal, flagrantly self-indulgent, unabashedly self-absorbed, proudly self-sufficient, completely unashamed of her conspicuousness, and disdainful of the undifferentiated hordes around her. Momoko pushes this to a still higher level of snobbery; she never identifies with Harajuku, where Lolita fashion originated, and takes pains to note that she buys her ensembles in Daikanyama (the location of Isobe's outlet), an upscale, sophisticated Tokyo neighborhood. Thus, Momoko considers herself above the hordes of noncomformist youth at Harajuku, including other Lolitas. She is a Lolita's Lolita.

The Lolita identity presents such a concentrated expression of romanticism that it cries out for a mimetic interpretation. Where does it fit within René Girard's analysis of the "Romantic lie"?[6] Unabashedly derivative, it proclaims originality. Mediated down to the finest detail, it expresses nonconformity. Transparently inauthentic, it asserts authenticity. Duplicated enthusiastically among thousands, it boldly broadcasts individuality. What are we to make of Momoko's Lolita incarnation?

A hasty mimetic analysis might identify it as pseudo-narcissism. In Girard's exposition, the pseudo-narcissist feeds off the attention he or she attracts, all the while cultivating the impression of not needing it, of being self-sufficient. This in turn draws more admiration and further facilitates the façade; admirers imitate the pseudo-narcissist's self-regard.[7] Cutting off the admiration will reliably destabilize the narcissism, something that Girard observes in *As You Like It* and *Twelfth Night*.[8]

"Pseudo-narcissism" is among Girard's most brilliant interpretive concepts, yet it fails to fully account for Momoko or any other Lolita. As noted, Momoko does not surround herself with fawning admirers and appears quite content to be alone, to be in relation instead with her clothes, her accoutrements, with her mediators, with beauty itself. The lack of attention or admiration will in fact (and this is quite important) *strengthen* the conviction that her tastes are superior, that she is a transcendent being. As noted, Momoko is shown several times walking up into the sky, on a river of magic sparkles, leaving the dull, ugly earth behind. Thus, the Lolita raises pseudo-narcissism to a level that seems to comprise a new category altogether. To understand it we need to move on, as both Girard and the film do, to the sacred.

It is no coincidence that Momoko, and Lolitas in general, have chosen the court of Versailles as the model for their aesthetic. The rococo exists under the shadow of the guillotine that will follow it; it is the brief, effervescent coda preceding revolutionary violence. The dress that shoots Momoko in the heart, precipitating her rococo transformation, is headless, as are all the dresses in the film that appear on display or on tailor's dummies (the center of focus in four scenes, including that one).

But Versailles, the French Revolution, and particularly Marie Antoinette are fixed in the popular mind in Japan primarily through *The Rose of Versailles*, a spectacularly popular manga series from the 1970s.⁹ It has been adapted continually in anime and film versions, and most notably in a smash hit musical version by the famous Takarazuka all-female revue. *The Rose of Versailles* tells the story of Marie Antoinette and her protector Oscar, a woman raised as a man who becomes the commander of the Royal Guard. Oscar ultimately sides with the revolution in the storming of the Bastille and dies in battle, and Marie Antoinette, of course, dies at the guillotine.

The position of *The Rose of Versailles* in Japanese popular culture can hardly be overstated, and it is hard to imagine any Japanese person who is not familiar with it, but especially a girl like Momoko. Just as important as the characters and story are the splendor, and particularly the costumes, as they appear in manga, anime, and musical versions of *Rose*. The frilly ensembles of Marie and the other ladies at court have come to define extravagant feminine beauty for generations of girls, and not a few men, while Oscar's androgynous beauty has had a similar impact regarding the masculine ideal, and both have undoubtedly influenced a number of "visual" rock bands.¹⁰

Without question, Lolita fashion in general, and *Kamikaze Girls* in particular, draw very heavily on *The Rose of Versailles*. Though never explicitly mentioned, it is impossible not to see this element of *Kamikaze Girls* once it is noticed—it is "hidden in plain sight." Specifically, in *Kamikaze Girls*, Momoko is the comic counterpart to Marie Antoinette, and Ichigo the comic counterpart to Oscar. Ichigo's mussy androgynous hairstyle closely matches Oscar's, and her blue kamikaze jacket (a central item in the film) matches Oscar's uniform. She often takes on the role of Momoko's protector, especially in the latter half of the film. Roses are ubiquitous in the film. Novala, the novelist's pen name, means "wild rose," and in Japanese reproduces "the roses of" in the title ("no bara") phonetically ("Nobara" → "*Berusaiyu no Bara*"). The book is almost certainly his paean (albeit a whimsical one) to *The Rose of Versailles*. In the film, roses appear prominently on the headless dresses already mentioned. The first thing Momoko is shown embroidering in her middle school club is a rose, and later her expert stitching of roses will be a key element in the story. A bright red rose also appears on the breast of Ichigo's school blazer.

That Momoko does not acknowledge these debts is a howling omission, as well as an obvious clue. To exposit constantly on rococo and Versailles without once mentioning Marie Antoinette, the French Revolution, or *The Rose of Versailles* is quite a feat; it amounts to ignoring the elephants in the room. In the movie, Momoko never mentions Marie Antoinette at all. In the novel, interestingly, she mentions Marie Antoinette once, only to casually dismiss her, insisting that her real model is Madame du Pompadour, mistress of Louis XV.[11] But again, a girl like Momoko could not possibly have grown up in Japan without reading or seeing *The Rose of Versailles* and thus being very familiar with Marie Antoinette and the French Revolution. To put it more bluntly, and more generally, Momoko, and Lolitas in general, are modeling their subcultural identities on Marie Antoinette through the mediation of *The Rose of Versailles*. Thus, Momoko, and by extension all Lolitas, are denying the primary sources of their subcultural identity.

This puts us back on the familiar ground of mimetic theory; Momoko's real mediators are profoundly influential yet absolutely denied, even to Momoko herself. Though Momoko cannot avoid the fact that her Lolita identity is in some way derivative, she can do the next best thing: she can misrepresent the way in which it is derivative. Momoko is a Lolita (or so she tells herself) because of her unique appreciation of beauty, because rococo is a superior way of life, because she studies eighteenth-century Versailles, because she discovered the best designer, because she spends the most money buying his outfits. It could not possibly be because she is imitating Marie Antoinette, and it must absolutely not be because of a comic book she read as a child.

More importantly, once we understand that each Lolita is in fact a little Marie Antoinette, the peculiar intensity of this subcultural identity becomes more comprehensible. It is not pseudo-narcissistic so much as it is pseudo-sacrificial. The Lolita appropriates the sacred aura of Marie Antoinette, of the beautiful, young, pampered, vain, passionate, selfish, self-indulgent, tragic victim. Herbert Plutschow has persuasively outlined the vital role played in Japanese culture by tragic victims, military or political figures that were vanquished or executed.[12] Honoring them (and often ultimately deifying them) was essential to establishing and maintaining legitimate authority in Japan up to the Edo period (1603–1868). Failure to do so adequately was believed to result in plagues, misfortunes, and natural disasters.

The fact that there have been almost no female victims of comparable historical stature in Japan could account for the attraction many Japanese women feel for figures like Joan of Arc and Marie Antoinette. It is certainly clear, at any rate, that the latter has taken on the status of the tragic victim in the pop imagination through the mediation of *The Rose of Versailles*. This confers on Marie Antoinette a certain sacred aura, particularly among girls and young women, but also among males who have contributed so much to the Lolita aesthetic, including androgynous "visual" rock groups, designers, and Novala Takemoto himself, author of *Kamikaze Girls* and himself a designer and cross-dresser. Marie Antoinette is the female divinity (largely unacknowledged) of the Lolita subculture. The Lolita identity thus presents a fascinating modern validation of Girard in the divinization of the scapegoat, Marie Antoinette.

The identity also draws on the dynamic of scapegoating in revealing ways. The Lolita self-designates as a conspicuous object of attention that is already a sacralized victim: because the Lolita is striking and unique, she is a potential scapegoat; conversely, because she is a potential scapegoat, she must be strikingly unique. It is an impressive win-win strategy that appropriates the sacred aura of scapegoating to create a personal bubble of transcendence. The Lolita adopts in a sense the purest form of romanticism: the strategy of Jean-Jacques Rousseau (claiming authenticity through victimhood) in the very unlikely form of a Marie Antoinette. Eric Gans's observation about Rousseau could apply equally well to Momoko, who puts the same dynamic to work on a practical level; Rousseau "demonstrated the heuristic power of the victimary mechanism as a means by which the individual can conceive itself at the scenic center."[13] "Rousseau's intuition folds the singularity of the Christian revelation back into a symmetry that appears blasphemous from a Christian perspective but is in reality its triumphant generalization: in order to be oneself the/a center, to know oneself as akin to the son of God, one must experience unanimous persecution."[14] By making herself the conspicuous center of attention, yet one also fashioned in the image of the scapegoated tragic victim, the Lolita creates in herself the ultimate romantic.

However—and this is quite important, because scapegoating is no mere hypothetical possibility for a Japanese teen—the Lolita manifests a certain audacity that will tend to discourage or at least defer scapegoating. Certainly in the film, Momoko is definitely not the type that will be bullied in school, as will become clear when we compare her with Ichigo. The aura of attention around the Lolita is a defensive parameter. In theory, any hypothetical scapegoating would merely confirm her superiority, while in practice any actual scapegoating will tend to be indefinitely postponed. The Lolita thus self-designates as a sacred being, unapproachable, untouchable, a scapegoat that preempts actual scapegoating by appropriating the sacred aura first, before any scapegoating can take place.

Ichigo and the *Yanki* Identity

One reason *Kamikaze Girls* should be known and appreciated beyond its fan base is that fans tend to valorize the film as a paean to youthful nonconformity and miss the movie's real insights. Nowhere is this more evident than in the invocation of the proverb, "The nail that sticks up gets hammered down" (appearing on the film's US site).[15] At first glance this might seem a fair encapsulation of the film's message, as well as of the scapegoat mechanism as it is understood in mimetic theory. However, the proverb fails to describe either Momoko or Ichigo aptly and is in some ways nearly the opposite of the truth.

Rarely in the film are youths persecuted, unless it is by other youths. Further, as we have seen, "sticking up" as a Lolita is a fairly reliable strategy for not getting "hammered down" as a scapegoat by these other youths. Conversely, as will also be seen, Ichigo is not hammered by her middle school peers for being different, but for wanting to be the same, for wanting to belong. And, as with Momoko, Ichigo's noncomformist incarnation, rather than attracting persecution, is a more or less successful (though not absolute) defense against it.

Momoko and Ichigo come at their subcultural identities both *to* opposite extremes and *from* opposite extremes. Unlike Momoko, Ichigo has an idyllic middle-class upbringing. She discovers its deficiency when it fails to prepare her for the brutality of high school, where her smiling innocence and eagerness to be accepted immediately mark her out as the class scapegoat. These are haunting and disturbing scenes—Ichigo smiling desperately while suffering repeated humiliations—the more so for being slipped in almost inconspicuously in a comic context, when Momoko gives an accelerated summary of Ichigo's life story. Almost as if in compensation, Nakashima will devote an entire film to a life that unfolds as an unending tale of victimization in his next movie, the unbearably sad *Memories of Matsuko* (2006).[16]

Ichigo is saved from perpetual victimhood through identification with a girl biker gang, a crowd of antisocial victimizers. She has her own defining moment of rebirth when she encounters Akimi, the gang leader of the Ponytails. Akimi mediates the birth of Ichigo's *yanki* identity in the same way that Isobe's dress mediated Momoko's definitive Lolita transformation. And just as Momoko scrupulously constructs her Lolita identity, Ichigo also spectacularly reinvents herself: mussed-up hair and disheveled school uniform; *kamikaze* jacket (the source of the English title for the film); black nail polish, dark lipstick, and drawn-on eyebrows; a noisy, souped up, garishly modified scooter; a devotion to the rebellious songs of Yutaka Ozaki (though she was already a fan); and above all, foul language, deficient grammar, an aggressive swagger, and a thoroughly intimidating demeanor.

The key interest animating the plot in *Kamikaze Girls* is the unlikely friendship that develops between Ichigo and Momoko, both of them as far from normal as it is possible for either to be, and thus twice as far from each other. As mentioned, Ichigo's androgyny, contrasting so sharply with Momoko's exaggerated femininity, draws comically on Oscar in *The Rose of Versailles*. The friendship certainly has quirky twists and turns, but it follows a relatively standard (and well executed) story arch for "odd couples," wherein each comes to challenge the other's assumptions.

Among the assumptions Momoko challenges is biker mythology, particularly the dubious urban legend of Himiko, who is said to have united girl bikers in Kanagawa prefecture, preached against social hierarchy, and successfully led a battle against gangsters. Interestingly, the

Himiko legend is presented immediately after the story of Ichigo's bullying in school and transformation into a *yanki*: a segue from scapegoating to mythology. Himiko's symbol is a golden dragon that was embroidered on her jacket by Emma, another legendary figure. Himiko has become a sort of patron deity of girl bikers everywhere, though her whereabouts are unknown. (Significantly, and almost certainly not coincidentally, Himiko is also the name of a shaman queen, a real historical figure who ruled a large kingdom during Japan's Iron Age. Queen Himiko is only spottily attested in history and, like Ichigo's mythological biker, is also shrouded in legend.[17] The name Himiko has cultural resonance and establishes symmetry with the subliminal aura of the regal sacred around Marie Antoinette.)

Momoko remains highly suspicious of the veracity of Himiko, and after a certain point even the word "legend" (*densetsu*) itself is enough to provoke her eye-rolling disdain. However, the cartoonish Himiko legend (actually presented as a cartoon in the movie) becomes a linchpin in the plot and an important element tying together the film's overall anthropological vision.

Scapegoating, Myth, and Sacrifice

A gang member named Miko assumes leadership of the Ponytails after Akimi gets pregnant and marries. Miko then orchestrates a merger with another local Ladies gang. Ichigo, who opposes the gang's new authoritarian tendencies, is ordered to undergo a ritual "challenge," that is, a collective beating by gang members. Ichigo is the scapegoat whose victimization will seal the unity between the two gangs. Thus, the gang that once rescued Ichigo from scapegoating is now itself Ichigo's scapegoater. When Momoko comprehends what will happen she rushes to help Ichigo, though it is unclear what she will be able to do. This is the stage for the dramatic climax of *Kamikaze Girls* and brings the film full circle to the opening scenes, when Momoko was shown riding determinedly on a scooter. The fight scene is filmed on location within view of an enormous statue of Buddha (the Ushiku Daibutsu, a local landmark) and in a large dirt lot (now a graveyard).

Ichigo, no longer the child who submitted passively to bullying with a desperate smile, stands up defiantly to the gang and specifically to Miko. The back-and-forth confrontation between them is hackneyed and bombastic, but Ichigo's essential objection boils down to this: "We were freer as a small gang; now we're just like everyone else, making rules and pushing people around." It is the objection of primal egalitarianism against hierarchical annexation; it is a complaint against civilization.

Miko then invokes Himiko, who she says personally commanded her to unite the gangs of Ibaragi prefecture. In other words, Miko is claiming mythological legitimacy and to be an oracle of girl gangs' key mythological figure (though Himiko is said to have preached egalitarianism). Since Ichigo cannot simply walk away from the gang, there is nothing left but for her to face her "challenge," to undergo ritual victimization. Ichigo puts up an impressive fight, but of course she is hopelessly outnumbered.

Momoko, who has rushed to the scene to rescue Ichigo, watches the commencement of the beating helplessly. When her dress becomes splattered with Ichigo's blood, she screams, and a member of the other gang (whose members have been observing the scene impassively) tosses Momoko contemptuously into a mud puddle. Momoko rises from the puddle in her most spectacular incarnation yet. She launches herself into the action in a reckless act of self-sacrifice, grabs a baseball bat, swings her way wildly through the startled members of Ponytails, and faces down Miko herself.

Momoko then proceeds to brazenly rewrite the Himiko legend. She presents herself as the daughter of Himiko, the legendary gang leader, and Emma (now suddenly a man), the legendary embroiderer who stitched Himiko's golden dragon. She announces that she herself is her father's best apprentice and as proof points to Ichigo's kamikaze jacket (which Momoko expertly embroidered earlier in the film). If Miko makes herself an enemy of Himiko's daughter, Momoko threatens, every biker girl in East Japan will hunt her down. Momoko allows Miko (and the rest of the stunned gang) to have Ibaraki prefecture, but only if they promise not to lay a finger on her friend.

Thus, Momoko invents a new chapter of the Himiko legend and writes herself into it. She is able to create a sacred aura that designates

Ichigo and herself as untouchable. It must be among the most impressive on-the-spot improvisations (and personal transformations) portrayed in film, and the picture of a Lolita facing down a biker gang is hilariously funny. It is also a stunning success. Ichigo and Momoko ride off together in a show of proud contempt, leaving the crestfallen gang in shock. The scapegoating is averted, unification presumably goes forward, and—excepting a large amount of lost face for Miko and the gang—everyone wins.

As Momoko and Ichigo discuss what has just happened, the truth comes out. Ichigo explains that Miko and the gang fell for Momoko's outrageous improvisations because Miko herself was lying. Himiko could never have told Miko to unite the gangs because Himiko doesn't exist. Himiko is a fiction created by Ichigo herself in a fabricated diary she sent to a biker magazine some time ago. It subsequently became an urban legend that underwent further elaboration. The entire Himiko legend, not just Momoko's embellishment, is bogus, though every biker girl believes it.

We ought to catch our breath here, in these fast-paced but unmistakably sacrificial scenes, to tease out their mimetic significance. Among its notable aspects is that it quotes very heavily from the opening sequences of Stanley Kubrick's *2001: A Space Odyssey* ("The Dawn of Man"). In fact, Takemoto's novel was published in 2002. The story thus marks a sort of expiration date for Kubrick's prematurely ambitious vision of the future. We are still very far from having a manned mission to Jupiter, yet we are not very far at all from the bands of protohumans that beat each other with blunt instruments. At any rate, viewers familiar with Kubrick's film are clearly meant to be aware of the parallels in the two scenes, as they are numerous and obvious:

1. The biker girls wield blunt instruments, just as the protohumans in *2001* gripped their newly acquired bone clubs.
2. The brown dirt landscape closely matches that in *2001*, including Momoko's puddle, separating the two biker gangs precisely where the puddle in *2001* separated the rival groups of apes.
3. *2001* contained a tall, oblong, metal artifact that mysteriously contributed to hominization (though this preceded the clubbing scene);

Kamikaze Girls likewise has the enormous statue of Buddha of very similar proportions standing placidly in the background.

4. In both *2001* and *Kamikaze Girls*, there are multiple club wielders but only one actually clubbed (one of the outsider apes in *2001*, Ichigo in *Kamikaze Girls*).
5. Johann Strauss's "Blue Danube" waltz accompanies the ballet of machines in space immediately after the clubbing scene in *2001*, and in *Kamikaze Girls* it is actually the background music for the fighting (Strauss's music, as mentioned, is also Momoko's ringtone).
6. The scene of confrontation in *Kamikaze Girls* is a graveyard (this is clear in the novel but not in the film), while the parallel shots in *2001* constantly show dry bones, including those of the protohumans' progenitors.

These multiple parallels with cinema's most iconic depiction of human origins indicate that Nakashima is dealing with something of fundamental anthropological significance. He is not just paying comic homage to Kubrick but having an extended dialogue with him. And it could be argued—without denying Kubrick's groundbreaking iconography—that *Kamikaze Girls'* anthropology is the more substantial of the two. From the standpoint of mimetic theory, the differences of *Kamikaze Girls* from *2001* will seem more striking than the similarities:[18]

1. The group violence comes near the end rather than at the beginning of the film. That is, it is a flash point building up from ongoing social dynamics: a sacrificial crisis.
2. Unlike the bands of apes in *2001*, the two groups in *Kamikaze Girls* are not fighting, but uniting.
3. The one being clubbed is from within rather than from without the group doing the clubbing.
4. While the alien artifact in *2001* is featureless, more or less unconnected to the intraspecies violence that takes place, and has a limited and somewhat ambiguous role in hominization (apparently inspiring protohumans to use tools), in *Kamikaze Girls* the artifact is actually visible *at* the scene of violence, and is specifically sacred. It has a human form, benign face, and meaningful gestures: the *Raigo-in* or

"reasoning mudra" in Japanese Buddhism.[19] The gently raised open palm could also be considered a sign of peace, a universal gesture for averting conflict.
5. From the standpoint of generative anthropology, another difference will stand out: there is a nonviolent rather than violent resolution, in which language and symbols (the reconstituted Himiko myth) are exchanged in the place of violence.[20]

The "scenic center" is depicted quite dramatically when Momoko designates herself as sacred and walks contemptuously through the biker girls. Momoko is untouchable, inaccessible. They back away from her, opening up a circle that moves along with her.

Ironically, the explicit inclusion of the sacred in *Kamikaze Girls* makes human origins *less miraculous* than the "secular" obelisk makes it in *2001*. No mysterious alien artifact is needed to explain anything that we are seeing in *Kamikaze Girls*, and what we are seeing is by implication a reenactment of something that has gone on since the dawn of man. Hominization in *Kamikaze Girls* is connected with religion, language, and symbolic substitution, and these are connected in turn with the problem of violence.

Kamikaze Girls, seemingly irreverent toward religion in this scene, is in fact being irreverent toward Kubrick's ponderous and somewhat preposterous anthropological vision. In *2001*, intraspecies violence is simply the regrettable though inevitable consequence of alien intervention, the breaking of eggs necessitated by the omelet of human progress. It is a remote and pompous concession to violence, corrected in Kubrick's next film, *A Clockwork Orange* (with which *Kamikaze Girls*, with its costumed biker gangs, also shares some obvious kinship).[21] Violence is much more central to hominization in *Kamikaze Girls*. At the same time, the solution to violence is equally central, making the scene both more and less violent than the opening of *2001*. Rather than an all-out clash between gangs, violence can be channeled onto an unfortunate scapegoat. Then, rather than being discharged upon the scapegoat, the scapegoat can be put off limits by the invocation of the sacred.

The clashing religious symbolism in *Kamikaze Girls* (Buddhism in the enormous but pacific Ushiku Daibutsu, folk warrior mythology in the Himiko legend) makes perfect sense in a Japanese context; the negotiation between Shintoism, the animistic folk religion, and Buddhism, the transcendent imported creed, is one of the oldest arguments in Japanese civilization. It is often hard to tell, even on temple grounds, where one religion ends and the other begins. Is Buddhism the aggrandizing faith that stifled the authentic folk religion of Japan? Or is it rather Shinto that is the authoritarian mythology, aggrandizing more and more of the oppressed ancient peoples under its hierarchical gods, with Buddhism being the more generous and liberating creed? Or is it a little of both?

The struggle is reflected in Miko and Ichigo's standoff (freedom vs. authority, smallness vs. bigness, autonomy vs. unity). Who was Himiko? Himiko preached freedom and equality, but after all she was a leader herself and eliminated gangs' autonomy by uniting them all. Who is Himiko's rightful heir? In characteristically Japanese fashion, the solution in *Kamikaze Girls* is religious accommodation. Ichigo and Miko both get what they want and establish irresolution as the long-term solution.

Kamikaze Girls's funky and somewhat conventional youth movie denouement may disappoint Girardians, as it presents no authentic conversion in the manner of Cervantes, Stendhal, Dostoyevksy, or Proust. Neither Momoko nor Ichigo abandon their subcultural identities. Momoko goes to work in Isobe's studio, though she cannot decide whether she wants to make clothes or just buy them. Ichigo has a brief, comical stint modeling Isobe's dresses (she launches the brand to fame by creating an aggressive new Lolita image), then returns to working on bikes and riding solo. The younger versions of Momoko and Ichigo (Momoko the detached, cynical elementary school child, Ichigo the smiling, innocent fourteen-year-old) are shown at the side of the street, watching in approval as their mature incarnations pass by. In the end, the film appears to validate the fans, who are drawn to it precisely as a celebration of individualism and romantic self-expression.

Having invested so much in deconstructing "romantic lies" and sacrificial mythology, does the film finally fall right back into them? In fact, Nakashima should be viewed here as making reasonable and perhaps inevitable concessions to the youth movie genre. Youth movies, if they are to be more than an amoral pander, should perform a certain ethical function. In this case, the function is to speak honestly about the pains of growing up, the problems of belonging and acceptance, the realities of bullying, the importance of friendship and self-sacrifice, the possibilities and limits of self-expression, the delicate task of surviving socially while defining one's personal differences, and the importance of finding one's niche in the world. These very elements, which may keep *Kamikaze Girls* from being a perfect lesson in mimetic anthropology, contribute a warmth and humanity to the film that also keep it from being merely bleak or discouraging. In the end, the film stays true to its genre.

This makes it all the more impressive that Nakashima is able to explore so much mimetic truth in such an unlikely vehicle. *Kamikaze Girls* remains an insightful treatment of imitation, mediation, myth, ritual, and sacrifice. Its conventional denouement notwithstanding, the film unfolds in many ways almost like a dramatic exposition of mimetic theory. Though the film is far too much a product of its time to be anything like a timeless masterpiece, it is too substantial in its anthropological vision to be dismissed as a mere historical artifact. This engrossing and inventive film deserves a larger audience.

Notes

1. *Shimotsuma Monogatari* (Kamikaze Girls), DVD, directed by Tetsuya Nakashima (Tokyo: Shogakukan, 2004); Novala Takemoto, *Shimotsuma Monogatari* (Kamikaze Girls) (Tokyo: Shogakukan, 2002); Novala Takemoto, *Kamikaze Girls*, trans. Akemi Wegmüller (San Francisco: VIZ Media, 2008).

2. *2001: A Space Odyssey*, DVD, directed by Stanley Kubrick (1968; Burbank, CA: Warner Home Video, 2001).

3. Much of the influence came from androgynous Japanese "visual" rock bands, particularly Malice Mizer, which perfected the dark, decadent gothic Lolita look in the 1990s and became well known in France. Mana, Malice Mizer's cross-dressing guitarist (also a designer) eventually started a new band, Moix dix Mois, specializing in the same baroque-themed rock and gothic Lolita look. Moix dix Mois is still active and has toured Europe. The band is possibly better known in France than in Japan.

4. Novala Takemoto, *Kamikaze Girls*, 8.

5. Ibid., 50.

6. The first and still best explication is René Girard's *Deceit, Desire, and the Novel*, trans. Yvonne Freccero (Baltimore: Johns Hopkins University Press, 1976).

7. See, for instance, René Girard, *Things Hidden since the Foundation of the World*, trans. Stephen Bann and Michael Meteer (Stanford, CA: Stanford University Press, 1987), 368–82.

8. René Girard, *A Theater of Envy* (Herefordshire, UK: Gracewing, 2000), 100–120.

9. Riyoko Ikeda, *The Rose of Versailles* (*Berusaiyu no Bara*), 10 vols. (1972–1973; repr., Tokyo: Shueisha, 1982).

10. See note 3 above.

11. Novala Takemoto, *Kamikaze Girls*, 6.

12. Herbert Plutschow, "The Tragic Victim in Japanese Religion, Politics, and the Arts," *Anthropoetics* 6, no. 2 (Fall 2000–Winter 2001), http://www.anthropoetics.ucla.edu/ap0602/japan.htm

13. Eric Gans, *The Scenic Imagination* (Stanford, CA: Stanford University Press, 2008), 51.

14. Ibid., 52.

15. *Kamikaze Girls*, US Official Site, http://www.kamikazegirls.net (accessed November 2, 2012).

16. *Kiraware Matsuko no Issho* (Memories of Matsuko), directed by Tetsuya Nakashima (Tokyo: Amuse Soft Entertainment, 2006).

17. See, e.g., *Encyclopedia Britannica*, 15th ed., s.v. "Himiko." Chicago: Encyclopedia Britannica, 1988.

18. For a useful account of human and cultural origins as Girard hypothesizes them, see *Things Hidden*, 84–125.

19. Mark Schumacher, "Mudra: Hand Gestures with Religious Meaning," *A-Z Photo Dictionary of Japanese Sculpture and Art*, http://www.onmarkproductions.com/html/mudra-japan.shtml# (accessed November 17, 2012).

20 For an explanation of the "originary scene" as Eric Gans hypothesizes it, see his "A Brief Introduction to Generative Anthropology," http://www.anthropoetics.ucla.edu/gaintro.htm (accessed November 3, 2012).

21. *A Clockwork Orange*, directed by Stanley Kubrick (Burbank, CA: Warner Brothers Pictures, 1971).

PART 3

MIMETIC THEORY AND THEOLOGY

CHAPTER 10

BACK TO THE FUTURE

The Prophetic and the Apocalyptic in Jewish and Christian Settings

SANDOR GOODHART

Prologue

It has often been said that Judaism is about prophetic thinking and Christianity about apocalyptic thinking, and there is of course much truth to that claim. But if Judaism reads prophetically, I would maintain, it does so necessarily in the wake of disaster, in order to understand the steps leading up to it and to foresee new ones lest one fall prey to them accidentally. And I would also maintain that if Christianity reads apocalyptically, it too is disaster-based and already premised upon prophetic understandings of both what has passed and what is coming down the road.

In other words, the two, in short, are "entangled" and are, as one might say today in the parlance of contemporary theoretical physics, two sides of the same interpretative coin. The apocalyptic is a reading from within the prophetic, a special case of the prophetic, in which devastation is the expected outcome of the dramas underway. The same understanding of the prophetic is operative in each of these cases, which may be expressed by the following formulation. The prophetic, we may say, is the recognition of the dramas in which human beings are engaged and the naming in advance of the end of those dramas in order that human beings may choose whether to go there or not. Defining the two in this fashion sets them diametrically at odds with more popular accounts in which they are opposed as distinct species of prediction or fortune-telling. The word "prophetic" is often invoked, for example, in popular discussions to designate in retrospect an idea or event that first occurred in the past but now appears fulfilled by some other present occurrence. And the word "apocalyptic" is similarly invoked to speak about some catastrophic future occurrence forecast at a prior time and that now seems to have taken place in accord with that earlier prediction—often in a rhetorical framework of "I told you so" and as a means of chastising those who did not pay sufficient heed to that alleged warning.

What is at stake in what we are suggesting, on the other hand, is never what will inevitably, or unavoidably, come to pass but rather what will follow necessarily should the drama underway continue to its natural and forgone conclusion, a conclusion always generally known in advance and never in any doubt. The prophetic, and the apocalyptic as a species of the prophetic, is a return to a genuinely futural orientation, a future that is authentically open, that is inevitable should the dramas it designates play themselves through to their expected outcomes but that need not do so, that have the capacity not to be played out. People can choose to follow them to their conclusion, but can equally choose not to do so should some other drama prove more attractive and better serve the circumstances at hand.

Now, there are many parts to this formulation of the prophetic I have offered—which is in the first place essentially a Greek definition rather an Hebraic or a Christian one—and a great deal more to be said about each part than can be developed here. But my purpose in setting this definition, in this context, as an interpretative construction shared at a profound level by both Jewish and Christian readers, is that it appears to be plentifully in evidence in René Girard's last book, *Achever Clausewitz* (2007), or, as it is rendered in English, *Battling to the End* (2009).[1]

Part One: Girard

Girard's work is nominally a book-length conversation about the unfinished treatise of the nineteenth-century Prussian military officer, Carl Von Clausewitz, which has come down to us with the title of *On War*. This is a treatise in which the author, in somewhat of a rational Aristotelian fashion, attempts to develop the principles of warfare as he understood them within the Napoleonic Era in which he wrote and fought. What fascinates Girard about this book, and indeed what attracted him to it in the first place, is the writer's treatment in particular of reciprocity or "reciprocal action," which, the author claims, appears to have a life of its own once it starts and, as such, exceeds the more commonly known Clausewitzean idea that war is "the continuation of politics by other means." Indeed, the treatment of reciprocity Girard finds in the text leads him to reverse that more familiar principle and to argue that in context of the book we have, politics is in fact an extension of warfare pursued in a slightly less intense context, a position which brings Girard in proximity to that of Michel Foucault, who famously makes something of the same claim in his lectures in the Collège de France and elsewhere, albeit to very different theoretical ends.[2]

But the real thrust of Girard's view is larger. For Girard wants to claim that Clausewitz's discovery of this runaway principle of violent reciprocity at the beginning of the nineteenth century is in effect a biblical reading, a recognition and confirmation of the ancient prophetic reading of the Christian scriptural book of the apocalypse, namely, the Book of Revelation.

In other words, in Girard's view, the ancient Christian writers already recognized the dramas in which they and their Jewish and Christian contemporaries were engaged and were naming in advance the end of those dramas in order to decide whether to proceed unimpeded to those ends or not. Clausewitz was simply registering, in Girard's view, whether unconsciously or not on Clausewitz's part, the unexpected fulfillment of such prophetic accounts.

In the following quotation, for example, Girard defines the appreciation of such coming disasters as "prescience":

> Christianity is the only religion that has foreseen its own failure. This prescience is known as the apocalypse. Indeed, it is in the apocalyptic texts that the word of God is most forceful, repudiating mistakes that are entirely the fault of humans, who are less and less inclined to acknowledge the mechanisms of their violence. The longer we persist in our error, the stronger God's voice will emerge from the devastation. This is why no one wants to read the apocalyptic texts that abound in the Synoptic Gospels and Pauline Epistles. This is also why no one wants to recognize that these texts rise up before us because we have disregarded Revelation. Once in history *the truth about the identity of all humans* was spoken, and no one wanted to hear it; instead we hang ever more frantically onto our false differences.
>
> Two world wars, the invention of the atomic bomb, several genocides, and an imminent ecological disaster have not sufficed to convince humanity, and Christians above all, that the apocalyptic texts might not be predictions but certainly do concern the disaster that is underway. What needs to be done to get them a hearing? (Girard, *Battling to the End*, x)

"The apocalyptic texts might not be predictions but certainly do concern the disaster that is underway." The whole of what we want to say is contained in those words. In the face of "disaster," we cling to "false differences." We misread the ancient texts as predictions and fail to see them as "prescient"—a profound reading of the very crises we are in the process of enacting, crises about the ownership of our own violence and its mechanisms, and mechanisms that derive, Girard explains elsewhere, from the very sacrificial structures that at other times have formed the basis for the genesis of the sacred.

Now what interests me in this essay is how Jewish this understanding remains, both Girard's understanding of the ancient (and modern) texts, and the understanding internal to the Christian scriptural writings.

To demonstrate that idea, I want to turn in the remainder of the essay to Jewish conceptualizations of the prophetic.

Part Two: Buber

Martin Buber, Franz Rosenzweig, Gershom Scholem, Abraham Joshua Herschel, Emmanuel Levinas, Yehezkel Kaufmann, Michael Fishbane, and a multitude of others have all expatiated extensively upon prophetic thinking in the rabbinic tradition, indeed, upon the rabbinical tradition as an example of prophetic thinking. Sometimes that thinking shows up as the prophetic tradition explicitly, as it does in the case of Buber.[3] Other times it shows up in discussions of messianic thinking—which is another version from a Jewish perspective of end-of-time thinking—as it does more commonly in the work of Gershom Scholem.[4] But in all cases it is a matter of diachrony or diachronic thinking, of thinking toward a future orientation rather than any sort of synchronic construction. For present purposes, I will concentrate initially upon two texts in this connection: Buber's "Prophetic, Apocalyptic, and the Historical Hour" and "The Dialogue between Heaven and Earth."[5] Then I will turn to one of the most famous texts of the scriptural canon, the Book of Isaiah (which in many ways originates this discussion) in order to ask what precisely a Jewish reading of that famous scriptural passage offers our more general understanding of the prophetic and the apocalyptic in these larger Jewish and Christian studies contexts. And finally I will return to ask about the status of Girardian thinking in this context.

In the two texts cited above, Buber distinguishes fairly radically between the prophetic and the apocalyptic. The prophetic derives for him quite simply from the writing of the Hebrew prophets: Isaiah, Jeremiah, Ezekial, and the like. "What good are all your sacrifices?," the prophet asks repeatedly, throughout what is commonly called First Isaiah. If you keep on going this way, in the way you have been acting, if you keep moving along the road you have been traveling, disaster is the inevitable result.

The prophetic, in other words, for Buber is an "if/then" structure. It may look like fortune-telling. It may have that appearance. You may think that the words are saying what will inevitably happen. But in fact there is always a hidden clause at work: if you do not give up the way in which you have been acting.

A good example is the Book of Jonah. "Forty days more and Ninevah will be destroyed," Yonah ben Amittai proclaims. If you continue your evil ways, if you continue doing what it is you have been doing, then here is what will happen. But if you give it up, if you give up that path, then suddenly everything changes. Who knows but that God may relent of the destruction he has planned for you and put aside such terrifying designs. The people, of course, in the case of the Book of Jonah, do repent and their repentance is of an unprecedented nature. And if Yonah is unhappy with that repentance and God's giving up of his planned destruction, it is not because Yonah has not known that God is a compassionate God, full of mercy as well as justice (indeed, as he says, he has known that), but for reasons of a more personal nature, reasons from which the book appears to take some distance and upon which it offers some criticism.

On the other hand, the apocalyptic for Buber is another matter entirely. It is almost mythic in structure. It begins in the present and justifies that present retrospectively, in an almost etiological fashion, as the fulfillment of earlier predictions. For Buber the apocalyptic approach is represented most fully by the originally joint Book of Nehemiah and Book of Ezra. The catastrophe occurred because you have done something wrong, the people are told, because you have sinned in some way that made God angry. You brought all this on yourself, the writers seem to say.

A good example of the poverty of this perspective in Buber's view is the Book of Job. The opening of the Book of Job is about myth. Satan and God plot Job's difficulties to satisfy a bet between them. The behavior of the friends at the human level parallels this position. You must have done something wrong. Evil comes only from evil. If evil is the result, evil is also the cause. But I am innocent, Job protests, in what Buber regards as the third major movement of the book. From divine play with human fate, to flippant formulaic responses of well-meaning but naive friends, Job protests his innocence. I have done nothing to bring this about. And for Buber the lesson, available in this reading process turned site of instruction, is completed only when we hear from God Himself that the answer to human suffering is creation, a creational principle we may only glimpse in the present context but which nonetheless orders everything.

We may not understand how creation answers human suffering, Buber admits. We may need to introduce Jewish ideas such as anti-idolatry to do so, ideas more plentifully displayed in the Book of Isaiah, for example, for the answer to become evident. (We recall that Job from the rabbis' point of view in the midrashim is regarded as "not Jewish.") But the instruction in any event is scripted in advance: from myth, to formulaic responses, to protestations of human suffering, to creation, the path for Buber is clear. The apocalyptic is but one step along the way and in the view of the friends as in the minds of the author of the Book of Ezra and Nehemiah—in Buber's view—it has been perverted out of all proportion. It has been taken as a counter logic to the prophetic as a whole of which it is in fact only a part and in fact a small one.

But it may be that we need to turn elsewhere in scriptural texts to identify instances where the apocalyptic is given a more positive and robust treatment. In the Book of Isaiah, for example, the modality of the apocalyptic is given considerably more status and in fact is identified with the prophetic perspective itself in the first thirty-nine chapters. Let us turn, then, to Isaiah, and in conclusion we will return to Girard and larger Jewish and Christian usages of it.

Part Three: Isaiah

The Book of Isaiah is traditionally regarded as made up of two parts. Chapters 1 through 39 are said to constitute the various Isaiahan takes on the days leading up to the fall of Jerusalem said to occur in 586 or 587 BCE. And chapters 40 through 66 are said to constitute a postexilic perspective, the writings gathered under the rubric of the Isaiahan school once the unthinkable has occurred. Sometimes the last eleven chapters, 56 to 66, are identified as a third division supplementing these two, but that idea is by no means universally accepted.

It is hard for us today to imagine just how disruptive that event (or series of events) in 586–587 BCE was to the Hebrew psyche. It was the incommensurate par excellence, the unsayable or unimaginable itself. How could one conceive the possibility—let alone the reality—that the Temple at Jerusalem could be overrun? That after generations of independence, the community would be forced to live under the thumb of foreign powers thousands of miles from the regions in which they are raised? It inaugurated an entirely new mindset, a mindset with which, I would suggest, we are still grappling, a mindset that dislodged itself from the stable physical cultural manifestations in which other cultures of the region found their solace (think of Egypt or Babylon or Sumeria) and developed a view of the text as homeland.⁶ If I have recourse on occasion to the idea that the Holocaust is not entirely new, that disaster has been lurking behind Scripture for as long as there has been Scripture, that Scripture as a whole is a kind of "book of destruction" (to use Geoffrey Hartman's phrase) or the "writing of the disaster" (to use Blanchot's phrase, *l'écriture du désastre*)—it is to this series of events that I refer.

The Book Isaiah is thus in many ways the proof text of Jewish scriptural writing. It is the veritable origin of the text, the text being written while the writings we know as Scripture were being gathered and constituted.

And it is from the constructed two parts of this book, First Isaiah and Second (or Deutero-) Isaiah, that I would suggest the concomitant notions of the prophetic and the apocalyptic may effectively be distinguished. The Book of Isaiah is unquestionably prophetic throughout. Its language is the same language used in the Book of Job—"Where were you when I created the Heaven and the earth?" "Did you lock in the sea with doors?"—minus the discussion of anti-idolatry, which is what is missing from its more famous counterpart. In the first part of Isaiah, the future of the road they are traveling is articulated: here is the consequence of your actions. And in the second part, the future of the path they are pursuing is again articulated, although the end of the path they are traveling is conceived there somewhat differently.

But since in both cases the future is conceived in somewhat dire terms, we could qualify both perspectives equally as apocalyptic. What good are all your sacrifices, the prophet cries out. They will only end in destruction. They do nothing to forestall that destruction they were designed to thwart, and in fact given the time you take pursuing these wasteful activities, they take away energy and resources that could otherwise be used to divert that impending disaster.

In part two, the circumstances are no less dire. The prophet's theme here is comfort—"comfort, comfort my people, says the Lord," says the prophet. But before that redemptive moment, much that is unsettling is likely to occur. The servant of Yhwh, the servant of the Lord, Israel, the house of Ya'akov, the community of those who have owned their election, their infinite responsibility for other individuals, which is to say, those who have chosen to live in accord with the commandments, with the Instruction or Teaching handed down by our beloved teacher, Moses Rabbeinu, will undergo great hardships.

If we consider the servant—the family of Ya'akov, Israel—in the manner of a single man, then the drama is clear. It has several parts. We will throw him out, exclude him from our community. But it will really be our sins to which in effect he will be bearing witness. Since in fact he will have done no violence, his exclusion will only come to serve as a teaching tool, reminding us of our own violence. It will serve to unite us, since by his stripes will we be healed. It is hard not to think of a young rabbi from the town of Nazareth several hundred years later being highly impressed by these ideas and taking upon himself to illustrate them, making them his life's project as it were, Torah incarnate, so to speak. The word of God made flesh.

In this context at least, then, the prophetic and the apocalyptic are one and the same. Jews read the anti-sacrificial perspective of First Isaiah and the redemptive structure of the coming Kingdom of Yhwh in consequence of have already suffered "double" for their sins. They will therefore, not unlike Job, merit "double back" at the moment of their redemption, the moment when the one who redeems you, who stands as surety for you (as described in the Book of Ruth), answers for you when your number is called. And Christians similarly read the anti-sacrificial perspective of First Isaiah and the coming (and trying) fate of Israel or Jacob (the Christian name for Ya'akov), of the servant of the Lord in the final days. The Jewish prophetic deemphasizes the coming disaster (or the recently past disaster) for an emphasis upon the changes still capable of being made, and the Christian apocalyptic mode emphasizes those dire consequences of our current behavior, deemphasizing what may be done in the interim. The two perspectives remain nonetheless dual approaches to the same fundamental orientation. The Christian reads from within the Jewish perspective and not about it, even if at times the reading fails to recognize that Jewish prophetic apocalyptic perspective as its own and mistakenly identifies Jews (and Judaism) as foreign to its own internal program.

And even if at times it adopts the midrashic perspective that the Isaiahan servant of the Lord is the literal son of God, and reads from within that perspective the prophetic midrashic view.

Part Four: Strong and Weak Readings

The prophetic and the apocalyptic, in other words, in both their Judaic and Christian settings, have both a weak and a strong sense. The weak Judaic sense of the prophetic is a matter of prediction or fortune-telling, for example, the way the rabbis sometimes read Joseph's dreams. He dreams that they were binding sheaves in the field and that his sheaves stood up and those of the others bowed down to it. The rabbis read the dreams as predictive of Joseph's ascendancy in Egypt, when he will serve as right-hand man of Pharoah and the distributor of the Egyptians' daily bread. The weak Judaic sense of the apocalyptic is reflected in Buber's explanation of the Book of Ezra/Book of Nehemiah or parts of the Book of Job, where the people read their chastisement by the prophets to mean they must have done something wrong to bring this about.

Concomitantly, the weak Christian sense of the prophetic is sometimes invoked by Christians reading Hebraic writing. Isaiah 52–53, for example, is famously read as predicting the coming of Jesus five hundred years later. And the weak Christian sense of the apocalyptic is invoked in reading the Book of Revelation not as an account of Christianity (or its future "failure," to use Girard's word) but as literal predictions of end-of-time events yet to take place.

There is, however, also a strong Judaic sense of the prophetic. The Joseph story, for example, may be read as the record of the desires of the father enacted in the behavior of the children—both Joseph and his brothers and the violent and sacrificial dynamics in which they become engaged—rather than anything to do with Egypt. And there is a strong Judaic apocalyptic mode, although Buber seems not to have much use for it. "Forty days more and Ninevah will be destroyed" is undoubtedly prophetic language. But it is also apocalyptic language. It is about the coming disaster, the crisis forecast to obtain should we continue behaving as we have been. And the anti-sacrificial language of the major prophets is nothing else if not forecasts of a coming destruction, should the contemporary and repeated warnings not be heeded.

And, a strong Christian sense of the prophetic is evident in the Gospel—for example, Jesus in John 8: here is where your accusations are leading, rocks on the shore of the sea which are fragments of the blood of exclusionary behavior. In bringing the woman before me, a woman caught in the shame of adultery, do you not do the same thing that she did? And are you not subject by Talmudic law to the same punishment for not stopping her from committing it? And are you not attacking me in doing so, accusing me of betraying the Mosaic law if I do not enforce this violent consequence? Rather than counterattack, however, Jesus literally removes himself from the line of fire. He stirs the rocks with his finger, as if to say, here is the future of stoning: countless acts of violence. Here is the language of the covenant, descendants as numerous as stars in the sky or grains of sand along the shores of the sea. This is where your violence leads. And when they don't get it, he stands up and says, "Okay, he who is without sin, let him be the first to cast a stone," repeating exactly the same lesson. They already know by Talmudic law (since they have brought the woman to him as a group) that there must always be two witnesses to any act of violence, and that first-person confession is never acceptable (so that there needs to be two witnesses other than themselves). Therefore, if they nominate themselves in response, they already transgress the law they say they invoke. Nor is the woman free of the danger of such transgression, for he never says to her "you are innocent" (indeed, he never challenges their assertion of her guilt) but rather "go and sin no more."

And there is finally a strong Christian sense of the apocalyptic: a reading of the Book of Revelation as an account of what's coming down the road rather than any mysterious figures from science fiction or fantasy, an account of the future of the revelation developed in the letters and the texts of the synoptic Gospels.[7]

It is, in fact, I would argue, when weak and strong senses are set in opposition to each other that trouble is born, whether that opposition is given voice within Judaism, within Christianity, or between them.

Why should one view be considered weak and the other strong? Why should reading Isaiah 52–53 as predictive of the specific person of Jesus be considered weak, while reading the same passage as reflective of the dramas afoot in Second Isaiah (in the previous songs of the servant of YHWH, for example, transformed midrashically into the drama of a single individual)—even if Jesus would subsequently appropriate such dramas as a script for his own life—be considered strong? To some extent, of course,

I am echoing here the distinction Walter Benjamin makes regarding a "weak messianic power" in his famous "Theses on the Philosophy of History," although in a different context and to different ends.[8]

To respond at length would require a more thorough development than I can undertake here. Suffice it to say for the present that there appear to be four criteria at work: predictivity, retrospectivity, freedom, and fulfillment.

Let me take one example included above: the interpretation of Isaiah 52–53 as the prediction of the coming of Jesus specifically five hundred years later. What is wrong with that reading? It appears odd in the first place as an historical prediction. How would people of the time of Second Isaiah (in the immediately postexilic moment in Babylon or Jerusalem) know in advance that five hundred years later (in the time of the end of the Second Temple) an individual would come along named Jesus from the city of Nazareth whose experiences would duplicate the dramas sketched in Isaiah 52–53?

In fact, of course, they wouldn't. Saying so is equivalent to saying in 2016 that in the year 2516, Blubbety-Blub will come along and it is Blubbety-Blub to whom the text refers in 2016. The determination is made retrospectively, not prospectively, and that retrospectivity is substituted for the prospectivity desired in and attributed to the 2016 account. The 2016 account is designated subsequently as predictive, but in fact it is both more than predictive and not predictive enough. It is more than predictive since it is in fact based on what historically will take place (since it has in fact already taken place). But it is also not predictive enough, and too limited in its scope, since it excludes all other possible candidates for the messianic agency it identifies. What if another figure five hundred years after Blubbety-Blub should come along and reorganize everything once again? How does the 2016 account know that the 2516 appearance is the unique appearance of such a figure, a singular messianic event? And on what basis does it exclude other figures who have come along after 2016 but prior to 2516, others who, in retrospect of 2516, have come to count as "false" messianic or prophetic figures?

What, then, would a prophetic account of the same text look like? It would be a genuinely prospective reading. It would begin in the present—2016—and forecast on the basis of known diachronic cultural patterns the inevitable conclusion of the dramas that are afoot. Its determinations would be absolute since they would be the dramas in which the culture has traditionally and continually participated. But they would also be infinitely open and free since those dramas—and therefore those endings—need not be invoked or, if invoked, need not be completed. Other dramas may intervene and other conclusions may obtain this time around. If the ending foreseen should in fact come about, then that ending fulfills the prediction only to the extent that it satisfies it rather than completes it once and for all. And the possibility (indeed, the necessity) of new fulfillments at some time in the future remain open.

Prospective rather than retrospective, absolute and specific rather than sketchy and relative, free rather than determined and constricted, and fulfilling though not completing once and for all, such prophetic reading would proceed above all contextually. It would read in terms of the texts, languages, cultural dramas, and practices already afoot in the circumstances to which it is assigned. In the above example, it would read in accord with the proto-rabbinic Jewish cultural milieus of the ancient sixth century, a reading that I have tried to suggest Jesus himself later chooses as his adoptive path, just as others around him choose other perspectives from the surrounding Jewish culture.

Why then is the weak reading important? Why is weak prophetic reading not just a false reading and able to be dismissed as such? Because it introduces the terms that are genuinely important, although without setting them in the right relationship to each other. It gives you the terms that need to be brought into relation, even if it gets wrong what that relationship should be.

Weak reading retains, in short, the structure of myth that serves above all and primarily the community from which it derives and for which it works as a narcissistic projective defense and etiological justification of the current situation rather than the open and freedom-based structure of the prophetic as we have tried to describe it.

Which brings us back to the work of René Girard.

René Girard reads in *Battling to the End* from a strong apocalyptic sense that shares fundamental affinities with the strong prophetic sense in both Judaism and Christianity. Within Christianity, those affinities derive from a young rabbi in Nazareth who is indisputably Jewish and at the same time indisputably at the center of Christian thinking, a young rabbi whose own personal affinities seem to have derived from a prophetic voice he identifies simply as "the prophet," in which prophetic and apocalyptic senses are fairly indistinguishable from each other.

Girard's reading of Clausewitz, then, as stumbling upon an understanding of reciprocity that conforms to the deepest prophetic insights of Christian scripture (which in turn conforms to the deepest prophetic insights of the writing that some six centuries earlier founded the text-centered thinking and practice from which the rabbinic perspective contemporary with Christian writers derived) opens new doors for us. It ushers in a new appreciation for Judaism, for Christianity, for the prophetic, for the apocalyptic, and for their interaction (in weak and strong varieties) throughout the history of western Europe, in which the dynamics of mimetic behavior, sacrificial violence, and their exposure in the religious texts of our culture (that Girard describes so compellingly) play themselves out.

It is to that history of the mimetic, the sacrificial, and their violent conflation in the context of biblical scripture and their prophetic and apocalyptic understanding that I would suggest Girardian research of the future might—dare I say "profitably"?—be oriented.

Notes

1. René Girard, *Achever Clausewitz* (Paris: Carnets Nord, 2007). The English version is *Battling to the End: Conversations with Benoît Chantre*, trans. Mary Baker (East Lansing: Michigan State University Press, 2009).

2. Clausewitz's treatise remains unfinished (which is why Girard plays on that idea with the title word "achever," which means among other things "finishing" or "completing") and was never published by the author in its entirety as a stand-alone document. Hence my reference to "the book we have." For the reference to Foucault, see, for example, Michel Foucault, *Society Must Be Defended: Lectures at the Collège de France, 1975–76*, ed. Mauro Bertani and Alessandro Fontana, trans. David Macey (New York: Picador, 2003), 15.

3. See, for example, Martin Buber, *The Prophetic Faith* (New York: Collier, 1985).

4. See Gershom Scholem, *The Messianic Idea in Judaism, and Other Essays on Jewish Spirituality* (New York: Schocken, 1995).

5. See Martin Buber, *On the Bible: Eighteen Studies*, ed. Nahum Glatzer, with an introduction by Harold Bloom (New York: Schocken, 1982), 172–87, and Martin Buber, *On Judaism*, ed. Nahum Glatzer (New York: Schocken, 1967), 214–25.

6. See George Steiner, "Our Homeland, the Text," *Salmagundi*, no. 66 (Winter–Spring 1985), 4–25.

7. Charles Mabee is developing what seems to me a brilliant prophetic reading of the four horsemen which in my view is indistinguishable from the strong apocalyptic reading.

8. See, for example, Walter Benjamin, "Theses on the Philosophy of History," in *Illuminations*, ed. Hannah Arendt (New York: Schocken, 1969), 253–64.

CHAPTER 11

READING THE ANTICHRIST TYPE

Christian Apocalyptic Typology and Girardian Mimesis

THOMAS RYBA

The Controversy Surrounding Biblical Typology and the Apocalyptic

Biblical typology—like the notion of the apocalyptic—is a widely contested concept, and there is less agreement about it as a literary form than there is agreement about the prophetic and apocalyptic genres. The controversialists engaged in this contest form three camps: (1) There are those who reject the idea and approach outright, usually on the basis of its obsolescence. These include scholars such as Bultmann, Irwin, Baumgärtel, van Ruler, Smart, Barr, Fohrer, Haag, and Gese; (2) There are those who argue that in its traditional form it is problematic, so that it is important to find more precise scientific substitutes for it. Scholars such as Phythian-Adams and Hebert prefer "homology"; Barth, von Balthasar, Pannenberg, Pohlman, and von Rad (with qualification) prefer "analogy"; Rowley prefers "patterns"; and Hanson prefers "parallel situations"; and (3) there are those scholars, such as Fritsch, Lambert, Goppelt, Moorehead, Ellison, von Rad, Baker, myself, and others, who think the traditional notion is unique (and thus warranted) but requires explication.[1]

Most often, those twentieth-century theological approaches affirmative of apocalyptic have emphasized its positive dimensions, arguing that it should be construed optimistically as a revelation of the openness of history to the unpredictable novelty of God's redemptive grace. In this, they emphasize the connotations of "apocalyptic" that are connected to the gnostic meaning of "apocalypse" as revelation according to a hidden code. Girard, on the other hand, has more pessimistically placed emphasis on the ominous connotations of the word, to the meaning of apocalyptic having to do with unavoidable catastrophic conflict.[2] Because Girard's more pessimistic appraisal dovetails with a specific Christian apocalyptic type—which has been my own part-time preoccupation for the past couple of years—in this essay I intend to propose a description of how apocalyptic typology and the type of the Antichrist function as well as how mimetic theory fits into these mechanics.

Among those who recognize typology as truth-expressive biblical communication, there is disagreement about whether there ought to be any limitation on it, or whether typology is an entirely open creative project. For example, one camp of defenders sees its application as virtually unlimited, with the effect that the reader is encouraged to be profligate in the discovery of types, so that any reading of the Bible is turned into raw material for engendering an unlimited number of tropes. Representative of this approach are works such as Ada Habershon's *Study of the Types*, a popular book that has been reprinted many times since its initial appearance in 1898, one in which the author begins with a vague and unexpressed pre-apprehension of what types are and then moves on to discover that a type may be expressed by any two biblical things brought into relation to one another in any way.[3] This reckless multiplication can sometimes be found in the patristic fathers as well, though generally they control typological production better than their Protestant critics claim. At the other extreme are the defenders of the type, who argue that the only admissible varieties are those which already appear in passages of scripture and especially in passages where *tupos* or cognates are used.[4] The moderate view is one that steers between either of these extremes.

As to its origins, typology is not a uniquely Christian invention, though it has been sometimes assumed to be such.[5] Rather, a large number of scholars have recognized its Old Testament origin, connecting it with prefiguration, ordination by God, or correspondence when the things connected by such relationships are individuals, institutions, and historical events.[6] As a kind of trope, types are most intimately connected with the prophetic and apocalyptic biblical genres in function and purpose.

Given all of these complications, is it then possible to specify exactly what a type is? Even as they set out to define its characteristics, some biblical scholars are reticent to provide too much precision, recognizing as they do the role of the Holy Spirit in illuminating both the author of this trope and its interpreter.[7] Cognizant of and in agreement with this last condition, I would rather opt for a description that provides the greatest specificity possible.

My intention in this essay is to explore the relationship between Christian typology and apocalyptic and to argue that apocalyptic typology functions prophetically,[8] but in a narrow sense. My chief concern will be the prophetic mechanics (or function) of typology according to the distinction between form and content. To explain an apocalyptic type's formal structure, I will draw on features of the Kantian notion of hypotyposis, the Weberian notion of an ideal-type, and the Husserlian notion of a manifold. To explain an apocalyptic type's content, I will have recourse to the Girardian theory of mimetic rivalry. Finally, I will argue that apocalyptic typology is not without renewable theological significance because, understood along the above lines, it can become a perennial optic for social criticism.

What Are Biblical Types?

The answer to this question can be approached either according to the field of meanings connected to the related biblical words (*tupos, tupikos, hupotupikos*, and so on) or according to the structural characteristics which all types have in common. I will take these up, each in turn.

The semantic field of tupos: A preliminary survey of the constellation of related biblical words makes it apparent that the semantic field of *tupos* is broad.[9] Most often, the Greek word *tupos* (type) signifies a pattern or an example, particularly in the sense of paradigmatic example, but it can also signify a characteristic mark, an image, or a representative structure or form.[10] The related term *tupikos* is more directly connected to prophecy and is employed only once (1 Corinthians 10:11) in the sense of a cautionary example or warning.[11] Other important, related terms are *antitupos*, the copy or anticipation of a true archetype, and *hupotupōsis*, an outline, adumbration, or underlying example that is "to be filled in or completed."[12] In a number of places, *tupos* also has the sense of an example that foreshadows, but—except for a couple of New Testament passages—is not a technical literary term.

Should anyone imagine that typology is confined to the New Testament as a form of retrospective discovery of Old Testament analogues, von Rad and Eichrodt have forcefully argued that typology is already present in the thought of the ancient Israelites. More recently, in a way consistent with the notion of a concrete analogical hypotype, mentioned below, G. W. Lorein has extended the Antichrist-type to the material of the Old Testament and the Intertestamental period, though his summary of the commonalities in this extension is disappointing.[13]

Some common characteristics of types: Overarching possible thematic deployments of typology is a further set of common structural characteristics.[14] These structural features are especially important for anyone who hopes to interpret types systematically.

First, biblical types manifest an analogical structure by which a copy and original are compared. Second, biblical types entail fulfillment along a series of instantiations from type to antitype (or ectype to archetype), whether these instantiations are historical or metaphysical. Third, biblical types are semantic forms that express increasing fulfillment in two senses: (a) there is a qualitative intensification or escalation (Goppelt's and von Rad's *Steigerung*) of the attributes present in the type, and (b) there is quantitative increase in the features fulfilled. Fourth, biblical types possess a sequential *Vorbild-Nachbild* (form-imposing vs. copy-formed) structure. In serial realizations of the type, it is also possible that what functions as the form-imposing type has already been pre-formed by another form-imposing type. In this case, other members of the series have a similar dual function, except for the original form-imposing type, whether that original (*Urbild*) is construed as archetype or antitype. Fifth, types fall into two categories: they are either historically sequential (diachronic) because they terminate in a historical fulfillment—which is badly named as "antype" (being the ultimate *Vorbild* for the series)—or they are ontologically sequential (diaontic) because they terminate in a perfection of being (which I will call the ontotype).[15] Historically, sequential types are also discovered in one of three ways: (a) retroactively, through a backward reading from their fulfillment; (b) prospectively, according to an anticipated fulfillment; or (c) dialectically, moving backward and forward from retroactive discovery to prospective fulfillment. Sixth, biblical types are accretive—they accumulate features as their penultimate fulfillments occur. Seventh, biblical types are teleologically structured. They are designed to direct the intentionality of their interpreters to see fulfillment in series of persons, events, and realities as connected with salvation history and/or the metaphysical structure of the cosmos. As intended, they are not fantasy, nor are they simply constructs of human consciousness. Rather, they are inspired semantic forms that call attention to real features of history (and being) and share a "secret affinity" with them.[16] Eighth, and finally, biblical types are often morally hortatory (or paranetic). They have a moral edge to them. Either they encourage positive imitation of moral qualities or behavior connected with the type or they are cautionary in discouraging sin or behavior connected with the type.[17]

A Phenomenological Interpretation of Biblical Types

The biblical and classical notions of a type, the Kantian notion of hypotyposis, the Weberian ideal-type, and the von Radian interpretation of biblical types are genetically related ideas. They form a sequence in the history of ideas, each idea being dependent on its predecessor. Put another way, the classical notion of type—as native to the Bible and ancient Greco-Roman culture—is unfolded to different purpose in each subsequent development, though those developments are partially dependent upon one another. It is for this reason that each may be seen as making a contribution to an explanation of how biblical typology functions.

Kant's notion of hypotyposis and biblical typology: In the *Critique of Judgment*, Immanuel Kant makes a stipulation that is useful for an understanding of the phenomenology connected with the reading of a trope.[18] There he describes a process of the exhibition of meaning which he terms "hypotyposis." According to Kant, hypotyposis consists in making a concept sensible in one of two ways, either schematically or symbolically: schematically, when the concept is expressed directly through a corresponding intuition whose content is sensorially filled; symbolically, when the concept, having no adequate sensible intuition, can only be thought by reason "in terms of the form of the reflection rather than the content" (*Critique of Judgment*, §59:351).[19]

What Kant has in mind is the difference between schematic hypotyposis as the demonstrative expression of a concept or type through concrete qualities versus symbolic hypotyposis as the expression of a type through an analogy that takes the rule used to reflect upon a sensible object only to apply it "to an entirely different object, of which the former [object] is only a symbol" (*Critique of Judgment*, §59:352). Typical of the Kantian philosophical style, this distinction, as perspicacious as it may be, is nearly inscrutable. It can, however, be made clearer through a couple of examples.

A schematic hypotyposis (or the corresponding hypotype) is a metonymic structure in which the individual qualities express the structure or schema without exhausting it. Symbolic hypotyposis is an analogical structure, where the individual qualities associated with two objects are not intended to express the sensorial content of the schema of those objects but to stand for a purely formal similarity shared by each.

Symbolic hypotyposis prevents a literalistic reading of biblical tropes that would otherwise transfer anthropomorphic, anthropopathic, or anthropopaic attributes to God. Symbolic hypotyposis is already recognized—though not named such—by both Christian theologians and the rabbis, the rabbis interpreting it in a way very close to Kant's intention. Like Kant, the Christian fathers and Jewish rabbis employ it to express the moral exemplarity and transcendence of God in relationship to humankind.

But the dichotomous nature of Kant's distinction seems to leave a possibility unrealized. There must also be a mediate form of hypotyposis between the schematic and the (purely) symbolic, because if it is possible to compare schematic hypotypes as analogues, then there must be a kind of hypotyposis that compares the sensorial content of these concrete realizations according to general structural similarities. I would argue that this is an overlooked kind which might be named "concrete analogical hypotyposis." It is this kind of hypotyposis that will allow us to account for the ability of a type to collect the specific similarities between types in a general form.[20]

In concrete analogical hypotyposis, two kinds of hypotyposis are operative, making a single type: schematic hypotyposis in two concrete expressions of a schema and analogical hypotyposis as the formal comparison of the schema that unites the two schematic hypotypes. Here, the concrete analogical hypotyposis will always require the schematic hypotyposis, but the reverse is not the case because it is impossible for the former to establish an analogy without concrete analogates. This substantiates what von Rad and others have said about biblical typology being an instance of the broader human talent for analogical thinking.[21]

Schematic hypotyposis is operative in prophetic writings and typologies, where the sensuous predicates connected with prophecies or types are realized in historical fulfillments; however, these predicates, historically instantiated, are *not* exhaustive of the prophecies or types. Thus, if the type possesses a set of quality placeholders that correspond to its possible characteristics, then concrete historical individuals or things may be seen to realize a subset of these characteristics. But it is also possible that a prophecy or type be read according to concrete analogical hypotyposis, when the general form of the analogy across schemas allows the interpreter to anticipate features which might occur in its next historical realization. In the case of the Antichrist, a particular instantiation—say that of the historical Nimrod, Nebuchadnezzar, Antiochus IV Epiphanes, Nero, Domitian, Frederick II, or Hitler—represents a particular "filling-in" of the schema of a type, without yet being the ultimate fulfillment of it. It is concrete analogical hypotyposis that operates comparatively across different types, and these anticipate but do not disclose their final term, *the* Antichrist who will fulfill the series. Concrete analogical hypotyposis seems to be related to what the patristics and medievals call the "spiritual sense" of the scriptures—especially in the form of allegory—a sense that must always be construed as dependent on and consistent with the literal meaning.

Concrete analogical hypotyposis is also operative in the analogy that unites the schemata of Kant's three *Critiques*. It is the formal analogy which collects (in the first *Critique*) the categories of understanding and their sensorial fillings, (in the second *Critique*) the categorical imperative and the specific moral acts which realize it, and (in the third *Critique*) the idea of beauty and its concrete embodiments.

Weberian ideal-types and biblical typology: What I have called concrete analogical hypotyposis—aside from its compatibility with the demands by von Rad, von Balthasar, Pannenberg, and others that typology be construed as a kind of analogy—also seems to be another name for what Max Weber called an "ideal-type."[22] Some of the features of Weber's type anticipate the reading of biblical typology provided here. Unlike Weber's ideal-type, however, biblical types are not scientific instruments, even though there are some commonalities.

According to Thomas Burger, ideal-types should be considered according to three aspects: (1) their logic, (2) their content, and (3) their function. In their logic, ideal-types are abstractions from reality in an "idealizing or exaggerating fashion."[23] This means that if the conditions prescribed by the ideal-type were fulfilled by the phenomena, they would behave as the type predicts. However, phenomena are too complex to behave exactly the way the idealization of the type predicts. The divergence of phenomena from the ideal-type measures the other factors that come into play in the real behavior of people.[24] The "substantive content" of ideal-types describes norms and plans that humans decide to follow in specific social situations and the acts and thoughts which follow from these.[25] These maxims are the general expression of the goal-oriented behavior typical of humans. Here, the formal properties of the type are like a Kantian maxim; its examples are similar to the concrete application of the maxim. Finally, the function of ideal-types is heuristic; it is to confirm, in particular circumstances, what kinds of "motives or action maxim" are active in the minds of the actors.[26] The Weberian examples of things that may be types—economy, city, bureaucracy, state, and so on—are not rigorous scientific concepts based upon inductive discovery because they are not constructed to disclose identical causal sequences present in all phenomena. Rather, they designate a serial order which more closely or more distantly collect the properties of the constellation of phenomena in question.[27]

The Weberian ideal-type is like the biblical ideal-type in that both form a serially ordered thought-image. Both are alike in that the phenomena they typify are instantiations of general structures of goal-directed behavior, though each type is employed to a different end. In this, they are like the relation between the content and form of the Kantian hypotypes. But though biblical typology is interested in the embedded structure of behavior as a moral warning or recommendation, Weberian ideal-types are employed not to recommend behavior but to predict and understand it. Biblical and Weberian types both also involve a one-sided exaggeration or intensification. It is my hunch that this is the origin of von Rad's claim that the biblical type involves an exaggeration of features, but it is also clear that von Rad's exaggeration means either (a) the excessive contribution of one of the type's historical instances to its meaning or (b) the progressive historical increase in some of the type's features. For Weberian ideal-types, the exaggeration is the specification of a particular schematic quality as a heuristic for explanation. The features of the biblical type do not principally function as prognostications—as they do for Weber's ideal-type—but they add to the scope of the type after the emergence of an historical instance expressing them. Biblical types are cumulative; they grow in significance until they achieve fulfillment in their antitype. In contrast, the Weberian type is a whole cloth at the beginning of the scientific project. It is assembled in advance of its application, and it confirms its features in historical instances.

Additional Husserlian precisions: It is probably not an accident that the process of thinking entailed by schematic hypotyposis may be thought of the as noetic complement to the Husserlian notion of "definite manifold," if that process is allowed to range across a whole world.[28] (And so what Weber thought difficult [or impossible] to conceptualize, Husserl provides the vocabulary to accomplish.)[29] Husserl defines a definite manifold as a finite set of concepts and propositions that are "determinate modalities of something in general."[30] It determines *"completely and unambiguously on pure lines of logical necessity the totality of all possible formations in the domain, so that in principle . . . nothing further* remains *open within it."*[31] This is very close to the notion of "a book on the world."[32] As it stands, however, it is too large a conception to be useful in explaining the biblical notion of a type. However, if a biblical type can be cashed out in terms of its propositional content—in other words, if it can be described in terms of its logical form and possible concrete qualitative fillings—then we might say that the biblical type is a small subset of propositions in that book. But how it marks out propositions which are eternally true for that world and how it is interpreted by the reader of the scriptures as referring to that world are two different things.

As it is experienced by those of us who are time bound, a type establishes a horizon of meaning that approximates (but incompletely characterizes) the object which it delineates.[33] Husserl thinks that this horizon of meaning can be sectioned into an internal horizon which is responsible for the typification of the meant object and an external horizon which is the context of its meaning. Though a meaning's internal horizon is relatively stable, the variability that a meaning possesses is a function of its external horizon or context, and there are contexts and typifications of meaning which are at odds and/or are incompatible with other sets of types.

How a type functions may instructively be contrasted with how a work of fiction functions.[34] A work of fiction establishes an imaginative secondary world, a mapping of a series of descriptions onto a possible world. Its author, if he is adept at conveying that world as consistent and vivid, engages the reader in an act of willing suspension of disbelief. This suspension of disbelief is intensified by the author's leaving certain features of that world vague and by his inviting the reader to concretize these features imaginatively. The context of this engagement is the awareness on the part of the reader that this is how fiction is supposed to work, though sometimes readers of novels are swallowed up in the fiction they love, and their willing suspension of disbelief metamorphoses into positive belief in the imaginary world.

It may be that types and prophecies are read in ways that have affinities with the reading of literature, but there are important differences. The suspension of disbelief, which is required for a novelistic world to achieve believability, is premised on the imagination's supplying concrete images where no description is provided. Literary, or constructive-imaginary, readings encourage the reader to flesh in the attributes of a character or scene when the details are left indeterminate. This corresponds to providing the frame for the Kantian schematic hypotype but allowing the reader to imagine the sensuous content.

Against this, apocalyptic prophecy proscribes such constructive-imaginative readings because they introduce unwarranted details. Constructive-imaginary readings of apocalyptic are always disastrous for predictability because they force upon the type a premature fulfillment. They preclude the type's extension to future events and thereby truncate its meaning. The result is that they predict a premature final fulfillment of the Apocalypse in the present, a fulfillment which (thus far) has proven to be false.[35] Constructive-imaginary readings of apocalyptic prophecies are a species of what A. N. Whitehead has called "the fallacy of misplaced concreteness."[36]

A type, in contrast, maps out a smaller segment of meaning than a work of fiction. It is not tied to an imaginary world intentionally, but it is supposed to map onto a segment of an actual world, a segment relative to the temporal experience of the reader and possessing a past, present, and future. Its expected form of intentionality is, from the start, that of belief, not the willing suspension of disbelief. Moreover, the contextual horizon for a type is not fictionally constructed. Rather, the type takes its context from the present actual world of its interpreter and the past, actual, antecedent horizon of sacred history. Like the work of fiction, features of the type are purposively kept undefined, but with the type—as is the case with the reading of prophecy—this is not an invitation for its interpreter to supply these details when the type does not explicitly indicate that its interpreter should do so. Quite to the contrary, the descriptive limitations on the type are supposed to be brakes on its interpreters' flights of fancy.

A type is in dialectical relationship to the salvation history that contextualizes it. The noetic acts involved in the reading of the type establish correspondences between past and present events in salvation history. These count as partial fulfillments of the type. The type also licenses the anticipation of future fulfillments, but in contrast to the concrete historical realizations, these anticipations are analogous, and relatively indistinct and vague, before the fact of their partial realization. They are known only as the historical events unfold. In this, biblical types are like what I have termed the concrete analogical hypotype.

Fulfillment in the meaning of a type must not be construed simply as the correspondence between an emergent event and its precise prediction. Fulfillment is also the emergence of new meaning; it is the novel discovery that the emergent event realizes unanticipated possibilities in the open future horizon of the prophecy. The purpose of the type is *to predict vaguely* and *be fulfilled concretely*; its purpose is to lead the interpreter to a series of licit interpretations that confirm its predictive intention while not being detailed, scientific prognostications. Rather, the fulfillment of a type is the realization that what was obscure has become concrete in the present. Ultimately, the licit interpretations produced will be recognized as a series of progressive fulfillments, but only retrospectively. This series reaches its final fulfillment in the antitype that is vaguely intended through each partial fulfillment and not fully pre-apprehended. In Husserlian terms, the type opens a horizon of partial fulfillments that can be indexed to real historical things, but a type may, as well, also possess a final future term at some indefinite historical point. The fulfillment of the type is not completely pre-given but is discovered in the present to which it is relevant.

When the interpreter of a type overloads it with details that it will not bear, he reads it as fiction and not as prophecy. And as he does this, he produces a false, illusory reading. This is pretty much the false way of all frustrated chiliastic expectations.

Summary formalization of the notion of a type: A type can be analyzed on the basis of the noetic horizon of the type and its noematic horizon. These are correlative notions that mutually condition one another. The noetic horizon refers to the way the type is understood as actively grasped. It involves the mental acts connected with the "reading" of the type. It is what Ingarden—had he addressed the notion of a type—would have called the cognition of the type.[37] Thus, this aspect may be understood as the cognitive formality of the type. On the other hand, there is the regular or relatively invariant content of the type that is encompassed within the noematic horizon of the type. This content is a potential that is teleologically pitched toward future fulfillments. This aspect of the type may be understood as the material or factual filling of the type.

It is possible to summarize the features of a type as follows:

1. A type is a relation between its (a) predicative words, (b) qualities, (c) respective quality magnitudes, and (d) things.

2. A type does not refer to a single thing but picks out many things, each of which may be said to be an instantiation of some of the type's qualities, some qualities having greater salience than others. We may say that a type is a trope whose relations to its instantiations is injective or many-to-one, that is to say that its predicative words single out different-sized sets of qualities in different things belonging to the same category.[38]
3. A type's fulfillment is progressive in the fulfillment of salient qualities both quantitatively and qualitatively.
4. The type also has built into it an expectation of fulfillment; this expectation is analogous to eschatological fulfillment, even when the type is not an eschatological type per se. In this way, typological thinking carries in it a similar intentional structure to that of eschatological thinking. This means that as historical instantiations of the projected ultimate fulfillment are realized, a deeper understanding of the original "promise" of the type becomes apparent.
5. A type is not simply a prophecy because a prophecy's validity is proven by the prophecy's coming true, either conditionally or not. However, a type functions like a prophecy, inasmuch as it anticipates future things as constituting fulfillments of it, but these will be partial until the realization of its antitype.[39]

The Antichrist—Both Antitype and Streptotype

Having sketched how typologies function, I would now like to explain in what sense the Antichrist may be understood as both antitype and streptotype. As we have seen, one kind of typology functions not only as indefinite prediction but as an optic for recognition. If diachronic typologies are connected as the fulfillment of the type in the antitype, it is also the case that though pointing to their antitype, they also admit intermediate forms.[40]

Right and wrong ways of reading the Antichrist: Now, there are right ways and wrong ways of reading the Antichrist. Wrong is to think of it as a trope whose time has passed. This incorrect understanding goes against the fact that types are configured to refer to historical things and the fact that its application to historical persons has already succeeded in a limited way. To read a type without understanding that it is about historical realization is a denial of the semantic import of prophecy. However, when it is granted that the trope has historical application and historical individuals *can* be identified with the Antichrist-type, then there are three possibilities for the way this identification may pan out: (a) there may be error in the identification; (b) the historical individual may be identified as merely one of a series; or (c) the historical individual may be identified as the final member in a series, the ultimate fulfillment of the apocalyptic prophecy or type.

Error in identification entails that though the type of the Antichrist may be associated with a particular human individual, the realized properties are not sufficient and/or not appropriate for the classification of that individual as a fulfillment of the type—not sufficient when the features of the identification are few and not particularly salient, nor appropriate when the features are fantastic accretions that have no justification in the structure of the type. In this case, the reading of the type does not meet a minimum threshold and thus is a false reading. As an example of insufficient typing (even as one of the little antichrists) might be the identification of a narcissistic and authoritarian leader of some country. It may be that this leader does indeed share a subset of traits with the Antichrist-type, but these traits together, as a constellation, are simply not enough to warrant the identification.

Historically, there have been many indefensible readings of the Antichrist, and many of these have bordered on the absurd. This is especially so when the characteristics of the type have been fancifully expanded.[41]

Another equally inadmissible approach to the reading of the Antichrist is the simple point by point reversal of the characteristics of the Christ to which the type is opposed. Though such a point by point negation is rarely carried out comprehensively, there are limited and unjustified applications of it in some interpretations of the Antichrist-type.

As a type, the Antichrist describes a series with intermediate realizations and a final fulfillment. Its function—like subjunctive prophecy—is principally cautionary, hamartiological, and diachronic. Its function is also historical. Types are not about fancy but future fact. This means that though many evil historical individuals have admissible associations with intermediate historical realizations of the type, they point to a final fulfillment. But in the interim, each realization functions as another cautionary warning about what happens when the Christian community fails to stand in solidarity against evil. When this solidarity is not great, then little antichrists achieve some limited supremacy. It may be that final antitype to which these antichrists point—*the* Antichrist—can be indefinitely deferred; but as a limit type, his historical arrival signals the general reprobation of humankind and the culmination of mimetic violence, symptoms which herald the end of the *aion*. But it is generally accepted that there are forces at work that hold the Antichrist back. In the New Testament, 2 Thessalonians 2:3–9 implies that the arrival of *the* Antichrist is held back by the power of someone mighty, and church fathers such as Tertullian, Lactantius, and others attributed the forestalling of the end both to the (imperfect) rule of law (or the secular Imperium) and to the grace of God as a mercy to faithful Christians.[42]

In the history of Christianity, in the middle patristic period and beyond, the views of the relevance of the apocalyptic writings fall along a spectrum. The spectrum is defined by imminent chiliastic expectation at one end, and that of deferred chiliastic expectation at the other.

Imminent chiliastic speculation is phenomenologically associated with the cyclical experience of successive expectations, frustrations, legitimations of the delay, and then with the cycle beginning again with restored expectations. That this imminentization of the eschaton can be "coked-up" again and again in the lifetime of a community (let alone a single individual) seems irrational, but it is probably a symptom of the intensity of alienation they experience.[43] Nevertheless, it is a pattern one sees repeated in connection with denominations within which anxiety about the world is great. This may be related to disengagement of their values and theology from that of the wider culture.

In contrast, other Christian traditions have domesticated the arrival of the Apocalypse either by (a) a strategy of discontinuity which interprets and thereby displaces the Kingdom of God to another plane of metaphysical existence so that it becomes the Kingdom of Heaven or (b) a strategy which shows the marks of acceptance of the worldly order by the immanentization of the eschaton.[44] The latter eschatology dissolves the frightening challenge of the eschaton according to a particular interpretation of the "now-and-not-quite-yet" structure, arguing that the Kingdom of God is indeed coming, though it will be built by

Christians on earth. For all practical purposes, apocalyptic chiliasm has been rejected by Roman Catholic theologians. This means that without the outright denial of the Second Coming, most contemporary Roman Catholic writers on eschatology opt for one or the other varieties of the domestication of the apocalypse.[45]

Although some scholars of the New Testament have argued that the "deferred" eschatology of the later epistles of St. Paul as well as the Gospels of Luke and John signals an indefinite deferral of the apocalypse, and that this is the original move that establishes the broader tendency, I do not see that the evidence must be interpreted quite this simply. It may be true that each work possesses the now-and-not-quite-yet structure of realized eschatology. But this does not automatically exclude the justified expectation of a horrific final apocalypse as well as little apocalypses along the way. A particularly good case in point is the First Epistle of John. This writer's treatment of the Antichrist demonstrates that a deferred apocalyptic need not necessarily be coupled with the eschaton's domestication.

How, then, ought we read the Antichrist?: The right reading of the antichrists/Antichrist begins by allowing the biblically delimited passages to establish the qualitative placeholders for the description and then see whether individual historical figures fit this general form. If they do, their concrete realizations allow us to add features to the type that could not otherwise be anticipated in the structure of the original general type. We are greatly aided in reading the Antichrist-type—in contrast to other apocalyptic types connected with it—by what the scriptures say about him and also what they indicate to be his characteristic negations of the Christ. What one can establish, I think, is a reading which is not simply a point by point reversal of the Christ-model, but rather a reversal of only the salient features of that type. I call this partial set of antithetical characteristics the *streptotype* (from *strepho-* or *streptos/strepsis-*, meaning "to twist" or "a twisting" and *tupos*, "type"). Thus, a streptotype is a type that twists the features of the type against which it negatively models itself, against which it creates a negative, mimetic double.[46]

Because the Antichrist streptotype requires a reading that is not a mechanical negation or reversal of Christological virtues and powers, it requires a reading which interprets this type as a twisting reconfiguration of them into a new form. A proper reading of the Antichrist must be limited by the parameters of the biblical trope supplemented by biblical

Christology, so that at base the reading of the Antichrist will be a biblically based anti-Christology. This presupposes that before we go any further, we first assemble a complete description of the trope on the basis of this biblical Christology. However, if theology has any merit as a "science" for discovery of truths implicit in scripture, then its scientific elaboration of scripture will also allow us to extend the Antichrist-type in a way that is more developed than that which is contained within scripture, but one that avoids the kind of baseless speculation which in the past has often characterized the interpretation of this type. This entails a reading of the Antichrist that would take classical Christological and biblical descriptions, together, as the basis for a streptological reading. I think this new theological extension will have some theological and hamartiological implications that have not before been made explicit. It will also have implications for Christian social responsibility and action. One of the grounding behavioral assumptions supporting these implications must be the Girardian mimetic theory.[47]

The start of this new approach to the reading of the Antichrist begins with the premise that this trope refers to something historically identifiable according to the pattern "past-and-now-and-not-quite-yet." This is an attempt to reinstall eschatological expectation at the heart of this trope, something that seems to be demanded by the very notion of type in the scriptures. But it has practical implications for present Christian action as well.[48]

Alien to this application is the desire to stir up yet another false expectation of the premature arrival of the end of things, which is much more common among fundamentalist denominations than among the Roman Catholic or Reformation traditions. Such false expectations are almost always coupled with hopelessness about the evil of the world, a hopelessness that borders on despair. *No Christian*—except one *in extremis—wants to live during the reign of the Antichrist*. A genuine apocalyptic desire, in the present generation, can only be proclaimed by those already at or beyond the threshold of despair. In the present, the only Christians who are capable of pleading maranatha! without any modicum of insincerity are either those who are already in the throes of a great persecution or those whose awareness of their collective impotence in (what they see as) an evil world causes them to roil and fulminate in a hell of resentment, a hell of their own making.[49]

Even so, I think we deny the pattern of the partial realization of little antichrists in John's epistle only at our own peril. The belief that both God and the Father of Lies are at work even in the new age begun by Christ's First Coming establishes a caution as well as a moral charge for Christians. This cautionary purpose is in conformity with some of Jesus's eschatological parables in the New Testament.[50] And it sets before us a renewable task. It shows us the work we must do to hold back the forces of anomie, and it warns us also not to be duped by the power and glory of leaders who would claim equivalence to God. In short, the type of the Antichrist functions as a powerful condemnation of anti-idolatry refracted through a Christian lens.

Essential to Paul's teaching is the implication that the Antichrist and related tropes must be preserved as a potent form of Christian social criticism. Clearly, I am not proposing that we spill gasoline on an already inflamed and uncivil public discourse. I think moderation is prudent. At the same time, I think the Antichrist-type has great revelatory value for Christian moral witness, and it is in that spirit that it should be applied. Christians are warranted in taking the "already-but-not-yet" structure of apocalyptic eschatology seriously: we *should* actively look for the little antichrists around us. Truth be told, I think we ought actively to cultivate this scrutiny. If we do take the Antichrist-type's historical applicability seriously, then (with the benefit of 20/20 hindsight) we are able to see that the fact that there have really been little antichrists is a part of this trope's ongoing significance, at least until the final antitype in the series can be deferred no longer. For the Christian, the Antichrist-type is a prophetic reminder that the man of lawlessness will appear at the nadir of the righteousness in the world. The Antichrist-type is a wake-up call to forestall his arrival; the apocalyptic narrative is an exhortation to endurance in hope, should an antichrist appear.

Notes

A much longer (and slightly less developed) version of this essay was presented at the conference "Dangerous Liaisons: Theology, Social Sciences, and Modernity," Warsaw, April 12, 2012, sponsored by the Institute of Sociology, University of Warsaw, and the (Polish) Centre for Thought of John Paul II.

1. See the very useful discussion (and bibliography in need of updating) in D. L. Baker, *Two Testaments: One Bible* (Leicester, UK: Inter-Varsity Press, 1976), 239–43.

2. In the variant of this essay presented in Warsaw in April 2012, I discussed the biblical conception of apocalyptic at greater length. Although apocalyptic is a form within many biblical literary units—in gospels, epistles, prophetic books, and so on—it also constitutes a separate literary subgenre, the apocalypse. Apocalypses typically fall into two varieties, those that emphasize spirit flight resulting in gnostic revelations and those that emphasize the near triumph of evil over the people of God. Sometimes these varieties are found mixed in a syncretistic aggregate. Among special literary features of apocalypses are pseudonymous and anachronistic authorship, internal *de re* and *de facto* claims to authority, the embedding of ancient prophecies in a contemporary narrative, symbolic and typological encrypting of prophecy, and—because of this encrypting—a prophetic revelation that was understood only as it began to come to pass. Among the thematic features of apocalypse are the foreordination of human history and accompanying pessimism about the power of humans to avert the final catastrophe, apparent assertion of (near) dualism between the forces of good and evil, symmetry between cosmic conflict and earthly conflict, the incursion of supernatural actors into history, the expectation of divine intervention near the end of the narrative to avert catastrophe, the resurrection (or expectation of the resurrection) of the dead, and the arrival or establishment of a new order in creation.

3. The newest reprinting (its twentieth!) is Ada R. Habershon, *Study of the Types* (Grand Rapids, MI: Kregel, 2001).

4. I am reticent to enter a dog in this fight, although I will admit—and I think it also will become apparent—that my sympathies are on the side of the limiters of the type as a hermeneutical tool. My concern is to provide a description of what biblical typology is, so that I can use this description to guide me in a correct interpretation of the significance of the Antichrist as a type.

5. Von Rad is the expert at marshaling this evidence against Goppelt, who claims it is a New Testament creation, but Goppelt, I think, defines typology too narrowly. See Gerhard von Rad's *Old Testament Theology*, especially the second volume (cited below, note 17).

6. Baker, *Two Testaments*, 242–43.

7. Von Rad put this very strongly when he says that for the handling of particular texts, no norm of typological interpretations can pedagogically be set up because "it cannot be further regulated hermeneutically, but takes place in the freedom of the Holy Spirit." Gerhard von Rad, "Typological Interpretation of the Old Testament," in *Essays on Old Testament Hermeneutics*, ed. Claus Westermann, trans. J. L. Mays (Richmond, VA: John Knox, 1963), 38.

8. Like Sandor Goodhart, I think apocalyptic is a subgenre of the prophetic. Among the important features of biblical prophetic are (1) irresistibility (Jeremiah 20:7, 9; Amos 3:3–8); (2) certainty (Jeremiah 26:12ff.); (3) direct or indirect attribution of the utterance to YHWH (Ko 'amar Yaweh!) (Deuteronomy 18:9–22); (4) *conformity of prophecy to doctrine*; (5) the necessity of predicted events (foretelling: Jeremiah 28:15–17); (6) subjunctive modality (forth-telling: Jeremiah 18:7–10); (7) cautionary, hortatory, or paranetic purpose; (8) limitation in scope and detail; and (9) incomplete determinacy implying a strategic choice on God's part, a choice to divulge only part of a future to prevent its being known and changed. The apocalyptic subgenre possesses seven of the nine features: 1, 2, 4, 5, 7, 8, and 9.

9. The semantic field of a word (and its cognates) carves out a sector of a world and the states of affairs therein. See N. C. W. Spence, "Linguistic Fields, Conceptual Systems, and the Weltbild," *Transactions of the Philological Society* 60 (1961): 87–106. See also Thomas Ryba, *The Essence of Phenomenology and Its Meaning for the Scientific Study of Religion*, Toronto Studies in Religion 7 (New York: Peter Lang, 2001), 6–9.

10. Baker, *Two Testaments*, 251.

11. The passage requires quotation to establish the prophetic sense: "Nor let us act immorally, as some of them did, and twenty-three thousand fell in one day. Nor let us try the Lord, as some of them did, and were destroyed by the serpents. Nor grumble, as some of them did, and were destroyed by the destroyer. Now these things happened to them as an example [*tupikōs*], and they were written for our instruction, upon whom the ends of the ages have come. Therefore let him who thinks he stands take heed that he does not fall" (1 Corinthians 8–12). *Antitupos* here reverses the convention that scholars use in defining it, and *hupotuposis* gives Kant the semantics of the word for his philosophical interpretation. See the discussion that follows.

12. See Richard M. Davidson, *Typology in Scripture: A Study of Hermeneutical Τύπος Structures* (Berrien Springs, MI: Andrews University Press, 1981), 173–74.

13. Lorein's scholarship is very careful and provides much useful data for the theologian. Unlike the theologian, however, he refuses to do a "backwards" (or temporally dialectical) reading of the Antichrist-type and instead opts for a historically progressive reading of the data. This means he discovers only the least common denominator shared by the sequential types in literature preceding the New Testament and by the New Testament Antichrist-type. I would argue that the view of biblical typology which I have presented here requires the cumulative addition of each type's features, including a diagnosis of the motivation of each. Lorein's description of these common features follows: "The Antichrist is a

man who will appear at the end of time, wholly filled with Satan. He will be an arch deceiver, as a tyrant (unjust, murderous) and as a false god (turning himself and others away from all existing religion). Other descriptions are "man of lawlessness," "Beast," and "false prophet" (the latter only for his religious aspect)." See G. W. Lorein, *The Antichrist Theme in the Intertestamental Period* (London: T & T Clark, 2003), 29 and throughout.

14. Davidson, *Typology in Scripture*, 397–98. Though the examination of its semantic field gives us a sense of the meaning of *tupos*, the context of its usage warrants New Testament scholars to associate it with a set of theological themes as well. Davidson's laudably careful study of these contexts establishes five of these uses: (1) a hermeneutical deployment, (2) a Christological-soteriological deployment, (3) an ecclesiological deployment, (4) a prophetic deployment, and (5) an eschatological deployment that includes apocalyptic types. Against the claims of some scholars, Davidson shows that there is, indeed, a hermeneutical deployment of typology in the Old Testament. As an interpretive device, a type is used to signify the historical correspondences between Old and New Testament, persons, events, and institutions. The Christological-soteriological deployment especially occurs in those contexts where cultic practices or persons (sacrifice or priesthood) find their fulfillment in Christ, just as Old Testament realities are seen as being positively or negatively fulfilled in the salvific promise of the new covenant. The ecclesiological deployment occurs whenever an Old Testament person, event, or institution finds fulfillment in the individual worshippers, the community, or the sacraments of the Church, while the prophetic deployment involves an anticipatory presentation or prefiguration of New Testament persons, events, or realities by corresponding things in the Old Testament. In each of these anticipations, a divine design is referenced that includes some specific details of the anticipated fulfillment, this fulfillment rolling out without violating human freedom of choice. Even so, the prophetic anticipation connected with prophetic types also possesses a strong *devoir-être* (there must needs be) structure. This suggests an ineluctable necessity operating through God's providential plan while simultaneously presuming the freedom of human response to the evangelical message. Here, paradoxical compatibilist presuppositions would seem to be hardwired into prophetic types. Finally, the deployment of eschatological types builds on the determinist characteristics of prophetic deployment but connects Old Testament persons, events, and realities with their ultimate fulfillment in the New Testament. In such tropes, this fulfillment is associated with either the arrival of the new *aion* or the events at the end of time. As such, eschatological types may be considered confluent with the apocalyptic.

15. Diachronic types are types that are developed and intensified across time. Diaontic types are types that are instantiated across orders of being.

Biblical types, when diachronic, are types that find their expansion and fulfillment in later history, in their antitypes, as the traditional description would have it. Here, the type anticipates and is fulfilled in the antitype. Biblical types, when diaontic, are concrete mimetic instantiations of a heavenly archetype. In the diaontic type, the earthly ectype is fulfilled in the heavenly archetype. Diaontic types may also have a temporally horizontal development that is equivalent to an incomplete diachronic fulfillment, but they are different in that they begin according to a divine model in the first instance. Though Plato would not have admitted the objects signified by diaontic biblical types as forms or eternal objects, and though the metaphysical explanation of their ingression and function in the Platonic and Neoplatonic philosophies is distinctive—because the biblical text makes no provision for similar metaphysical explanations—the diaonticity of the Platonic forms and the diaonticity of heavenly tabernacle in the Bible are analogous.

16. The English divine, Archbishop Trench, expressed this presumed affinity beautifully: "The parable or other analogy to spiritual truth appropriated from the world of nature or man, is not merely illustration but some sort of proof. It is not merely that analogies assist to make the truth intelligible. . . . Their power lies deeper than this, in the harmony . . . between the natural and spiritual worlds, so that analogies from the first are felt to be something more than illustrations. . . . They belong to one another, the type and the thing typified, by an inward necessity; they were linked together long before by the law of a secret affinity." R. C. Trench, *The Fitness of the Holy Scriptures for Unfolding the Spiritual Life of Men* & *Christ the Desire of All Nations*, Hulsean Lectures, 1845 and 1846 (Cambridge: Cambridge University Press, 1859), 12–14, cited in D. L. Baker, *Two Testaments*, 254.

17. Some examples of universally recognized types in the Old Testament are in Isaiah, Garden of Eden is a type of the New Paradise (Isaiah 9:1–2; 11:6–9); in Hosea, the Exodus wandering in the wilderness is a type of the predicted wandering of the Jews in the future (Hosea 2:16–17, 14–15; 12:9–10; Jeremiah 31:2); also related to the Exodus, in Deutero-Isaiah, is the type of Exodus as anticipating a new Exodus (Isaiah 43:16–21; 48:20–21; 51:9–11, etc.); across many prophets the figure of David is a type of the once and future King, Messiah, or deliverer of Israel (Isaiah 11:1; 55:3–4; Jeremiah 23:5; Amos 9:11, etc.); in the Pentateuch, Abraham is the type of the faithful (Genesis 15:6), Moses is a type of the prophets (Deuteronomy 18:15, 18), and the manna in the desert is a type of God's loving provision for his people (Exodus 16:9–27). These types sometimes have continuity with New Testament types as well, especially the types of Abraham, David, and manna. See Baker, *Two Testaments*, 243–44, and von Rad, "Typological Interpretation of the Old Testament," 20–21; Gerhard

von Rad, *Old Testament Theology*, vol. 2, trans. D. M. G. Stalker (1960; New York: Harper & Row, 1965), 329–34.

18. Though I reject many of the presuppositions of Kant's, his exposition of the distinction between symbolic and schematic hypotyposes does have utility for the explanation of the meaning of scripture, in general, and the meaning of the type of the Antichrist, in particular.

19. Immanuel Kant, *Critique of Judgment*, trans. Werner Pluhar (1790; Indianapolis: Hackett, 1987). Numbers after the section number refer to the Akademie edition numbers in margin.

20. A schematic hypotype can be represented by an equation: $x + y = z$, where x, y, z are variable placeholders and +, = are the functors or regular formal features. In a schematic hypotype, the sensorial content may be variable (x, y, z), though they are fulfilled by specific sensorial contents (a, b, c). In a symbolic hypotype, an analogy is established between the formal features of two schemas, one sensorial, the other unknown or projective. Thus, an analogy is intended between $x + y = z$ and $?_x + ?_y = ?_z$, where the terms of the analogies are the functors and a set of concrete sensorial fillings are known in the first form (a, b, c) but are nonsensorial (and thus transcendent) in the second ($?_x, ?_y, ?_z$). Here the analogy is what is important as a means for taking the formal structure of a schematic type as a model for another structure whose material contents are transcendental predicates that are sensorially unknown. In the symbolic hypotype, a schematic hypotype stands for (or symbolizes) another type, which transcends sensation. In what I am calling a "concrete analogical hypotype," two (or more) schematic hypotypes are joined together in a supervening type, so that all of the formal features and all of the material contents are combined.

21. As Gerhard von Rad has it, "Typological thinking is an elementary function of all human thought on interpretation.... Without this interpretive, analogical sort of thinking there would be no poetry. The poet ... sees the often insignificant, obvious things and recognizes in them ultimate value.... The theological or pseudo-theological presuppositions of this poetic mode of interpretation ought to be of interest to theologians, too, for concern here is continually with revelations, and with the belief that the world which surrounds man possesses transparence." "Typological Interpretation of the Old Testament," 17–18.

22. The individual ideas and ideals of actors, the actors' evaluations of these notions, and the subjective choices made on the basis of such evaluations make up an "intensively infinite manifold that cannot qualify as a coherent object of scientific knowledge." Guy Oakes, *Weber and Rickert: Concept Formation in the Cultural Sciences* (Cambridge, MA: MIT Press, 1988), 29. Cultural values, on the other hand, establish the general types within which the constitution

of behavior can be approached, but subjective meaning is not simply cultural meaning. Ideal-types provide the means for establishing the intelligibility of actions in culture, by being instruments by which cultural objects may be understood in accord with the interests of the social sciences. Ibid., 29–31.

23. Thomas Burger, *Max Weber's Theory of Concept Formation: History, Laws, and Ideal Types* (Durham, NC: Duke University Press, 1987), 154.

24. Ibid., 155.

25. Ibid., 154.

26. Ibid., 155.

27. Weber's classic definition of the ideal-type is in his essay "'Objectivity' in the Social Sciences": "An ideal-type is formed by the one-sided *exaggeration/accentuation* (*Steigerung*) of *one* or *more* points of view and by the synthesis of a great many diffuse, discrete, more or less present and occasionally absent *concrete individual* phenomena, which are in accordance with those one-sidedly emphasized view-points, and which are arranged into an internally consistent *thought-image*. In its conceptual purity, this thought-image cannot be found empirically anywhere in reality. It is a *utopia*." Max Weber, *The Methodology of the Social Sciences*, ed. and trans. Edward Shils and Henry Finch (New York: The Free Press, 1949), 90 (mutatis mutandis).

28. One node of intellectual transmission of Kant's idea of the manifold to Husserl was probably his teacher Leopold Kronecker, when Husserl was a mathematics graduate student. See Gottfried Martin, *Arithmetic and Combinatorics: Kant and His Contemporaries*, ed. and trans. Judy Wubnig (1972; Carbondale, IL: SIU Press, 1985), 89–93.

29. Burger, *Max Weber's Theory of Concept Formation*, 157.

30. Edmund Husserl, *The Crisis of European Sciences and Phenomenology*, trans. Davis Carr (Evanston, IL: Northwestern University Press, 1973), 45–46.

31. Edmund Husserl, *Ideas*, vol. 1, trans. W. R. Boyce Gibson (London: George Allen and Unwin, 1976), 204.

32. Thomas Pavel describes a book on the world broadly as "a complete set of propositions true *in that world*" (emphasis added). This allows a notion of truth relative to possible worlds. But Alvin Plantinga thinks there is something odd about this. For him, truth *simpliciter* is associated with actual worlds, so that, for Plantinga, a book on the world can only be a set of propositions which are true *simpliciter*. Plantinga's definition is more precise in that he associates a book on a world with an actual world. Truth for possible worlds is a truth that would obtain only if such worlds were actual. For possible worlds, truth values are in the subjunctive mode. Alvin Plantinga, *The Nature of Necessity* (Oxford: Clarendon Press, 1974), 47, and Thomas Pavel, *Fictional Worlds* (Cambridge, MA: Harvard University Press, 1986), 51.

33. This horizon may be divided into two parts, the act (or noetic) horizon of the meaning, and the object (or noematic) horizon of the meaning, and these can be divided further into antecedent, co-present, and consequent horizons.

34. For those interested in my attempt to give a phenomenological description of how fiction, suspension of disbelief, and possible worlds fit together, see Thomas Ryba, "Husserl, Fantasy and Possible Worlds," in *Phenomenology and Aesthetics: Approaches to Comparative Literature and the Other Arts*, ed. Marlies Kronegger, Analecta Husserliana 32 (Dordrecht, Netherlands: Kluwer Academic, 1990), 227–37.

35. The work of pop theology, *The Late Great Planet Earth*, by Hal Lindsey, is well-known. Lindsey's book is an incredibly specific eisegesis of the biblical apocalyptic texts. Its thesis has gone through multiple revisions and multiple recastings since this book was first published in 1970. Despite changes made to the thesis of the book to fit the ever-changing geopolitical scene, the scenario set forth in Lindsey's book has never been realized in any significant detail. For this as a paradigm of the fallacy of misplaced concreteness in reading apocalyptic literature, see Hal Lindsey, *The Late Great Planet Earth* (Grand Rapids, MI: Zondervan, 1970).

36. Alfred North Whitehead, *Science and the Modern World* (Cambridge: Cambridge University Press, 1926), 64, 72.

37. See Roman Ingarden, *The Cognition of the Literary Work of Art* (Evanston, IL: Northwestern University Press, 1973), esp. 3–93.

38. Assuming that the number of qualities realized in two instantiations is the same, if more salient qualities are realized in one of its instantiations in comparison to another, that instantiation is closer to "fulfillment." (Such an instance better fulfills the type than the other.) Two fulfilling instances of a type possessing the same number of qualities having the same salience can be further differentiated and (in theory) scaled on the basis of the respective perfection of those qualities. However, fulfillment is also a matter of the accretion of related qualities, so that there can be a quantitative increase in features that make the antitype's realization more concrete. Types are read as singling out sequences of things that can be scaled with respect to fulfillment.

If the type is an ontotype, that scale is arranged according to the number of properties realized in instances (ectypes) as approaching the perfection of the archetype. If a type is pitched toward an antitype, then that type falls into a temporal series of subtypes. Generally speaking, the later instantiations of the type—which are intensified by numbers, salience, and magnitude of qualities—are closer to fulfillment, that fulfillment being represented in the last instance in the series, their antitype.

The antitype, though not fully pre-apprehended in its particularity, is the end anticipated in—or viewed through—the serial reading of its instances. I think we can understand this as indicating that the type of the Antichrist—like other biblical types—is anticipatory in expecting a set of partial realizations, some of which have already been historically realized. In other words, a type must be taken to signify real historical personages as well as a final one in the series. Membership in a projective series entails that a historical individual will possess enough properties encoded in the idea that the intending of that individual constitutes a penultimate fulfillment of the type or prophecy. Being the final member of the series entails that the historical individual is the maximal fulfillment of the type or prophecy and that he is also the last in the series.

39. To make what I have suggested a bit clearer, it is helpful to think about the idea of a type in terms of what I. M. Bochenski has termed "a semantic complex." A semantic complex is a relation across words, things, properties, and relations.

40. By scholarly convention, an antitype (*anti-* + *tupos* = before the type, before the types that emulates it) is the preeminent type in a series of fulfillments; it is the exemplar for the series. There is also a less conventional use of the term—mostly in literary studies—which stipulates another meaning of antitype, and that is one which takes the prefix "anti-" as meaning "against." In this sense, an antitype is a type formed against or as a reversal to another type that it models negatively. Certainly, this is the way the prefix is used in the title "Antichrist," but this meaning is not the convention in biblical studies. Nevertheless, it is clear from the scriptural passages that employ the term "Antichrist" that it is to be used in both senses. The term "Antichrist" designates a series of anticipations, the little antichrists in 1 John 2:17–23, but it also represents the fulfillment—*the* Antichrist—who is to come at the time of the apocalypse. It is also clear, however, that "antichrist/Antichrist" with both significations is to be taken as the obverse of the Christ. The challenge, I think, is to develop an interpretive strategy that will allow us to flesh in this type as a reversal of the type to which it is opposed.

41. Bernard McGinn has provided a very interesting taxonomy of the inappropriate speculations about the physiognomic features of the Antichrist, which is an object lesson in how not to think of the Antichrist. From a series of Eastern texts from the third century CE, a catalogue of the expected physical characteristics of the Antichrist was built up so that his advent could be recognized by the kind of hair (fiery, gray, black, spiky, etc.), head (large, bald, three-crested), eyes (bloody, dead, on a stalk, etc.), pupils (two in his left eye), bodily marks (sickle of desolation, mutable signs, the marks "α-τ-χ"), and so on. No doubt,

there were interpretive codes beyond these speculations, but what makes them bad readings of the type is that they do not proceed according to the type's biblical meaning but use it as a springboard into unwarranted speculation. Also, their sheer variety and inventiveness cause them to be noncomparable. Bernard McGinn, "Portraying Antichrist in the Middle Ages," in *The Use and Abuse of Eschatology in the Middle Ages*, ed. Werner Verbeke, Daniel Verhelst, and Andries Welkenhuysen, Mediaevalia Lovaniensia (Leuven, Belgium: Leuven University Press, 1988), 1–48; Bernard McGinn, *Antichrist: Two Thousand Years of the Human Fascination with Evil* (New York: Columbia University Press, 2000), 68–70, 72–73.

42. This is mentioned by Blumenberg and Agamben in connection with Paul, Tertullian, and Lactantius, but it is a view not limited to these three figures in the patristic period. Chrysostum, Severian of Gabala, Theodoret of Cyr, Basil the Great, and Cyril of Jerusalem all have explanations of this delay. See Colossians 1–2, Thessalonians 1–2, Timothy, Titus, Philemon. Peter Gorday, ed., *Ancient Christian Commentary on Scripture*, New Testament 9 (Downers Grove, IL: InterVarsity Press, 2000), 110–11; Giorgio Agamben, *The Time That Remains*, trans. Patricia Dailey (Stanford, CA: Stanford University Press, 2005), 108–12; Hans Blumenberg, *The Legitimacy of the Modern Age* (Cambridge, MA: MIT Press, 1985), 41–42.

43. A classic case study of this imminentization of the eschaton in connection with a flying saucer cult can be found in Louis Festinger, Henry Riecken, and Stanley Schachter, *When Prophecy Fails: A Social and Psychological Study of a Modern Group That Predicted the Destruction of the World* (New York: Harper Torchbooks, 1964).

44. This is Eric Voegelin's happy phrase that I remember from my college days. At political gatherings of young conservative students in those days, one could see wonks sporting buttons with the legend "Don't immanentize the Eschaton!"

45. A good example of this trend is the view of Zachary Hayes, OFM: "The parousia is not a return of the Lord who has been absent from the world since his resurrection, but the final breaking through of the victorious presence of divine grace that has been present continuously throughout history, and in a special way since the death and resurrection of Christ. The *parousia* is not so much a question of Christ coming back to the world, but the world arriving at its goal with God in Christ. It may be unfortunate to use the term 'second' coming at all, since the usage seems to distinguish from a 'first' coming in the incarnation. . . . When the emphasis is placed on [*parousia* as] 'presence,' then the whole history after the death of Jesus is the mystery of his abiding presence or *Parousia*." Zachary Hayes, *Visions of the Future: A Study of Christian Eschatology*

(Collegeville, MN: Liturgical Press, 1990), 162–63. In defense of his view, which is a bit more nuanced than this passage suggests, Hayes does admit that apocalyptic thought creates a tension which is a call to conversion (35), and he identifies it with the later eschatological views of Rahner. See Hayes's full volume.

Notable exceptions to this tendency can be found among liberation theologians. An especially compelling presentation of how apocalyptic texts empower the destitute in trying times, how apocalypticism is thematically related to liberation theology, and how apocalyptic intentionality may be compared to the kataphatic and apophatic poles of mystical theology can be found in J. Matthew Ashley, "Apocalypticism in Political and Liberation Theology: Toward an Historical *Docta Ignorantia*," *Horizons* 27, no. 1 (Spring 2000): 22–43.

46. R. W. Brown. *Composition of Scientific Words: A Manual of Methods and a Lexicon of Materials for the Practice of Logotechnics* (Washington, DC: Smithsonian Institution Press, 1956), 821.

47. In a paper I read at the 2005 COV&R conference in Schoenstatt, Germany, titled "Optics of the Antichrist," I sketched some of the Girardian contents to the notion of the Antichrist-type, among them the relation between mimetic theory and concealment, scandal, and hypocrisy. I intend to augment the present essay, the version of it presented in Warsaw, and the paper presented in Schoenstatt with an extensive treatment of Satan's mimetic rivalry with God. These I am in the process of turning into a book of the same title as the 2005 paper. Unfortunately, limited time does not allow me to revisit these treatments.

48. Jürgen Moltmann's affirmation of the living significance of apocalyptic and its relation to history (contra Karl Löwith) has an apt application to the Antichrist-type:

> The relation [of apocalyptic] to every future is certainly not that of a recounting [of what is wholly settled]; it is essentially an anticipation through the medium of the imagination, because the future has not yet happened. There can be no ultimate telling of the ultimate future, but only divine promises and human expectations. Nevertheless, just as there is future in the past, so there could also be past in the future. Can we not by way of scenarios describe what in the future will pass away? Can the Christian hope for the victory of God's justice and righteousness not 'tell' of the passing away of the powers of injustice and death? . . . Here too we must distinguish: *the negation of the negative* can be told [this means] to take up our German proverb once more, an end with terror ends the terror without end that has been experienced here and now. The position of the positive—the new heaven and the new earth, and the heavenly Jerusalem—are anticipated

on the basis of the position already experienced— . . . but that position is broadened out into what is new and unimaginable. This is anticipation in the mode of remembered future, the mode of . . . fulfilled promises, the promise of creation and the promises in history. Telling and anticipation are interlaced, and cannot be distinguished . . . easily. [This is true in the reciprocal relationship between] the messianic anticipations of the future in what was promised beforehand to the apocalyptic narrative of the future past of the godless powers. (Jürgen Moltmann, *The Coming of God* [Minneapolis: Fortress Press, 1996], 140–41)

49. It is either generally missed (or not acknowledged) by the critics of biblical apocalyptic that the despair over the goodness of the order of the world is understandable in situations where persecution is so great that the wish to die is greater than the wish to live.

50. The parable of the wise and foolish virgins, for example, in Matthew's Gospel (25:1–13), is eschatological and apocalyptic.

CHAPTER 12

THE PLACE OF MIMESIS AND THE APOCALYPTIC

Toward a Topology of the "Far and Near," or Is René Girard a Postmodernist?

RICHARD SCHENK

In true love one must see oneself in the absolutely other. This must mean I would die in me to live in you. At the foundation of what I have named the self-consciousness of the absolute nothing, in which I am myself through the fact that in my foundations I see the absolutely other or, better, a Thou: here must lie the meaning of love. In my view the agape of Christianity has this meaning. Agape is not a yearning, but rather much more a sacrifice, the love of God and not the love of a human. This love comes down from God to humans rather than rising from humans up into God. . . . Just as Augustine puts it: I am myself through the love of God, i.e., through the love of God I am truly I.

—Nishida Kitaro, *Watashi to nanji*[1]

"Completing Heidegger": Gianni Vattimo and/or René Girard "Post-Schwager"?

The late Jesuit professor of systematic theology at the University of Innsbruck, Austria, Raymund Schwager (d. 2004), in whose honor this essay is written, made his own a great deal of the analysis and critique of sacrifice articulated by René Girard. In return, Schwager provided Girard a sense of the importance of letting stand a core of sacrificial imagery with which the crucifixion has been understood, arguably beginning with Jesus himself. Schwager's friendly critique allowed Girard, already in 1995, in a corrective to his own earlier work, to—as he said—"give credit to the decisive input from Schwager" by acknowledging as necessary a nuanced interpretation of the death of Jesus as a sacrifice.[2]

Some four years later, Girard accepted an invitation to discuss mimetic theory with the well-known postmodern theorist, Gianni Vattimo, who identified Girard's intentions constructively but somewhat too closely with his own programmatic and its reading of the later Heidegger. In order to articulate the difference between his own position and that of Vattimo, Girard once again stressed his debt to Schwager. Before discussing the greater discreteness that he—Girard, here in contrast with Vattimo—sees between text and interpretation, Girard first admitted that the basis for Vattimo's confusion was the unnoticed shift that he—Girard—had made in the wake of Raymund Schwager's critique:

> There is a misunderstanding between us [Vattimo and Girard], and it has several causes. One of these is obvious, and I am 100 percent responsible for it. In *Things Hidden since the Foundation of the World* (first published in 1978), I had decided not to use the word "sacrifice" in connection with the Cross. This decision has most probably influenced Vattimo's assessment of my work. Like many readers, he interprets my past rejection of the word "sacrifice" as a repudiation of orthodoxy, that I did not really intend. . . .
>
> The symbolic symmetry between archaic sacrifice and the cross cannot be meaningless from a Christian point of view. The attachment of orthodox theologians to traditional words, such as "sacrifice," even if it still needs to be explored, is never without reason. . . .

In an essay published in 1995 entitled "The Mimetic Theory and Theology," I rejected my former rejection of the word "sacrifice."[3]

One of the questions that first enticed Vattimo to look for an affinity between himself and Girard was the claim made by Girard himself that mimetic theory was necessary "to 'complete' Heidegger."[4] Vattimo gave this claim by Girard a sympathetic reading.

Consider the analogy between the apocalyptic view of modernity, which Girard gives in *Things Hidden*, and the "Overcoming of Metaphysics," as Heidegger describes it in his late works. For Girard and Heidegger, what is decisive and apocalyptic, meaning revelatory, in the present situation is the explosion of violence caused by the fact that in our time the will to power—or the mimetic rivalry—has become explicit and boundless.[5]

Completing the Logic of Place

The following reflections will explore the question of what it means not just generally "to complete Heidegger," but specifically to complete Heidegger's ontology of place, most particularly in his work prior to 1930. The focus on this seemingly restricted topic and period has two advantages. First of all, it corresponds to the initial years of contact with the Kyoto school of thought, documented not only by Hajime Tanabe's 1924 report on the phenomenological, hermeneutical, and neo-Kantian discussions of the lived world,[6] which first introduced Heidegger to the Japanese world, but above all in Nishida Kitaro's groundbreaking essay of 1926, "Basho" (Place), the "turn to the thinking of place" and Nishida's "breakthrough to a philosophy of his own";[7] followed by his 1932 essay, "Watashi to Nanji" (I and Thou), where Nishida associates the derivative sense of place-in-which with the social sphere;[8] and finally, in 1945, "Bashoteki Ronri to Shukyoteki Sekaikan" (The Logic of Place and the Religious World-View).[9]

A second feature of this strategy for comparing late Girard and Vattimo to the completion of early Heidegger's thought on place, especially in his 1927 magnum opus, *Being and Time*, is that it precedes both the "political" coloring of Heidegger's topological remarks in the 1930s and the "topophilic" celebrations of place in Heidegger's postwar writings.[10] While both these periods can be valued for including more expressly than had the early work the social dimensions of place, the connection of both to what was the most contagious and tragic expression of mimetic rivalry in the twentieth century leads to the kind of suspicions expressed by Emmanuel Levinas in *Difficult Freedom*:

> I am thinking of one prestigious current in modern thought, which emerged from Germany to flood the pagan recesses of our Western souls. I am thinking of Heidegger and the Heideggerians. . . .
>
> One's implementation in a landscape, one's attachment to *Place*, without which the universe would become insignificant and would scarcely exist, is the very splitting of humanity into natives and strangers. And in this light, technology is less dangerous than the spirits (*génies*) of the *Place*.
>
> Technology does away with the privileges of this enrootedness and the related sense of exile. It goes beyond this alternative. . . . Technology wrenches us out of the Heideggerian world and the superstitions surrounding place.[11]

The question of whether Heidegger's early philosophical topology can be "completed" amounts to asking, along Levinasian and Girardian lines, if the interpersonal and social dimensions of human existence, analyzed in Heidegger's work before 1930, point to a social topology, prior to the nationalistic or topophilic celebration of place, a topology that could help us today to diagnose and possibly to curb or cure the rivalries that exist not just between individual humans, but between cultural regions ("Gegenden") or economic zones, between the respect for human and for nonhuman creatures, as well as between the reverence due to humans and to God.

The early and constant assertion, stated in a formula prior to its phenomenal analysis, that human existence of this sort must be understood as "being in the world" (the term occurs more than three hundred times in *Being and Time*)[12] or, better, "being [a self] in the world," maps out well to the chapters of the first division: being-in as the theme of chapters 2 and 5, world as the topic of chapters 3 and 4. That the words "a self" (as opposed to the "others than self") do not appear as part of the formula is already a sign of the secondary importance attached to the tension between myself and other selves. The concern for authenticity and for being the author of my own attempts to be, the concern for my individuation with the highest possible degree of independence from all social constraints, dominates the portrayals of an existence vis-à-vis the following: whether the other be the weight (never the support) of tradition, the synchronic, deficient (never instructive) voice of public opinion, or the possibly well-meaning but always counterproductive consolation of those who would soften or expropriate my own being-unto-death. The other is seen almost exclusively as a threat to selfhood. Samuel IJsseling points out the indirect but tangible sense of mimesis behind the search for authenticity in *Being and Time*; the other is my rival rather than an external source of my full self.[13] Not surprisingly, then, the chapter on the social world (First Division, chapter 4) is one of the shorter chapters of *Being and Time*, while the previous chapter on the work-world and worldliness as such (First Division, chapter 3) is the longest and phenomenologically quite possibly the richest.

The theory of historically occupied place, as distinguished from uncharted, unclaimed, and infinitely divisible or expandable space, has grown into a field of considerable interaction between the humanities and philosophy in Western academic circles, especially in the last sixty years.[14] The terminology of the "spatial turn" of the positive sciences and their reception of a philosophically articulated topology came to prominence in the 1980s.[15] The older and younger philosophical debates and sources behind the spatial turn of the sciences were charted in the late 1990s by Edward S. Casey in *The Fate of Place: A Philosophical History* (1998).[16] In this study, which stretches from ancient to contemporary texts, Casey sees the seeds of a renewal of philosophical topology even in the midst of the three-hundred-year dominance of space-and-time over place; Kant, for example, drew attention to the bodily foundation of our ability to orient ourselves geographically. Casey gives special attention to Heidegger's growing contribution to the development of topological theory.[17] Together with most commentators on Heidegger's writings on place,[18] Casey discusses in greatest detail the contributions to the theory of place found in Heidegger's later works. This path led in 1935 to a political interpretation of place that was already set in the context of Heidegger's support for National Socialism, seeking an independent path for the Germany of that time between the "pincers" of Soviet collectivism and American individualism, underscoring "the work of the polis as the historical place in which all this [unconcealment of being] is grounded and preserved,[19] also as "the historical place, the there *in* which, *out of* which, and *for* which history happens."[20] The interpretation of "das Unheimliche" (Sophocles's "deinotaton") as violent rather than uncanny must be seen at least partially in the context of this shift away from the more individualistic and less political text of *Being and Time*.[21] The concrete political context of Heidegger's work in this middle period, including his work on philosophical topology, raises the question of what had been missing from the earlier work that might have made the political development of Heidegger's thought more constructive and less encouraging of the violent rivalry that reached one of its most fevered pitches in the shadows of World War II.

In that same year, 1935, Heidegger gave a lecture in Freiburg titled "Origin of the Work of Art," developing numerous topological examples and metaphors such as the open, the clearing, leeway and the space of conflict ("Spielraum" and "Streitraum"), the somewhere, the *topos*, the stead, the source, expansiveness, furnishing, outline, dwelling, cleft, and frame-work (Ge-stell). While less manifestly political than *An Introduction to Metaphysics* (1935), this lecture continued to stress the close association between place and community, the omission of which was one of the deficits of *Being and Time*.

What Casey sees as missing in Heidegger's writings from the 1930s was his earlier and later use of the word "Gegend," usually translated into English as "region," a theme which had assumed a moderate role in *Being and Time* and advanced to become a central theme in 1959 with the publication of "On the Conversation on a Country Path," which includes texts dating to 1944–1945. Here Heidegger suggests and attempts to build a technical terminology around the terms *Gegend*, *gegen*, *Gegnen* (regioning), *die Gegnet* (that-which regions), and *Vergegnis* (the relation of regionality to *Gelassenheit*). In its form as a recollected dialogue and even more in its thematization of pre-objectifying openness, the

"Conversation" has similarities with "A Dialogue on Language," occasioned by the visit in 1954 of the Tokyo University professor for German literature, Tezuka Tomio.[22] Ohashi Ryosuke begins his "phenomenology of place" with a reflection on *Gelassenheit*.[23] A similar, English "language game" could be developed around the terms "country," "contra," to "counter," to "encounter," and to "countrify." Also around 1950, Heidegger resumes from the 1920s alongside the discussion of region also the earlier dialectic of near and far. "Then that-which-regions itself [*die Gegnet*] would be nearing and distancing. . . . That which-regions-itself [*Die Gegnet*] would be the nearness of distance, and the distance of nearness." "To be in a region is to be 'moving-into-nearness,' as Heidegger translates Heraclitus's fragment passed down as a single word, *anchibasiä*, which Heidegger translates as "In-die-Nähe-gehen."[24] Casey recalls that, parallel to the notion of region, this couplet of near-and-far remains prominent in the lectures "The Thing" (1950), "Building Dwelling Thinking" (1951), and "Time and Being" (1961). At the same time, a derivative sense of *Gegend* as cultural, economic, and political region suggests a field where mimetic theory could address international exchange, comparison, rivalry, and friendship.

To recall briefly what is well-known about the topology of *Being and Time*: direction, distantiation and region (or realm) are three topological features at the core of the analysis of the work-world, whose practical goals and subtasks are ordered or directed to one another in good eudaimonistic fashion ("die Ausrichtung des Verweisungszusammenhangs"), the ultimate end and most midsteps of which must largely be forgotten if they are to be effectively pursued. Too much absorption in the anticipated but still distant happiness of the house we are building can delay the work on its floor, walls, and roof. On the other hand, "Ent-fernung," distance, including the tendency to diminish distance, to de-stance, so to speak, that is, the tendency toward nearness, is a necessary, but *in praxi* often exaggerated, dynamic, leading us in excessive distance into theoretical speculation or, and indeed to some degree always, to an excess of nearness and absorption in the present moment and in the next, most pressing task, overlooking what that task presupposes, why it is presupposed, or what proximate or even ultimate good it is which I hope to gain from it all. To become authentically temporal is to develop the horizons of past and future against their ongoing collapse into the horizon of present-day business. Antiquarianism and otherworldliness on the one hand, and workaholism and the plausible or even unfounded fear of burnout on the other,[25] would be other words for the extremes of distance and nearness in the work-world. The realm or *Gegend* of what all belongs to any given set of tasks is the prerequisite for recognizing beings within this work-world: the tools, the materials, and the conditions that are or at least should be on hand, *zuhanden*. Such beings that are or should be presupposed and taken for granted and ready-to-hand within the work-world are—unlike my colleagues, employers, competitors, customers, my tax-community, my alumni, or my co-workers—without the character of human existence. They are not thematized for themselves unless a problem arises: a tool goes missing, is broken, doesn't fit, isn't easy to use. When they are utilized effectively, they are taken for granted, nearly overlooked. "Die Umsicht," or circumspection—looking about—already knowing "about" what is to be done and how, but not pondering what the tasks, tools, and materials are all "about": this is the core of *umsichtige* existence in the work-world, an existence lost for the most part in its tasks, focusing on the task at hand, the next step, or the step postponed, too close to the things of this world to dwell on them, not so distant from them as to construct scientific speculation about them. It is here, occasionally, that existence stands now and again in wonder before the "Naturmächte," first showing themselves on the edge of the work-world as "the wind in the sails" or under the warp of the window or through the fabric of the wrong sweater.[26] The ontological difference reminds us that the way something appears at present is not necessarily the way it can be or ought to be; the facticity of what it is now does not yet or perhaps does no longer reveal the possibility of what it can or should be. One must first draw back from ontic closeness in order to approach ontological proximity.

Completing the Logic of Social Place

Already in *Being and Time*, Heidegger distinguishes from this sense of work-world, or "Umwelt," what he occasionally calls "Mitwelt," the social world, which for the most part is interwoven with the work-world. The example of the family dining table with its defined set of functions, its place in the house, and its set places for the residents was already discussed in the 1923 lecture, attended by Tanabe, on the *Hermeneutics of Facticity*, in order to show the intersection of place, work-world, and social world.[27] Taking care of business (*Besorgen*) in the Umwelt finds a structural parallel here in solicitude (*Fürsorge*), not just taking care of the needy, but concern about any other coexistents met in any social context (Mitwelt), though here, too, the never-ending pursuit of one's own fulfillment is the quasi-eudaimonistic root or basis of the caring of each existent (the to-be of care/*Sorge*).[28] The unavoidable tendency to inauthenticity, the turbulence (*Wirbel*) and downward plunge (*Absturz*) that Heidegger articulates in the fifth chapter of *Being and Time*'s first division (§38), usually with examples from the all-too-proximate, present, and pressing tasks of the work-world, cut off from past and present, would all have their social parallels and interactions: temptation, tranquillization, alienation, and entanglement. Some basic features of inauthenticity, such as idle chatter (*Gerede*), are essentially social; others, like curiosity (*Neu-gier*), are often social. But much remains without parallel, where the structural differences would be harder to identify: what kind of significance is implied here by the pursuit of happiness in which what is encountered is not just a tool or material, not merely of practical relevance (*Bewandtnis*), but a who, a vis-à-vis who cannot genuinely be instrumentalized as a good-for-me without also being acknowledged as a good-for-themselves. Not just tools, but also my coexistents—including many who have ceased to exist in their own right, but who are still *mitdaseiend* with those who mourn them[29]—must be understood as still belonging to that social world.[30] The "Ausrichtung," or directionality, must be of a different sort, less exclusively instrumental, and in its beginnings less exclusively the spontaneous projection of the subject. Admittedly, it is "also" because one desires to love the truly other and to be loved by another, not just to construct signs of love from oneself and to oneself, that one wills the flourishing of that other; the self is never without coexistence, nor is there a robust sense of alterity without a robust sense of selfhood. Heidegger was fascinated by the maxim of Johannes Duns Scotus ascribed to Augustine, *amo: volo ut sis* ("To say I love, implies the claim, I will that you should flourish").[31] One could recall here as well Alasdair MacIntyre's critique of the Aristotelian ideal of the *megalopsychos*, the great-souled man, who delights in doing and giving but expects that he will have little occasion to receive.[32] The significance of reception, recalling in particular what each human being has already received from many in the fragility of his or her early years, not only determines an obligation (not necessarily matched by a strong inclination) to act toward others and for others in their fragility, but reflects the mutual conditioning of spontaneity and receptivity in human life as a whole.

The tendency to nearness in the co-world will require for its flourishing a complex and never completed dynamic of distancing. Not the excessive distance of sheer indifference, of cultural tourism, or of medial voyeurism for disasters and crimes in faraway places as a means of entertainment ("Nothing happened today" expresses the disappointment that no disasters were reported that might amuse me in my own empty life),[33] nor the excessive nearness of societal immersion, but a nearness made possible—but not yet accomplished—by the acknowledgement of the otherness of others. Such acknowledgement of alterity is the necessary but insufficient condition of what the patristic and medieval Christian tradition called *timor castus* or *timor reverentiae*, the root of *pietas* (*pace* Heidegger,[34] and Vattimo as well).[35] Tellingly, the question was posed in *Being and Time* as to what is nearest to me (*das mir Nächste*), and how (ontically or ontologically), but not yet the question who is nearest to me or to whom I am the neighbor (*wer mir/wem ich Nächster sei*).[36] Prior to concrete encounters with coexistents, there is a sphere or region of the co-world that prepares us as essentially coexistent to meet the concrete other coexistent in a personally oriented place, to encounter the vis-à-vis, to strain to see or hear if someone is approaching, to ask who has my back and to guard against backstabbers; to seek out who is to my right or left; to become aware of who is over me, beneath me, at my side, who are my superiors, subjects, and peers (of equal stature); to ask in the midst of which crowds I am being swept along, to face my fear of the crowd that might someday stand against me; to mistake which groups surround me attentively or in oblivion, perhaps to ask too faintly who those coexistents are before me to whom I owe my existence or who those coexistents are after me to whom I owe a future account of my stewardship of their inheritance; to know who marches with me shoulder to shoulder, who lay or not lay beside me, and who lies in wait for me or others; to identify who seeks to trip me up or to raise me up, to overtake me and leave me behind, to raise a heel against me and plant a foot on my neck, or who has momentarily looked away or decidedly turned away, who are those from whom I have looked or turned away?

We will always want to know "who's in, who's out":[37] this unavoidable (in Heidegger's terms, "existential" and not just "existentiell") tendency to follow common social expectations ("das Man") presupposes a kind of nearness not yet prepared by preliminary distance. Those traits of the they-self ("das Man") that Heidegger articulates with subjection ("Botmässigkeit"), averageness ("Durchschnittlichkeit"), and leveling down ("Einebnung") are—all three—modes of faltering nearness, of proximity without preparatory distance. These three modes of unavoidable but destructive nearness are reminiscent of what Girard subsumes under the title of "political correctness," based on an excessive, synchronic accommodation to the mediatized public opinion of the day. But even what is translated as *distanciality* ("Abständigkeit"), the fourth articulated feature of "das Man," and close to what Girard identifies as "mimetic rivalry," presupposes a form of nearness that gives rise to competition and violence:

> In that with which we concern ourselves "environmentally" [the in-order-to world of work] the Others are encountered as what they are [for that work-world]; they *are* what they do.
>
> In one's concern with what one has taken hold of, whether with, for, or against, the Others, there is a constant care as to the way one differs from them, whether the difference is merely one that is to be evened out, whether one's own Dasein has lagged behind the Others and wants to catch up in relationship to them, or whether one's Dasein has some priority over them and sets out to keep them suppressed. The care about this distance between them is disturbing to Being-with-one-another, though this disturbance is one that is hidden from it.[38]

The experience of other coexistents as missing, or broken, as not finding they fit in or as difficult for others to live or work with—all that will again call attention to those who might otherwise have been taken for granted but will call for something other than their replacement as instruments and resources. *Being and Time* points to a very particular form of ambivalence, defined narrowly as the neglect of the thorough reflection of suggested possibilities, because one assumes (perhaps hears others say) that the idea is already old hat, long-known and therefore without merit. The rumor that there is nothing new about a work seeks to prevent its discussion. Like the desire for authenticity, this kind of ambivalence, too, suggests a social comparison, a form of diachronic distantiality.[39] Scandal and shame presuppose a nearness that is still incomplete. Before perfect strangers and before perfect intimates there is no longer either. Heidegger's later reference to the "missing" God ("Der Fehl heiliger Namen")[40] could well have been anticipated here for missing coexistents as well, those lost one by one or in catastrophes, natural or of human making. Missing presupposes the expectation of presence and place and is one of their modes. The deceased who are missed and mourned for are with us in a unique manner of coexistence; thus mourning, private or collective, can become an attempt to maintain the last remnants of shared existence.

In 1928 Heidegger amended the text of his final lecture at Marburg with a short, inserted note, in order to articulate the topological dialectic of nearness and distance in social terms that were only implied the year before in *Being and Time*: "The human being is a creature of distance! And only by way of the real primordial distance that the human in his transcendence establishes for all beings does the true nearness to things [persons, regions] begin to grow in him. And only the capacity to hear the distance summons forth the awakening of the answer of those humans who should be near."[41] The expressly interpersonal reference of the final sentence in this citation builds on the remarks of paragraph 10 of the lecture, where in comparison to Leibniz's monodology, "The Problem of Transcendence and the Problem of *Being and Time*" were both raised in order to develop the post-Cartesian intent of the analysis of world in Heidegger's magnum opus. Though Dasein had thematized only a formal or neutral dimension of human existence prior to anthropology or ethics (similar to the scholastic discussion of the *actus humanus*—intentional acts proceeding from reason and will—as opposed to every mere *actus hominis*), "existential spatiality" is meant to include from the beginning the inner possibility for the de facto dissemination into bodiliness and with that into sexuality.[42] Heidegger sees the dispersion ("Streuung"), the dissemination ("Zerstreuung"), and the two-foldness ("Zwiespältigkeit") of sexuality not only as given along with spatiality and bodiless, all rooted in what *Being and Time* termed thrownness ("Geworfenheit"),[43] but he stresses that, despite the seemingly negative overtones, the very nonangelic, nonmonadic multiplication ("Mannigfaltigung") that human existence implies here is a positive possibility of social place. "The essentially thrown dissemination of a still neutrally understood existence makes itself known *inter alia* in this, that existence is always co-existing with existence" ("dass das Dasein *Mitsein* mit Dasein ist").[44] Sexuality must be understood from the manifold modalities of bodily concretized, social spatiality, from the dissemination and extension into coexistence that human existence is by its very essence.[45] Read together with the fourth and final section of *Kant and the Problem of Metaphysics*,[46] which Heidegger published the next year, in 1929, this kind of bodily concretized, social extension is not the cause, but potentially the partial cure of the initial autism of our intellectual, voluntary, and vital capacities.

Such experiences of others at a distance are the condition of the possibility of experiencing them in a gratuitous closeness based on a new but only partial approximation. This attention presupposes a priori the desire for a kind of nearness-in-distance to other existents. Such distance is also a necessary condition for the experience of shared activity and passivity. Like the direction ("Ausrichtung") toward a manifold goal of seeing and being seen, letting see and letting be seen; of hearing and being heard, touching and being touched, of letting hear and letting be heard, letting touch and letting be touched; of knowing and loving and being known and loved, letting others know and love and letting them be known and loved: such multifaceted goals do not arise simply as the result of meeting others, but rather the encounter with others ("Begegnung") is made possible by a different kind of being "counter," a dialogical realm or region ("Gegend"/the country) prior to and preparatory for relationships with other individual existents, a place initially of no things, no concrete persons. As *Being and Time* puts it, albeit usually without explicit reference to place, "Dasein" is essentially "Mitsein," existence is always coexistence, even prior to concrete encounters with other existents ("Mitdaseiende").

Any hope for the fulfillment of selfhood ("Selbstsein") without the fulfillment of coexistence ("Mitsein"), or the reverse, will prove illusory; the illusion of the many perversions of topophilia, including the "Selbstbehauptung" of nationalism and racism.

The Dialectics of Interpersonal Topology in Girard and Vattimo

The project of completing the philosophical topology of social emplacement which Heidegger merely sketches prior to 1930 suggests that the outsider Girard assigns more weight than the insider Vattimo to Heidegger's call to find in the "real primordial distance that the human in his transcendence establishes for all beings," the path to the "true nearness to things" and to all which that implies. Although Vattimo praises the later Heidegger for seeking an alternative to the total will to willing, the comprehensive will to power, the will to form, reform and reveal the whole of reality, it is precisely Girard who shows the greater reluctance to grant to the contemporary subject the right to claim once again a freedom that would ignore the places already occupied by others. Girard acknowledges the greater distance that is needed for the path to, and as an abiding element of, genuine nearness. Despite a palpable desire to demonstrate as much agreement as possible, Girard and Vattimo identified their differences on a number of issues, five of which are recalled below:

1. At a formal level, Girard and Vattimo point out their differing desires to make their own,[47] or not,[48] something like the orthodox sense of the Christian faith. The difference arguably goes beyond preferences *de gustibus* for the avant garde or against such political correctness. While the Scheiermacher expert Vattimo sees in the continuation of the dogmatic understanding of Christianity the continued will to power and control, the rejection of dogma and moral precepts as a vis-à-vis even for the believer challenged by such dogmata leaves the field of faith an empty space that, as Girard points out, is then occupied in a manner strikingly similar to the common opinions of the nonbelieving society, living without much of a discretely identified past or future. The opportunities of productive non-contemporaneity

are lost along with its dangers. Existence remains coexistence, even when—or especially when—faith is reduced to the formula understood just in terms of the present, *caritas, non veritas*. Vattimo criticizes Heidegger's increasing exclusion of the faith traditions from his thought, but Vattimo's own description of weak faith bears marks of accommodation and approximation to the popular discourse of just our day, similar to what Girard calls political correctness and what Heidegger had claimed as the subjection, averageness, and leveling down to a public opinion that he had hoped could be, if not avoided, at least resisted. If biblical insights had first unmasked sacrificial mechanisms, as both Girard and Vattimo claim, then such a non-accommodated, at first more distant faith could still today generate new rationality, the proximity of new experience, and the widespread renewal of social change. Girard's critique of "interpretation without a text" is closer here to the Heideggerian task of resisting the collapse into the mere present of contemporary social fashions.

2. The biblical themes of the Decalogue and the apocalypse mark something close to the beginning and end of the biblical text. The theme of freedom in the biblical Decalogue (already Exodus 20:2), developing a narrative old enough to flow directly both into Exodus 20 and Deuteronomy 5, distinguishes between God and the many goods that, if treated as gods responsible for my final happiness, will be destroyed both in themselves and in their utility for me.[49] The recollection of Israel's liberation from slavery is tied to the prohibition to enslave other creatures through demanding they provide what only God can grant. To allow that God be God calls for a certain distancing from my claims for myself and upon other creatures, but in the interest of the intended good of both, to which I come closer via such distance. Even in light of Girard's response to Schwager, sacrifice retains an essentially destructive element, whether the victim be oneself or another. The maxim seems justified: that in the realm of practice, sacrifices imposed upon or elicited from oneself or others should be encouraged only when the flight from them would cause still greater harm or forfeit a still greater good, and that in the realm of theory, sacrificial metaphors and imagery should be avoided as long as this evasion does not lead to the loss of valuable insights.[50] The

text cited from Nishida at the beginning of these reflections suggests a field where this maxim can be tested: the hope of agape is that my vis-à-vis will live, even if that must be at the price of something like my own demise.[51] The diminution of violence cannot consist simply in enabling the freedom of subjects to act upon themselves or others, but in the freedom of creatures from being acted upon by them. Morality consists as much in checking my freedom as in exercising it; to flee from such *Selbsthemmung* is so to live at the expense of others, that even the profit to self will sour. Though fascinated by the idea of the divine *kenosis*, Vattimo stresses the parenetic function intended by Philippians 2 in regard to our exalted claims to truth rather than to our exalted claims to freedom; even though participatory, human *kenosis* is located by the text itself less in human knowledge than in human will.[52] Not in unbridled freedom, but at least in self-restriction or, where called for, even in self-emptying, a form of self-sacrifice, is the good of the other to be secured.

3. The core of apocalyptic knowledge, as it was articulated in Israel and the Christian church between the second century BCE and the second century CE, is centered in the hope for salvation for a history and a nature that cannot save themselves, a vertical hope from above, the hope of those who have lost hope in any organic, continuous progress of their own history from below.[53] Like the Decalogue, apocalypse focuses less on the power of the human will than on the protection of human and nonhuman beings from the destructive potential of that will. The narrative account, where God is portrayed as causally at work with his angels to actively punish human sin by bringing death directly by war, disease, and natural catastrophe, plausibly reveals the sense of mimetic rivalry aroused in the persecuted community that composed the text: the unlikely hope that persecutors should feel the pain of persecution. The pauses of rest between disasters that the texts relate serve as little more than the chance for the impious to experience still another discrete punishment. Read less literally, the poisoning of water, air, and earth are the all too familiar works of a falling humanity, which seeks its salvation in measures that are predictably counterproductive. The sacrificial Lamb who shares the sufferings of humanity shares, too, its concerns for the goods of

creation and can provide to both the revelation of God's love. Contrary to popular usage, the apocalyptic vision is one of hope for the world, though not for the so-called best of all possible worlds, rather for a world already sinking into the catastrophe that human activity has prepared for it. This Christian spin on eudaemonistic structures, beginning with the conviction that all human projects, though undertaken to fulfill humanity, will not singularly or collectively achieve that common goal, is at the heart of *Being and Time*'s analysis of the work-world, requiring a more detailed completion in the social world of human interaction. Reduced to the dynamics of its own limited resources, human coexistence, though likewise for the sake of beatitude, will also fall short of its goal. The distance to the hope of self-perfection from below prepares for the nearing hope in a salvation from beyond, one which demands respect for fellow creatures, human and nonhuman. In its respect for others, in its allowing that God be God, in its developing sense of resurrection as strictly God's salvation of the finite, finally, in its perception of human and nonhuman suffering and its hope to overcome both, apocalyptic is able to deepen and develop the essential of faith in the creator God and an awareness of the demands placed upon us to care for his creation. If God is both the fullness of the meaning of the world and an abiding mystery for our *pensiero debole*, then we must acknowledge the whole of creation as mysterious and precious.[54]

Shortly after the atomic disaster in Chernobyl, Peter Sloterdijk commented on the changed situation of our epoch with regard to the notion of apocalypse:

> Let me start with an unargued assertion: today's Alternative Action Groups are already children of the catastrophe. What distinguishes them from earlier generations and what recommends them as first-ever candidates for a culture of panic, is their experiential, expert-like attitude towards the potential for catastrophes, which really surround them on all sides. Viewed historically, they are arguably the first human beings to ever have developed a non-hysterical relationship to possible apocalypse. It is the first time, where one does not have to conjure up the demonic, in order to read the

flaming letters on the wall. World events have provided for it all, and amply so.[55]

4. It was a similar focus on the real vulnerability of the victim that led Girard to enunciate even prior to Fukushima his own remarks on the realistic, nonhysterical consideration of the apocalyptical:

> I don't want to compel anyone to turn apocalyptic or sprinkle her head with ashes, but I have children and grandchildren, and I have to admit I am fearful. I have the sensation that something increasingly frightful is occurring in our world. I began to think about what was in store for the world in 1945, when the atomic bomb was invented and used. . . . But in today's world we see that increasing numbers of people are prepared to die in order to kill innocent parties whom they have never seen before.[56]

It is Girard's concern for the suffering and the preservation of past or future victims of war that motivates his stance here, and the consequence drawn is for an increased self-control rather than a maximum exercise of human freedom. One could draw a parallel to Hans Jonas's *The Principle of Responsibility* (1979) in contrast to Ernst Bloch's *Principle of Hope* (3 vols.; 1954–1959).[57] Girard's ethics assign greater weight to the suffering of the victimized than to the sufferings of those who limit their own freedom to victimize. Girard and Vattimo agree that the privileged part of humanity is obliged to find ways to curb its claim upon global resources. While this self-restriction can demand sacrifices of the privileged, the flight from such sacrifices could easily cause still greater harm and forfeit still greater goods.

5. In comparison to Vattimo, Girard is initially more consistent but also more severe in his judgment of religions outside Judeo-Christian traditions. Only the Old and New Testaments reveal the scapegoat mechanism sufficiently; religions in general do not. Vattimo and the earlier work of Girard still echo the once stylish theoremata of the theological interpretation of Christianity as pure faith, free of religiosity. Girard's early position resembled the religion-critical wing of Christian patristic and medieval theology, admitting no sense of the

truth before Abraham (*ante legem*), who first (*sub lege*) received monotheism and inklings of the truth before that truth became evident in Christ (*sub gratia*). This scheme, which led to a kind of unsuspected and unsought rivalry between Christian and non-Christian religions within Girard's earlier work, became less stringent but far more nuanced after his turn post-Schwager. After "rejecting the rejection of the term sacrifice" for Christ's death, Girard begins to see even in pre-Abrahamic religions elements of the progressive revelation about scapegoating the innocent. Suspicions about the nonsalvific and even destructive character of sacrifice were harbored by sacrificial societies themselves. For this position, too, there were precedents in the religion-friendly wing of Christian patristic and medieval thought: it saw inklings or inspiration *ante legem*, revelation *sub lege*, and internally graced revelation *sub gratia*.[58]

What can be learned from Girard is the path to a kind of closeness, which still allows for a limited rivalry of allies and friends because it still presupposes the initial distance of a lasting acknowledgement of the other as other (what, as was noted above, Augustine—cited by Heidegger—called *timor castus*).[59] This lasting acknowledgement and reverence of the other requires a certain lasting self-restraint, something like a sacrifice, but—as Schwager suggested to Girard—a sacrifice that need not be ultimately destructive of itself or the other, a sacrifice that at its core is an affirmation of and intercession for the other that can be the fulfillment of a coexistent and the so-called pro-existent self (*pro homine*). It is the best of what Vattimo means by *kenosis* and *pietas*, but freed in large part from the need to deny the religiosity of rival religions, which cannot be reduced to religionless faith. It is perhaps not all too far from what "pre-metaphysical metaphysics" meant with the transcendentals and what Nishida meant by the priority of "immanent transcendence" before "transcendent immanence," and finally, perhaps, too, what fascinated Nishida about the return and new departure of Dostoyevsky's "silent as a dark cloud" of a Christ, who even as a voluntary victim leaves place and freedom for the Grand Inquisitor.[60] The place left open by neighbor for neighbor leaves a place for the nonpersonal as well, a place where "Naturmächte" can shine out in the midst of an otherwise instrumentalized world of technological work.⁶¹ This peace not just among religions but among regions—human and ontic—is needed particularly in our times, peace between an East and West of different strengths and different sources, peace as an alternative to monotone globalization, which might allow for peace between the world economy and natural resources, whether native to a region or imported. It is the gift of distance and letting others be in places of their own that the Godhead bestowed upon creation to make it an image of itself.

Notes

1. Nishida Kitaro, *Watashi to nanji* (1932; I and Thou), my translation into English from the German translation of Rolf Elberfeld: Nishida Kitaro, *Logik des Ortes: Der Anfang der modernen Philosophie in Japan*, ed. and trans. Rolf Elberfeld (Darmstadt, Germany: Wissenschaftliche Buchgesellschaft, 1999), 140–203, esp. 198–99. For the original text see *Nishida Kitarō zenshū* (1966), 6:341–427. Nishida included here a long citation from the Protestant theologian Heinrich Scholz, *Eros und Caritas* (Halle, Germany: Niemeyer, 1929), 49.

2. René Girard, "Mimetische Theorie und Theologie," in *Vom Fluch und Segen der Sündenböcke*, ed. Józef Niewiadomski and Wolfgang Palaver (Thaur-Vienna: Kulturverlag, 1995), 29. This essay is now available in English in *The One by Whom Scandal Comes* (East Lansing: Michigan State University Press, 2014), 33–45.

3. René Girard, "Not Just Interpretations, There Are Facts, Too," in Gianni Vattimo and René Girard, *Christianity, Truth, and Weakening Faith: A Dialogue*, ed. Pierpaolo Antonello, trans. William McCuaig (New York: Columbia University Press, 2010), 92–93.

4. Gianni Vattimo, "Heidegger and Girard: *Kénosis* and the End of Metaphysics," in Vattimo and Girard, *Christianity, Truth, and Weakening Faith*, 78. Cf. René Girard, *Things Hidden since the Foundation of the World*, trans. Stephen Bann and Michael Metteer (Stanford, CA: Stanford University Press, 1987), 265.

5. Girard, *Things Hidden*, 80–81. The text continues, "This explosion makes clear, for Girard, the basic victimary structure of all human culture; for Heidegger, it exposes the 'secret' of metaphysics, which is the forgetting of Being and the identification of it with beings, objectivity, and so on. The analogy between these two theories becomes evident if we consider that what motivates Heidegger's rejection of metaphysics is not a theoretical reason, as if metaphysics

were a false description of Being for which we had to substitute a more adequate one. Heidegger's rejection of metaphysics, as is clear already in *Sein und Zeit*, is motivated by the violence by which it reduces Being—and particularly human existence—to measurable objectivity and rationalized mechanisms."

6. Cf. Hajime Tanabe, "Die neue Wende in der Phänomenologie—Heideggers Phänomenologie des Lebens" (1924), in *Japan und Heidegger*, ed. Hartmut Buchner (Sigmaringen, Germany: Thorbecke, 1989), 89–108. Tanabe bases his description of the conversation among phenomenology, hermeneutics, and neo-Kantianism principally on his attendance at Heidegger's lecture in Freiburg in the summer semester 1923, now accessible as M. Heidegger, *Ontologie (Hermeneutik der Faktizität)*, GA (=*Gesamtausgabe*) 63 (1985; Frankfurt am Main: Klostermann, 1995). On Heidegger's phenomenological reading of Aristotle with which Tanabe was familiar, cf. the footnote by Buchner to Tanabe, in Tanabe's "Die neue Wende," 96n14, and the 1922 lecture, sent to P. Natorp as part of the successful application for the position in Marburg: M. Heidegger, *Phänomenologische Interpretationen zu Aristoteles: Anzeige der hermeneutischen Situation*, ed. Hans-Ulrich Lessing, in *Dilthey-Jahrbuch für Philosophie und Geschichte der Geisteswissenschaften* 6 (1989): 235–74.

7. See Rolf Elberfeld, "Einleitung," in Nishida Kitaro, *Logik des Ortes*, 8.

8. Cf. Girard, "Mimetische Theorie und Theologie," in *Vom Fluch und Segen der Sündenböcke*, ed. Niewiadomski and Palaver, 29.

9. The text is in *Nishida Kitarō zenshū*, 11:371–464; trans. Elberfeld in Nishida Kitaro, *Logik des Ortes*, 204–84.

10. For the distinction between topoanalytic and topophilic or "topophiliac," cf. Edward S. Casey, *Getting Back into Place: Toward a Renewed Understanding of the Place-World*, 2nd ed. (Bloomington: Indiana University Press 2009). For the first concept, Casey refers the reader to rough equivalents in Heidegger (the "topology of being" in *Aus der Erfahrung des Denkens*) and Gaston Bachelard's influential 1957 meditation, *The Poetics of Space*, trans. M. Jolas (Boston: Beacon Press, 1958, 32–34). Casey refers somewhat dismissively to a pre-philosophic, "later wave, stemming from the 1970s and frankly topophiliac in character, [that] was composed of ecologically minded geographers.... A recent undercurrent of architects, sociologists, anthropologists, ethicists and theologians, feminists and social observers is still gathering force.... Instead of succumbing to topophilia, I will pursue what Bachelard has aptly termed "topo-analysis'" (Casey, *Getting Back into Place*, xv; cf. 311). While topoanalysis attends to the structures by which all human beings orient themselves, topophila usually refers to a particular affection for a particular place or kind of place. In Heideggerian terms, "topo-analysis" is an ontological concept; "topophila," an

ontic one. As such, the latter activity, while not necessarily pejorative, is more vulnerable to patriotic and romantic instrumentalizations of the kinds that have drawn even topoanalysis into suspicion.

11. Emmanuel Levinas, *Difficult Freedom: Essays on Judaism* (Baltimore: Johns Hopkins University Press, 1990), 231–34. The passage continues, "Judaism has always been free with regard to place. . . . It is perhaps on this point that Judaism is most distant from Christianity. The catholicity of Christianity integrates the small and touching household gods into the worship of saints and local cults. Through sublimation, Christianity continues to give piety roots, nurturing itself on landscapes and memories culled from family, tribe and nation. That is why it conquered humanity. Judaism has not sublimated idols—on the contrary, it has demanded that they be destroyed. Like technology, it has demystified the universe. It has freed Nature from a spell. Because of its abstract universalism, it runs up against imaginations and passions. But it has discovered man in the nudity of his face."

12. Cf. Rainer A. Bast and Heinrich P. Delfosse, eds., *Handbuch zum Textstudium von Martin Heideggers Sein und Zeit 1* (Stuttgart-Bad Cannstatt: Frommann-Holzboog, 1980), 158–59.

13. Samuel IJsseling, "On Authenticity and Inauthenticity and the Problem of Mimesis in Heidegger," in *Heidegger, A Centenary Appraisal: The Seventh Annual Symposium of the Simon Silvernman Phenomenology Center*, ed. Edward S. Casey, Samuel IJsseling, Thomas Sheehan, and Jacques Taminiaux (Pittsburgh: Duquesne University, Simon Silverman Center, 1990), 13–27, with a brief reference to René Girard, p. 21.

14. Cf. as one example among many the series "transcript": Stephan Günzel, ed., *Topologie: Zur Raumbeschreibung in den Kultur- und Medienwissenschaften* (Bielefeld, Germany: transcript, 2007); Jörg Doring and Tristan Thielmann, eds., *Spatial Turn: Das Raumparadigma in den Kultur- und Sozialwissenschaften* (Bielefeld, Germany: transcript, 2008); Georg Glasze und Annika Mattissek, eds., *Handbuch Diskurs und Raum: Theorien und Methoden für die Humangeographie sowie die sozial- und kulturwissenschaftliche Raumforschung* (Bielefeld, Germany: transcript, 2009).

15. The popularization of the term owes much to Edward Soja, *Postmodern Geographies: The Reassertion of Space in Critical Social Theory* (London: Verso, 1989); Edward Soja, *Thirdspace: Journeys to Los Angeles and Other Real-and-Imagined Places* (London: Blackwell, 1996).

16. Edward S. Casey, *The Fate of Place: A Philosophical History*, pbk. ed. (Berkeley: University of California Press, 1998). Casey's more phenomenological works on the topic are *Getting Back into Place: Toward a Renewed Understanding*

of the Place-World, 2nd ed. (1993; Bloomington: Indiana University Press, 2009), and *The World at a Glance* (Bloomington: Indiana University Press, 2007).

17. Casey, *Fate of Place*, esp. chapter 11, 243–84.

18. Cf. especially Jeff E. Malpas, *Place and Experience: A Philosophical Topography* (Cambridge: Cambridge University Press, 1999); "Heidegger's Topology of Being," in *Transcendental Heidegger*, ed. Steven Crowell and Jeff Malpas (Stanford, CA: Stanford University Press 2007); *Heidegger's Topology: Being, Place, World* (Cambridge, MA: MIT Press, 2008); and *Heidegger and the Thinking of Place. Explorations in the Topology of Being* (Cambridge, MA: MIT Press 2012). Despite Malpas's critique of Casey's claim that Heidegger's approach to topology was "indirect," it is the latter who devotes greater attention to Heidegger's work in the 1920s.

19. Martin Heidegger, *An Introduction to Metaphysics* (Garden City, NY: Anchor, 1961), 160; cf. also 54–55. That this argument for the "polis" is more about the political than the urbane was clear two years earlier in the largely "topophiliac" (as opposed to "topoanalytic"; for the term, cf. Casey, *Getting Back*, xv) announcement: "Schöperische Landschaft. Warum bleiben wir in der Provinz?," in Martin Heidegger, *Aus der Erfahrung des Denkens*, GA 13 (1983; Frankfurt am Main: Klostermann, 2002).

20. Heidegger, *An Introduction*, 128.

21. Ibid., 123–39; Casey, *Fate of Place*, 261–66.

22. Cf. Tomio Tezuka, "Eine Stunde mit Heidegger: Drei Antworten," in *Japan und Heidegger: Gedenkschrift der Stadt Meßkirch zum 100: Geburtstag Martin Heideggers*, ed. Hartmut Buchner (Meßkirch, Germany: Thorbecke, 1989), 173–80.

23. Ohashi Ryosuke, *Zeitlichkeitsanalyse der Hegelschen Logik: Zur Idee einer Phänomenologie des Ortes* (Symposium 72) (Freiburg im Breisgau: Alber, 1984), §1:15–23.

24. Casey, *Fate of Place*, 271.

25. Juliet Schor, *The Overworked American: The Unexpected Decline of Leisure* (New York: Basic Books, 1991).

26. Cf. *Sein und Zeit* (16th Aufl.; Tübingen: Max Niemeyer, 1986) §15, 70 (*Being and Time*, trans. John Macquarrie and Edward Robinson [New York: Harper & Row, 1962], 100), where Heidegger already identifies "Naturmacht" in a regional ontology distinct from human existents, our work-world, and our theoretical observations:

> Hammer, tongs, and needle refer in themselves to steel [*sic*], iron, metal, mineral, wood, in that they consist of these. In equipment that is used,

> Nature is discovered along with it by that use—the Nature we find in natural products.
>
> Here, however (i.e., in the work-world of circumspection), Nature is not to be understood as that which is just present-at-hand, nor as the *power of Nature*. The wood is a forest of timber, the mountain a quarry of rock; the river is water-power, the wind is "wind in the sails." As the "environment" (the instrumental context we care about) is discovered, the "Nature" thus discovered is encountered, too. If its kind of being as ready-to-hand is disregarded, this "nature" itself can be discovered and defined simply in its pure presence-at-hand. But when this happens, the Nature which "stirs and strives" [*webt und strebt*], which assails us and enthralls us as landscape, remains hidden. The botanist's plants are not the flowers of the hedgerow; the "source" which the geographer establishes for a river is not the springhead of the dale.

A closer analysis of the "assailing" and "enthralling" of the "power of nature" discovered in but distinct from what is instrumental will wait for discussion until Heidegger's later works.

27. M. Heidegger, *Beiträge zur Philosophie* (*Vom Ereignis*), 1936–38, GA 65 (Frankfurt am Main: Klostermann, 1989), 98–99.

28. In his last Marburg semester, Heidegger seeks to distinguish the eudaimonistic "Jemeinigkeit" of *Being and Time* from its exaggeration into selfish egotism: *Metaphysische Anfangsgründe der Logik*, the fifth clarification in §10, GA 26 (Frankfurt am Main: Klostermann, 1978), 172.

29. Heidegger corrects only to some degree his disturbing suggestion that, at death, the *Mitdaseiende* are transformed into *Zuhandenes*, practical projects of *Trauerarbeit*: See *Sein und Zeit* §47, 237–41 (*Being and Time*, 281–85). This transformation into nonexistents is more easily imaginable with beings of a character other than Dasein and for the kind of existence forgetful of its essential coexistence.

30. Cf. *Sein und Zeit* §47, 238 (*Being and Time*, 281–82), where Heidegger is at pains to say in what sense and in what sense not death transforms coexistents into one last item of business that still needs to be taken care of/to get done with (*Gegenstand des Besorgens*) in the rituals of burial, or even "in the sense of what is just present-at-hand in the merely still present-at-hand of the corpse."

31. Cf. M. Heideggers Briefe an H. Arendt (May 3, 1925) and E. Blochmann (January 11, 1928), in H. Arendt und M. Heidegger, *Briefe 1925 bis 1975 und andere Zeugnisse*, 3rd ed. (Frankfurt am Main: Klostermann, 2002), 31, 269–70.

32. Alasdair MacIntyre, *Dependent Rational Animals* (Chicago: Open Court, 1999). Although in this work MacIntyre does not cite A. Gehlen, *Der Mensch, seine Natur und seine Stellung in der Welt*, 3rd ed. (1940; 1944; Bonn: Athenäum, 1950), 3, Gehlen's sense of the individual as *Mängelwesen* matches his sense of community as a more than equal compensation for human weakness and as the source of corresponding obligations.

33. Cf. Neil Postman and Steve Powers, *How to Watch TV News* (New York: Penguin, 1992).

34. Cf. Heidegger, *Sein und Zeit* §40, 190n1 (*Being and Time*, 235 and 492n4), with reference to Augustine.

35. Cf. Gianni Vattimo, *After Christianity* (New York: Columbia University Press, 2002). For a fuller sense of *pietas*, cf. Theodor Haecker, *Vergil, Vater des Abendlandes* (Leipzig: J. Hegner, 1938), 94–107.

36. Even in his later, directly topological works, Heidegger thematized the personal sense of "neighbor" more in terms of the second syllable of that word. Cf. M. Heidegger, "Building, Dwelling, Thinking," in *Poetry, Language, Thought* (New York: Harper & Row, 1971), 145–61. See 146–47: "The real meaning of the verb bauen, namely, to dwell, has been lost to us. But a covert trace has been preserved in the German word *Nachbar*, neighbor. The neighbor is in Old English the *neahgebur; neah*, near, and *gebur*, dweller. The Nachbar is the Nachbebur, the Nachgebauer, the near-dweller, he who dwells nearby." The intended sense of "nearby" is not elucidated here.

37. William Shakespeare, *The Tragedy of King Lear*, act 5, scene 3.

38. Cf. Heidegger, *Sein und Zeit* §27, 126 (*Being and Time*, 163–64).

39. Cf. Heidegger, *Sein und Zeit* §37, 173–75 (*Being and Time*, 217–19).

40. So the title of the 1974 "gift" to Hugo Friedrich; GA 13, 231–35.

41. Cited here from Casey, *Fate of Place*, 260–61, trans. from M. Heidegger, *Metaphysische Anfangsgründe der Logik: Im Ausgang von Leibniz*, GA 26, 285.

42. Heidegger, *Metaphysische Anfangsgründe der Logik*, GA 26, 173.

43. Cf. Casey, *Fate of Place*, 259–60.

44. Heidegger, *Metaphysische Anfangsgründe der Logik*, GA 26, 174.

45. Ibid., 174–75.

46. The final section, attempting to inscribe (or "retrieve") the foundations of metaphysics into a philosophic anthropology, does not yet have a parallel in the lecture from winter semester 1927–1928. Cf. M. Heidegger, *Phänomenologische Interpretation von Kants Kritik der reinen Vernunft* (GA 25) (Frankfurt am Main: Klostermann, 1977); M. Heidegger, *Kant und das Problem der Metaphysik*, 4th expanded ed. (Frankfurt am Main: Klostermann, 1973), xiii–xviii, 198–239. Heidegger suggests that the anthropological extension of his

reflections on imagination and temporality in Kant developed from his disputations with Ernst Cassirer at Davos in the spring of 1929.

47. Cf. René Girard, "Not Just Interpretations, There Are Facts, Too," in Vattimo and Gerard, *Christianity, Truth, and Weakening Faith*, 92–93.

48. E.g., Gianni Vattimo, *The Trace of the Trace*, in *Religion*, ed. Gianni Vattimo and Jacques Derrida (Stanford, CA: Stanford University Press, 1998), 79–94.

49. Cf. Christoph Dohmen, *Exodus 19–40* (Freiburg im Breisgau: Herder, 2004).

50. Whether ecumenism is thematized or not, Christian theology today cannot escape the context set by the ongoing disunity of the Christian confessions; theology is therefore always and unavoidably ecumenical. Given this author, from Germany's Catholic University, speaking before our gracious hosts here at International Christian University, it is best to state this common sense maxim explicitly, as it enunciates a goal of possible future consensus. Cf. Robert W. Jenson, *Systematic Theology*, vol. 1, *The Triune God* (Oxford: Oxford University Press, 1997), vii–x.

51. Cf. the epigraph at the beginning of this essay.

52. Cf. Gianni Vattimo, "Heidegger and Girard: *Kénosis* and the End of Metaphysics," in Vattimo and Girard, *Christianity, Truth, and Weakening Faith*, 78–87.

53. Cf. Karlheinz Müller, "Apokalyptik/Apokalypsen. Altes Testament: Die Jüdische Apokalyptik. Anfänge und Merkmale," in TRE [*Theologische Realenzyklopaedie*] 3 (1978; Berlin: De Gruyter, 1993), 202–50.

54. Thomas Joseph White, *The Analogy of Being: Invention of the Antichrist or Wisdom of God?* (Grand Rapids, MI: Eerdmanns, 2010).

55. Peter Sloterdijk: *Eurotaoismus: Zur Kritik der Politischen Kinetik* (Frankfurt: Suhrkamp, 1989), 102–3.

56. Vattimo and Girard, *Christianity, Truth, and Weakening Faith*, 42.

57. Cf. Hans Jonas, *The Imperative of Responsibility: Foundations of an Ethics for the Technological Age*, trans. Hans Jonas, with the collaboration of David Herr (Chicago: University of Chicago Press, 1984), with Ernst Bloch, *The Principle of Hope*, trans. Neville Plaice, Stephen Plaice, and Paul Knight (Cambridge, MA: MIT Press, 1986).

58. Cf. Richard Schenk, "Divina simulatio irae et dissimulatio pietatis. Divine Providence and Natural Religion in Robert Kilwardby's Quaestiones in librum IV Sententiarum." in *Mensch und Natur im Mittelalter*, ed. A. Zimmerman, Miscellanea Mediaevalia 21, no. [vol.] 1 (Berlin: De Gruyters, 1991), 431-55; and Richard Schenk, "Christ, Christianity, and Non-Christian Religions: Their Relationship in the Thought of Robert Kilwardby," in *Christ among the Medieval Dominicans: Representations of Christ in the Texts and Images of the*

Order of Preachers, ed. Kent Emery, Jr., and Joseph Wawrykow (Notre Dame, IN: University of Notre Dame Press, 1988), 344–63.

59. Cf. R. Schenk, "*Factus in Agonia*. Zur Todesangst Christi und der Christen," in *Christus—Gottes schöpferisches Wort: Festschrift für Christoph Kardinal Schönborn*, ed. Georg Augustin, Maria Brun, Erwin Keller, and Markus Schulze (Freiburg im Breisgau: Herder 2010), 401–28.

60. Cf. Nishida's essay, first published the year he died: *Bashoteki ronri to shukyoteki sekaikan*, translated by David A. Dilworth as *Nothingness and the Religious Worldview* (Honolulu: University of Hawaii Press, 1987), 282.

61. Heidegger, *Sein und Zeit* §15, 70 (*Being and Time*, 100).

CONCLUSION

CHAPTER 13

THE DRUM, THE *GAITA*, AND THE DESERT

Thoughts on How to Approach Conflicts with Mimetic Theory

MARIO ROBERTO SOLARTE RODRÍGUEZ
AND MERY EDITH RODRÍGUEZ ARIAS

In this essay, we analyze some ways of bringing together concrete solutions to armed social conflicts, in particular Colombia's, with mimetic theory. Even though there was a peace agreement signed between the Colombian government and the Revolutionary Armed Forces of Colombia (FARC) on September 26, 2016, there is not yet a clear path to implement it; also there are still several illegal armed actors present in the country, among them the National Liberation Army (ELN), new paramilitary groups, and drug-trafficking bands. In the conclusion, we examine those cases inscribed in the horizon of silence proposed by René Girard in *Battling to the End* (2010). Our use of the word "we" here is not rhetorical in that this essay is a dual-authored consideration written out of our proximity to the conflict (we are university professors in Colombia). The object of our consideration is the relationship between conflict resolution theory and mimetic theory as regards to Colombia's situation. At the same time, it also aims toward a level of generality appropriate to thinking about the Apocalypse and the way it affects every human being.

We come from Colombia, a country where violence seems to have no end, to Japan, where an extreme violence, an atomic bomb, ended a terrible war. In both cases, the immediate evidence of violence exposes a sort of reality we call "apocalyptic," the imminence of the violent destruction of existence. "Hiroshima" is the expression of the execution of the worst fears of a total war, as seen by Carl von Clausewitz and studied by Girard in *Battling to the End*. It inaugurates the nuclear era that corresponds to an apocalyptic consciousness. The apocalypse is the last threat of an image represented by violence moving toward the universal due to the fact that he who might destroy my life, my enemy, is potentially anyone, since in the apocalypse, violence escalates to an extreme in which humans can destroy each other because there are no institutions that can contain it. Further, due to the secularization of the world, we no longer count on any barrier to protect us from the imminence of violence. Thus, globalization is the oncoming of an era of violent reciprocity among antagonists, which reminds one of Schmitt's views on politics: "The specific political distinction to which political actions and motives can be reduced is that between friend and enemy."[1] In the face of this apocalyptic universe in which we imagine a destructive chaos has been imposed, it becomes possible to choose to pressure the apocalyptic imagination to produce victims among "enemies" or to recognize the enemy as nothing more than a symmetric other, other like me, upon whom the exercise of violence does not make sense.[2]

Within this apocalyptic horizon, however, the Colombian case may very well be understood under the category of "states of violence" proposed by Paul Dumouchel in his essay "Inside Out: Political Violence in the Age of Globalization."[3] What happens in places like Colombia is neither a war against another state nor a civil war, but violence that has become the state of existence in entire regions of the country.[4] The states of violence do not affect the entire society but are confined to parts of the nation's territory; outside those zones of violence, life is relatively normal. Dumouchel claims that in countries such as Colombia, Palestine, Iraq, Afghanistan, Somalia, and Democratic Republic of Congo,

These enclaves of violence sometimes have an important economic role or strategic value, and many different types of agents may participate in the hostile relations that characterize them: government troops (and more or less official paramilitary units), rebel forces, private security companies, local warlords, tribal combatants, troops from neighboring countries, and members of international peacekeeping forces. This incomplete list brings out two important features of states of violence. First, there is their internationalization: very rarely are the participants, the parties in the conflict, limited to citizens of one state only. Most of the time foreigners are involved. Second, there is the presence of nonstate actors, rebel troops of course, but also private security companies, the corporations that hire them, and organized crime. In fact, it is often difficult to distinguish between political conflict and large-scale criminal activities, as insurgents turn to various illegal activities to fund their operations. When that happens, winning often stops being the goal. The struggle itself becomes a form of economic enterprise. . . . The conflict thus gets integrated into the world economy. Simultaneously, this localized fighting, as long as it does not get out of hand, can serve the purpose of certain groups within the state and help them maintain their hold in power.[5]

The fact of violence discloses the decreasing capacity of the state to keep its monopoly of force and apply the empire of law democratically; globalization, as the most recent moment of secularization, has undermined that capacity of the states. This can be appreciated in the traffic of psychoactive substances, which is transnational. The criminal organizations, the insurgent groups, and the corrupt elites are interested in maintaining a fragile state in order to be able to cover their illegal activities and negotiate their position in the international system. Hence, the links between illegal economies, corruption, and the fragility of the state have become a vicious circle, in which a permanent state of violence makes society even more vulnerable due to the links between public relations, insurgent groups, and organized crime.[6]

Let us turn to approaches to conflict resolution. We have the goal of initiating a dialogue between conflict resolution and mimetic theory. We consider that conflict resolution theory has advanced methods and techniques of proven efficiency in the facilitation of ending social conflicts and promoting peace building. Peace education (understood broadly beyond the classroom) uses conflict resolution as a means to achieve a culture of peace. In that way, conflict resolution is understood as the conjugation of skills and tools that come from what is known as reflexive practice. Reflexive practice allows people to share what has been learned by experience; essentially what has been done in the field is turned into models and theories built from collective knowledge. Conflict resolution techniques allow people to remove themselves from the idea that they are conditioned to be violent and to understand that it is possible for both individuals and collectives to choose to build peace.

Conflict resolution has changed its approach since it was first conceived as a discipline. In the classic approach, it was believed that conflict resolution was to be achieved by those who had political power at the elite level, with the help of third-party mediators who also would be part of this elite. The premise was to reach agreements and sign accords that would by definition be followed by the people who were citizens or victims of the violence of war. It was an enforcing view. With time, as violence and the actors involved in it changed, so did the approach to looking for ways of making peace. The first and most progressive idea was that peace was to be sought and achieved by everyone in a society or collective; that is, that it was everyone's responsibility to create it and make it sustainable. All levels of society must be involved in peace building, not just the elites and leaders, not just combatants, but all people who in one way or another had been touched by the violent conflict. Conflict resolution starts moving toward a wider approach known today as conflict transformation, a concept developed in depth by John Paul Lederach.[7] Conflict resolution, as it is understood and practiced in more recent approaches, works to address the root causes of conflict at the same time that it works to manage the destructive and immediate effects of direct violence. With this approach, conflict resolution becomes a practice in which individuals at all levels are responsible for peace building and for working within the collective to make it sustainable. The basic idea of changing what does not work instead of eliminating it opens a door to Girard's concept of silence and how true transformative practices can only come from ethical relations. That is developed further in the conclusion of this essay.

If it is assumed that societies need to move toward a conflict transformation approach, then it is necessary to learn how to do peace. One of the most common misconceptions about peace is that people naturally know how to go from the drum of war to the *gaita* (bagpipe) of peace. Not only is it necessary to reflect upon one's self, to learn to hear the silence; we also need to be taught how to live in peace, how to forgive and forget, how to resolve our differences without violence. We need to be educated for peace.

During the last twenty-five years, Colombia has begun to understand the importance of working toward the empowerment of collectives for the construction of local peace by using conflict resolution techniques. We will examine three processes of reduction of violence in Colombia, two of which can be comprehended from the perspective of conflict resolution theory, while the last may be understood by posing the question whether a solution to conflict is possible through a renunciation of any kind of new violence.

The Drum

We will speak only of the war drums, which measure the timing of soldiers in military marches. Music, being one of the most elaborate expressions of culture, has very old links with violence, going back to the most primitive combats, where yelling and whistles gave way to the banging of shields, which was intended to create a sound that had the purpose not only of expelling the fear out of those who created it, but also of injecting terror in enemies. Later and up to our own day, military apparatuses have employed drums to give orders that were expected to be fulfilled by all within identical timing,[8] generating in combatants the spirit of a single body, of closed unity,[9] characteristic of armies. Thus, we speak of the drum to refer to solutions built on the exacerbated antagonisms of rivalry,[10] solutions that propose the elimination of the adversary.[11] The war drum times the solutions to violence that flow from military logic, no matter whose army is involved. Conflict resolution has worked if at least one of the rival armies renounces the continuation of armed fighting and decides to reinsert itself in civil society. Conflict resolution does this, for instance, through the role of conflict mediators, who use the traditional track one approach (the actors in the mediation are members of the elites of their respective groups). But we wondered about the changes produced in subjects who are immersed in these processes of conflict resolution: Does the conflict resolution process manage to change the perceptions of the causes that have been attributed to the conflict's origin, or is there any change in the conceptions of the individual and collective subjects who participated? That is, were they able to exit that logic of war or not? If so, then the origin or cause must have been blurred, and the rival must have disappeared as such in order to appear with a less evil face.[12] We believe there to be different cases and different levels of depth. For instance, in the 1990s in Colombia, several guerrillas surrendered their weapons and signed up for peace; Otty Patiño, an old leader of the M-19 guerillas, claimed that the difference between being at war and having decided for peace was the fact that the world could no longer be understood in terms of black or white, friend or enemy. In war, on the other hand, everything was clear, because you knew who was the enemy and what you had to do, but to exit the armed fight, a lot of creativity is necessary. It may be that the concept which best approaches this experience of renouncing the violence of the armed fight is that of "imperfect peace," proposed by Francisco Muñoz at Granada University. Imperfect peace stands for all those experiences in which conflicts have been regulated through pacific means. It presumes some sort of renunciation of the intentions or expectations of one of the groups in contention, but this renunciation is a voluntary act that responds to some sort of conviction or change in the understanding of the conflict's dynamics.[13] Another level is when the combatant is captured or defeated and accepts the logic of its conqueror, appropriating that logic as its own. This has frequently been the case in Colombia, where old combatants tell how they began changing sides without any problems of conscience or conviction, rather, on the contrary, denouncing and several times even executing their old partners. Also, old guerrilla leaders who were captured or surrendered when surrounded by the military or betrayed by their comrades were pronounced "peace promoters" by President Àlvaro Uribe's government, which meant using them to try to convince former fellow combatants to join the government's demobilization program and, by doing it, obtaining legal benefits.[14] Finally, there is also the disenchantment of war, which means ending the sacralization of one's own cause, one's own army, and one's own logic of war. Such is the case for the subjects who found themselves alone, dealing with their own violence without the magical protection that a just cause presumes and the religious-like structure of an army. Many people committed to the construction of peace in Colombia emerged out of experiences of that type, whether they were old combatants, sympathizers, or just people who have been victims of some sort of violence. These subjects have often seen death face-to-face and have been immersed in an apocalyptic universe in which the only options are forms of exercising violence; however, their experience in this exposure to violence has led them to renouncing violence. The most difficult question in these cases is how to build a community with the capacity to renounce violence.

The *Gaita*

The Spanish-named bagpipes, *gaitas* (which possibly had names such as *sharv*, in the indigenous lanugage Arhuaco, or *kuisi*, in Kogui), are a type of flute with a peak traditional to the northern indigenous peoples of Colombia. During the past five centuries, they have been kept as traditional instruments by the indigenous tribes but have also come to be part of the musical legacy of the Colombian Caribbean, combining with different sorts of African drums and Spanish instruments like accordions and guitars. They are symbols for the resistance of indigenous peoples and for the miscegenation that united the sons of African slaves to those of the conquerors and elder indigenous peoples. But its crafting is traditional; it is still made of cylinders of different canes, woods, or cactuses, mixed with bird feathers for the nozzle, beeswax and ashes or vegetal coal for the head. Following the indigenous understanding of the universe, Colombian *gaitas* are played in couples: one is a female and has five holes, the last of which leads the melody, and another one is male and has two holes that account for the harmony. These two flutes are played together, making a sort of harmony also used by other Amerindian peoples such as the Mayans. With the combination of indigenous music and

African music, different drums linked to traditional dancing were incorporated together with a sense of improvisation that remains characteristic of music in the north of Colombia. Since the nineteenth century, the indigenous *gaita* has been part of northern Colombia's cultural patrimony, becoming commonly employed during the twentieth century in rhythms such as *porro, puya, mapalé,* and *cumbia,* with, of course, the risk of being lost in commercial music.[15] *Gaitas* developed from being used in religious ceremonies of indigenous peoples to being part of celebrations and parties of rural communities in northern Colombia; in indigenous ceremonies, *gaitas'* music was played with no lyrics but with a mix of African and Spanish elements; diverse rhythms emerged that incorporated lyrics. Without a doubt, these traditional indigenous flutes are the most important musical instrument that Colombians have inherited from pre-Colombian cultures and that has reached our day as a clear example of the miscegenation and the forms of resistance to cultures and impositions of diverse powers that occur without, we emphasize, a recurrence of violence.[16]

Violence during the last forty years in Colombia has had several causes and expressions, but perhaps the most important one is the fight for territory. It has been a type of violence that has taken the rural communities away from their lands, ending in hundreds of thousands of deaths and several millions of people in a situation of internal displacement in what has constituted the worst humanitarian tragedy in Latin America. This violence has left towns deserted and wrecked, as if whipped by apocalyptic punishment. Nonetheless, against this violence, many communities have organized means of pacific civil resistance. We wish to highlight the case of the Corporación Desarrollo Solidario (Joint Development Corporation), created by inhabitants of ten towns in the north of the Departamento de Bolívar in a fertile and marshy area a few kilometers south of Cartagena de Indias. There, the resistance to a state of violence has taken the form of a search for economic alternatives that guarantee the food sovereignty of the communities, together with the strengthening of cultural traditions in which the music of *gaitas* and *tamboras* is highlighted. Thus, their direct nonviolent actions tend to be accompanied by traditional music, which is meant to draw attention to the identity of the inhabitants, the product of miscegenation.

Nevertheless, several questions come up. The first is, can cultural identity, understood as the articulation of diverse elements, be effective enough to resist the great powers that have stolen the land of the region? Do they have a rich enough culture to be able to exit violence without new appeals to more sophisticated forms of violence? The idea of a cultural identity as the articulation of the diverse may be a powerful element against violent unanimity; if carefully examined, this articulation is not sufficient, but it can be just a part of the conflict in which a completely westernized white elite does not recognize itself in those mixed traditions, even though it uses them for profitable purposes. Thus, the purported articulation in the music may imply several uses of the traditions. In some cases it is to resist, in others to profit, and that implies also that the harmony the music achieves carries in a hidden way the sequel of racial discrimination and discrimination of classes in a society formed by the establishment.

The value of the music of the *tamboras* and the *gaitas* is that they are symbols for the frolics of the community, opposed to that state of violence which dissolves the community through the murder of its members. Those ways of facing the state of violence set in contrast the hopes of the collective subject (the celebration of life in common) to the potency of death in war. Even if the *tamboras* and *gaitas* music is a form of resistance from their own culture, this way is weak in that it has not achieved enough weight to stop the state of violence, that is, the logic of violent inclusion and expulsion, which have permitted the survival of communities and their members immersed in the process of living their lives daily, carrying on their regular activities, in this state of violence. Part of the imposition of a state of violence consists in the fragmentation of communities and the imposition of mistrust, augmented by the sprouting of gangs associated with the mafia and the almost unavoidable mixture of old warriors reinserted in communities that were the victims of their military actions. Thus, the fight of the armies for the control of a territory, and the expansion of enterprise projects linked to the imposition of the hegemonic domination of one of them, is contrasted with the fragmented and terrified communities that declared their resistance through their culture.

The second question is whether these cultural traditions themselves have violent roots, roots which Girard has so well helped us understand.

We recognize the richness of cultural resistance to violence, which is the most common practice in Colombia for resisting violence. It may be enough to remember the traditional legend about the origin of the *gaita*: "The gaita was born of the hairs of Popuma, the princess who was buried alive, in the beaches of the country of Pocabuy." This ambivalence of the culture, which contains violence in both senses of the word "contain," is recalled by the poems of Tulio Apolinar Arroyo Avilez.[17]

> The Gaita
> is complaint,
> is rebellious yell
> immerse into the Mounts of María;
> !!!she was born of the hairs of Popuma,
> the princess who was buried alive!!!
>
> The left Indian of Gaita
> is a beautiful provocation
> its song sings a thousand voices
> its song full of sadness and joy
> is a song of liberation
> the gaitero and its fututos
> rattle with passion
> tell the language of music
> the country bleeds in sorrow
>
> Gaitas of Cardón
> whistles of cardenchas;
> gaita is Peace
> gaita hates violence.

The Desert

We have chosen the desert to talk about a God who speaks in the silence, and also God's silence in our apocalyptic era.[18] In the realm of conflict transformation, the desert is a fundamental part of the principles of action. The individuals have to live a process inside these principles that would allow the change to be sustainable over time and so that future conflicts are not just prevented from emerging but are also truly transformed for the collective. We wish to remember the words in an audience of Pope Benedict XVI, which began by quoting the prophet Hosea: "But alas that I shall attract her and I shall take her to the desert, and I shall speak with her heart" (Hosea 2:14):

> Silence is the environmental condition most conducive to contemplation, to listening to God and to meditation. The very fact of enjoying silence and letting ourselves be "filled," so to speak, with silence, disposes us to prayer.
> The great prophet Elijah on Mount Horeb—that is, Sinai—experienced a mighty hurricane, then an earthquake and finally flashes of fire, but he did not recognize God's voice in them; instead, he recognized it in a light breeze (cf. 1 Kings 19:11–13).
> God speaks in silence, but we must know how to listen.[19]

While the garden of Eden, the place of abundance, was the scenery for sin, the desert is the place for absolute sterility, a "dammed place, where there are no seeds, no fig trees, no vines, no cattle, not even water to drink" (Numbers 20:5). God speaks in the desert because our desires no longer find the excuse that there is no object of our desires, and perhaps no one else has desires for that object. That is, it's the ambit in which we find ourselves helpless, alone with the contingency of our desires (1 Maccabees 12–13). In the extreme, the desert awakens in us a desperate thirst, an anxiety for something to sate our emptiness, due to the dynamics of desire that only answer to desire, in which our anxiety peaks. It is for that reason that the desert is not so much the place to encounter God as to confront the dynamics of our desires. In the desert, we can go back to others and sink in pleasing idolatry that adores its desires and sacralizes them (Exodus 15, Numbers 11:14, Psalms 78 and 95); or in another sense, we can let the voices that invade and constitute our subjective existence be silenced and in the radical silence we can find ourselves with a loving God who welcomes our colossal contingency and gives it a way out of the captivity and slavery to which we submit when we passionately follow someone else's desires.

But if the silence of the desert opens up the possibility of meeting this loving God, it also takes us to the route of the silence of a God whose love is realized in the cross. Golgotha is not only the ambit in which the truth of human violence is revealed, but the place where our idols and God himself come to die. Without the support of our idols, through the process of collapse of the religious that is inaugurated by the crucifixion, we face having to live creating a loving memory of this crucified man, always remembering the compassion of the women who walked by his side, not giving into the contagious madness of considering him our expiatory goat.

It may be that the biggest weakness of the projects that blossom from their own cultural traditions is that they do not sufficiently achieve a reflexive and self-critical point of view. Reflection has validity in the field of theory, or put another way, placing the experience in terms of theory, but it very well may be that purely reflexive theory is not enough to escape violence. The reference to the desert answers the question of God, often asked by the victims, whether that question is expressed as a clear Oh my God! in the face of the horror of violence or expressed as the question of how could God allow this. In all this resounds the repeated question that has found no more answer than the silence of God, either to question the massive production of victims during World Wars I and II or the terrible Holocaust in which the Jewish community was subjected to those efficient machines of death that were the concentration camps, or the terrible massacre that the radical regimen of Pol Pot committed against its own people in Cambodia. But it's the same question the victims have yelled since ancient times, before the bloody empowerment of the empires, and which has accompanied human history in every culture. The question of whether God punishes violence seems logical and clear in the sacral universe. But after the violence has been exposed and reported up to the death of God himself on the cross, and the world has been disenchanted, the problem becomes different, not just because God does not sanction or legitimate the offenders,[20] but because he identifies himself with the victims, making himself a victim. The subject who has been able to think during his loneliness, in front of a God who keeps silence, can let the open possibility take him precisely because this man has died on the cross. It is about the experience of being forgiven, that is, of recognizing oneself as the subject of violence, recognizing further that the fragility of our own contingency is formed by the structures of the founding murder, for we are the sons of Cain: not just me, every me, but also each and every other person, in such a way that forgiveness becomes a collective structure of conversion to the possibility of the formation of a community linked by this reconciling grace.[21]

It is about a form of thought that consists in making the memory of this forgiving death of Jesus on the cross a reflexive and self-criticizing memory, one that is so compassionate as to apprehend the meaning of the presence of the women in Golgotha. Thus, the overcoming of the boundaries that cultures have to reduce violence can be a bet for a silent experience of inner confrontation, constituted by the loving and compassionate memory of the people who, like Jesus, have exposed the logic of violence and opened a road where rivalry may be gradually substituted with a compassion that brings to the present of our lives those life examples of which we make memory.

Notes

1. Carl Schmitt, *The Concept of the Political* (Chicago: University of Chicago Press, 2007), 26.

2. Robert Hammerton-Kelly, "An Introductory Essay," in *Politics & Apocalypses*, ed. Robert Hammerton-Kelly (East Lansing: Michigan State University), 1–28.

3. Paul Dumouchel, "Inside Out: Political Violence in the Age of Globalization," *Contagion: Journal of Violence, Mimesis, and Culture* 15–16 (2008–2009): 173–84.

4. Ibid., 180–81.

5. Ibid., 181.

6. Angélica Durán, *Organized Crime, the State and Democracy: The Cases of Central America and the Caribbean* (Madrid: FRIDE, in collaboration with the United Nations Department of Political Affairs, 2007), http://www.fride.org.

7. John Paul Lederach, *The Little Book of Conflict Transformation* (Intercourse, PA: Good Books, 2003).

8. Matt Dean, *The Drum: A History* (London: Scarecrow Press, 2012), 136–60.

9. Hegel's analysis of the French Revolution is done in terms of a process of an abstract road toward the universal that subjectivity takes, which rejects any particularization:

> Each individual consciousness elevates itself out of the sphere assigned to it . . . it grasps itself as the concept of the will . . . thus it is only able to realize itself in a labor which is a total labor. In this absolute freedom, all the social estates . . . are effaced. The individual consciousness . . . has sublated its boundaries, and its purpose is now the universal purpose, its language the universal law, its work the universal work (586). . . . Universal freedom can thus produce neither a positive work nor a positive deed, and there remains for it merely the negative act. It is merely the fury of disappearing (589).

G. W. F. Hegel, *Phenomenology of Spirit*, trans. Terry Pinkard, 2013 draft translation online at http://terrypinkard.weebly.com/phenomenology-of-spirit-page.html. Parenthetical numbers in the Hegel quotes in this note are paragraph numbers.

When constructing its own subjectivity by wanting what everyone wants, each subject loses all respect for the lone individuality of others, as particular beings with their own meaningless lives, and thus slips toward terror: "The sole work and deed of universal freedom is thus death, or to be precise, a death which has no inner amplitude and no inner fulfillment, since what is negated is the unfulfilled empty 'point' of the absolutely free self. It is therefore the coldest, emptiest death of all, having no more meaning than does chopping off a head of cabbage or swallowing a mouthful of water" (590). The religious effect of the revolution must be appreciated because after the violence that was unleashed as a destructive force, leaving out the fear of death that brings terror, individuals accept that the state can force them to fulfill roles in which "these individuals, who have felt the fear of their absolute lord and master—death—now once again acquiesce in negation and distinctions, put themselves into the various orderings of the social spheres, and return to a divided and limited set of works. However, as a result, they return back to their substantial actuality" (593).

10. Girard claims that Clausewitz defines "a duel as a 'trend to extremes' . . . the realities of war entail that 'hostile feelings' (battle lust) always ends up overwhelming 'hostile intentions' (the reasoned decision to fight). 'Even the most civilized people, in short, can be fired with passionate hatred of each other. . . . The thesis, then, must be repeated: war is an act of force, and there is no logical limit to the application of that force. Each side, therefore, compels its opponent to follow suit; a reciprocal action is started which must lead, in theory, to extremes.'" René Girard, *Battling to the End* (East Lansing: Michigan State University Press. 2010), 5.

11. Eliminating the adversary is one of the strategies of contending, which is one of the five approaches to conflict resolution in which one of the parties has high concern for self and little concern for others, so the use of violent means is acceptable. As presented in the introduction of Oliver Ramsbotham, Tom Woodhouse, and Hugh Miall, *Contemporary Conflict Resolution* (Cambridge: Polity Press, 2000), 6.

12. Realizing the importance of addressing both the underlying structural causes of conflict and the necessary changes in the individuals was one of the reasons why the field started to move from resolution to transformation.

13. Vera Grabe, "El abc pacífico: Aproximaciones a un estado de arte sobre la conceptualización de la paz," in *Aportes a una pedagogía para la paz*, ed. Vera Grabe (Bogotá: Observatorio para la paz. 2001), 24–25.

14. S. M. Céspedes, "Disposiciones, trayectorias e imaginarios sociales de Estado y ciudadanía en el proceso de reintegración de guerrilleros y paramilitares en Colombia," *Revista Colombiana de Sociología* 38, no. 1 (2015): 185–209.

15. José Ignacio Perdomo, *Historia de la música en Colombia* (Bogota: Plaza & Janes, 1980), 225.

16. George List, "Introducción a la música folclórica de la costa atlántica colombiana," *Huellas* 27 (1989): 44.

17. See http://revistadelfestivaldeovejas.blogspot.com.

18. According to Girard:

> *One can enter into relations with divine only from a distance and through a mediator: Jesus Christ*. This contains the whole paradox that we have to deal with. It contains the new rationality that mimetic theory seeks to promote. It proclaims itself to be apocalyptic reasoning because it takes the divine seriously. In order to escape negative imitation, the reciprocity that brought people closer to the sacred, we have to accept the idea that only positive imitation will place us at the correct distance from the divine.
>
> The imitation of Christ provides *the proximity that places us at a distance*. It is not the Father whom we should imitate, but his Son, who has withdrawn with his Father. His absence is the very ordeal that we have to go through. (*Battling to the End*, 119–20)

19. Benedict XVI, General Audience, Castel Gandolfo, August 10, 2011. See http://www.vatican.va/holy_father/benedict_xvi/audiences/2011/documents/hf_ben-xvi_aud_20110810_en.html. On the silence of God, Girard comments: "The *presence* of the divinity grows as the divine withdraws. . . . God's withdrawal is thus the passage *in Jesus Christ* from reciprocity to relationship, from proximity to distance. . . . The Incarnation was the only means available to

humanity to face God's very salubrious silence: Christ questioned that silence on the cross, and then he himself imitated his Father's withdrawal." Girard, *Battling to the End*, 122.

20. "Christianity . . . prevents people from blaming the gods for their violence and places them before their responsibility." Girard, *Battling to the End*, 118.

21. "Recognizing imitation and its ambivalence seems to be the only way of feeling that it is still possible to go from reciprocity to relationship, from negative contagion to a form of positive contagion. This is what the imitation of Christ means.

"However, this transition is not a given, and it is even less conceivable: it is on the level of a specific conversion, of an event." Girard, *Battling to the End*, 109.

CONTRIBUTORS

Jeremiah L. Alberg (PhD, University of Munich, 1993) is Professor of Philosophy and Religion in the Humanities Department of International Christian University in Tokyo, Japan, and director of its Center for Teaching and Learning. He is the author of numerous works on Jean-Jacques Rousseau and Immanuel Kant. His most recent book is *Beneath the Veil of the Strange Verses: Reading Scandalous Texts* (2013). He is serving as president of the Colloquium on Violence and Religion (COV&R).

Jean-Pierre Dupuy is Professor Emeritus of Social and Political Philosophy, École Polytechnique, Paris, and Professor of Political Science, Stanford University. He is a member of the French Academy of Technology. He chairs the Ethics Committee of the French High Authority on Nuclear Safety and Security. He is the director of the research program of Imitatio, a foundation devoted to the dissemination and discussion of René Girard's mimetic theory. Among his recent publications in English are *The Mechanization of the Mind* (2000); *On the Origins of Cognitive Science* (2009); *The Mark of the Sacred* (2013); *Economy and the Future: A Crisis of Faith* (2014); and *A Short Treatise on the Metaphysics of Tsunamis* (2015.)

Yoko Irie Fayolle is a PhD student in the graduate school of Language and Society, Hitotsubashi University (Tokyo, Japan), specializing in the philosophy of religion (German idealism) and Lacanian psychoanalysis. She received a master's degree in philosophy from the University of Rennes 1 (France) in 2010. She has published several articles, including "Vacation Homework: Problems after the End of History in Kojève, Sagan and Lacan" (*I.R.S. Les études lacanienne*, 2006) and "The Problem of Theodicy in Hegel" (*Proceedings of the Philosophical Society of Sophia University*, 2007).

Eric Gans (PhD, Johns Hopkins University, 1966) teaches nineteenth-century literature, critical theory, and film in the Department of French and Francophone Studies of the University of California, Los Angeles. He is the inventor of generative anthropology, a science of human culture. His recent books include *The Scenic Imagination: Originary Thinking from Hobbes to the Present Day* (2007), *Carole Landis: A Most Beautiful Girl* (2008), and *A New Way of Thinking: Generative Anthropology in Religion, Philosophy, Art* (2011).

Sandor Goodhart (PhD, State University of New York-Buffalo, 1977) is a professor of English and Jewish Studies at Purdue University, where he also directed the Jewish Studies Program. The author of *Sacrificing Commentary: Reading the End of Literature* (1996) and *The Prophetic Law: Essays in Judaism, Girardianism, Literary Studies, and the Ethical* (2014), he is a former president of the Colloquium on Violence and Religion (COV&R). He teaches, writes, and lectures widely on French theory, dramatic literature, and Jewish studies (especially on the Bible as literature and Emmanuel Levinas).

Shoichiro Iwakiri teaches French literature in the Humanities Department of International Christian University, Tokyo, Japan. He is a translator of numerous works, including René Girard's *Je vois Satan tombe comme l'éclair*, as well as a poet. His research interests are literature and modern and contemporary poetry, especially Baudelaire. His most recent work in English is "The Chrysalis Stage of Memory in Baudelaire," in *Fragments & Wholes: Thoughts on the Dissolution of the Human Mind*, ed. Kenjiro Tamogami (2013).

Mizuho Kawasaki (PhD, Kunitachi College of Music, 2016), is Research Assistant at Kunitachi College of Music in Tachikawa, Tokyo. He has received numerous honors, including the Raymund Schwager Memorial Award for outstanding paper at the 2012 COV&R Conference, as well as the Kizen SASAKI Prize from the Tono Culture Research Center in 2013. He spent a year in the doctoral program (Ethnomusicology) of Paris-Sorbonne University (Paris IV) as an exchange student.

Kunio Nakahata was born and raised in Chiba Prefecture near Tokyo in Japan. He received an MA for his study on Jean-Jacques Rousseau's thought and a PhD for his study on Hegel's *The Science of Logic* from Sophia University in Japan. He teaches philosophy, Christianity, religion, and ethics at several universities and colleges in Japan. His research interests are the philosophy of German Idealism, especially Hegel's logic, philosophy of world history, and theory of tragedy and comedy, as well as Western contemporary thought. He also does research in applied ethics, has authored several essays on bioethics, and has translated Norman E. Bowie's *Business Ethics: A Kantian Perspective* into Japanese. He reads the Bible and modern Japanese literature from the viewpoint of René Girard's theory. He also attempts to popularize philosophy by practicing philosophical dialogue every month at his philosophy cafe.

Andreas Oberprantacher is senior researcher in the Department of Philosophy at the University of Innsbruck, where he teaches political theory, social philosophy, and aesthetics. His tenure followed completion of research on the emergence of "illegal aliens" and the transformation of contemporary politics. He is currently acting secretary general of the Austrian Society for Philosophy and is involved in the Research Center Migration and Globalization at the University of Innsbruck. He has published widely in his fields of research. His latest English-language publications include "Holey Union: Contested European Frontier Zones" (*Journal of Conflictology*, 2014); "Breaking with the Law of Hospitality? The Emergence of Illegal Aliens in Europe vis-à-vis Derrida's Deconstruction of the Conditions of Welcome" (*Hospitality & Society*, 2013); and *Subjectivation in Political Theory and Contemporary Practices*, coedited with Andrei Siclodi (2017). He has been visiting professor and visiting researcher at universities in New Orleans (United States), Castéllon (Spain), Bangkok (Thailand), Pondicherry (India), and Taichung (Taiwan).

Mery Edith Rodríguez Arias (PhD, George Mason University, 2004) is Assistant Professor in the School of Law, Universidad Santiago de Cali. Her research interests are peacebuilding, reflective practice in conflict resolution, facilitation of dialogue strategies, comparisons of peace processes, conflict and peace in Colombia, and the impact of public policies on peace and conflict on the local level. She has published "The Peasant Patrols of Peru" in *Zones of Peace*, ed. Landon Hancock and Christopher Mitchel (2007). She and Mario Roberto Solarte Rodríguez are the main researchers for the research project Memories of the Future in the Middle Magdalena, sponsored by the Pontificia Universidad Javeriana, Bogotá, Colombia.

Thomas Ryba (PhD, Northwestern University, 1988) is the Notre Dame theologian-in-residence at Purdue University, where he has taught since 1990. He is the author of *The Essence of Phenomenology and Its Meaning for the Scientific Study of Religion* (1991) and editor, with George D. Bond and Herman Tull, of *The Comity and Grace of Method Essays in Honor of Edmund F. Perry* (2004). The author of numerous articles and an internationally known speaker, he recently served as the North American editor of the highly respected journal *Religion*.

Richard Schenk (PhD, University of Munich, 1986) is Professor of the History of Philosophy and Theology at the Catholic University Eichstätt-Ingolstadt, Germany, where he also served as president from 2011 to 2014. He is the author of numerous works on the theology of St. Thomas Aquinas and its contemporary implications. His most recent publication is *Soundings in the History of a Hope: New Studies on Thomas Aquinas* (2016).

Mario Roberto Solarte Rodríguez (PhD, Pontificia Universidad Javeriana, 1995) is Associate Professor in the School of Philosophy at the Pontificia Universidad Javeriana, Bogotá, Colombia. His research centers in the area of social philosophy, working particularly from the perspective of Hegel, Benjamin, and Girard. He also has collaborated in the Training Program for Policy and Citizens (CPAL) in Colombia. He and Mery Edith Rodriguez Arias are the main researchers for the research project Memories of the Future in the Middle Magdalena, sponsored by the Pontificia Universidad Javeriana.

Matthew Taylor has lived and worked for over three decades in Japan, where he is Professor of English at Kinjo Gakuin University in Nagoya.

He received a BA in English Literature from the University of Oregon and an MA in TESOL (Teaching English to Speakers of Other Languages) from Columbia Teachers College. He has co-authored EFL (English as a Foreign Language) textbooks on speaking and academic writing with Cengage Learning and Macmillan Languagehouse. He has written and presented talks on literature, culture, the interface between science and the humanities, language learning pedagogy, René Girard's mimetic theory, and Eric Gans's generative anthropology. His articles on mimetic theory have appeared in the journals *Contagion* and *Anthropoetics*, and he co-authored an essay in *Passions in Economy, Politics, and the Media: In Discussion with Christian Theology*, ed. Wolfgang Palaver and Petra Steinmair-Pösel (2005).

Anthony D. Traylor is Associate Professor of Philosophy at Assumption College, Worcester, Massachusetts. His scholarly interests include metaphysics, phenomenology (especially Heidegger), German Idealism, philosophy of religion, and mimetic theory. His published essays include "Reassessing Heidegger on *Existentia*" (*American Catholic Philosophical Quarterly*, 2001), "Violence Has Its Reasons: Girard and Bataille" (*Contagion*, 2014), and "*Vorhandenheit* and Heidegger's Predicament over Being-in-Itself" (*American Catholic Philosophical Quarterly*, 2014). He lives with his wife and five children in Princeton, Massachusetts.

INDEX

abandonment, state of, 11, 136, 142
Agamben, Giorgio, 143
   concept of base-life, 11
Alperovitz, Gar, 25–26
Anders, Günther, 5, 9, 22, 33, 34, 36, 38
   and Fourth World Conference against Atomic and Hydrogen Bombs, 35
   Hiroshima Is Everywhere, 36
   linking Hiroshima with Auschwitz, 24
   "Nagasaki syndrome," concept of, 27
   "Promethean discrepancy," concept of, 28
anime, 1, 11, 16, 139, 156
   and apocalypse, 142
Anscombe, Elizabeth, 24
Antichrist, 14, 192, 198–203
   how to read, 201–2
anti-idolatry, 14, 176, 203
apocalypse, 4, 13–14, 15, 20, 34, 36, 44–45, 53, 131, 145, 173–74, 196, 229–31, 246
   ante apocalypsis, 21
   blindness in the face of, 28
   bloodless, 139
   domestication of, 200–201
   final versus "little," 201
   gnostic meaning of, 187
   indefinite deferral of, 201
   narratives of, 142
   as our future fate, 27
   as undifferentiated violence at the limits of history, 145
apocalyptic, the, 2, 5, 11, 13–14, 16, 34, 42, 53, 171, 172, 186–87, 201, 217, 231, 246
   consciousness, 246
   eschatology, 203
   Girard on, 44–45, 60
   imagination, 246
   knowledge, 230
   language, 180
   loneliness, 137
   prophecy, 196, 199
   and the prophetic, 171–72, 175, 177, 179, 180
   strong and weak senses of, 180–81
   texts, 174, 200
   thinking, 171
   vision, 231
   See also typology
Arendt, Hannah, 23–24, 28, 33, 36, 38
Arias, Mery Edith Rodríguez, 15
Augustine, 215, 223, 233
Auschwitz, 23–24
autonomy, check, 6, 7, 58–63, 92, 166
   metaphysical, 59

bandon, 137
Benedict XVI, 255
Benjamin, Walter, 137, 182
Bernstein, Barton J., 26–27
Bible, the, 1, 19, 67, 187, 190
  as revelation of the scapegoat mechanism, 66, 232
Bloch, Ernst, 232
Bomb, the, 4–8, 20–22, 23, 25–28, 32, 37, 42, 44–47, 50, 52, 67–68, 72–75, 76, 80–83, 174, 232, 246
  as the *Aufhebung* of the violent arbitrariness of the old sacred, 46
  as intrinsically immoral, 24
  as returning humans to their originary state, 46
  as sacrament, 20, 35
Brodie, Bernard, 33
Buber, Martin, 175–77
  on the apocalyptic, 176
  "The Dialogue between Heaven and Earth," 175
  "Prophetic, Apocalyptic, and the Historical Hour," 175
Buddha, 112, 122, 163
  statue of, 150, 161, 164
Buddhism, 69, 103, 104, 165–66
Burger, Thomas, 193

Casey, Edward S., 219–21
catastrophe, 2, 3, 5, 34–36, 37–39, 61, 77, 136, 139, 176, 226, 230–31
Césaire, Aimé, *choc en retour*, 42
Charter Cities, 144, 145
Chernobyl, 38, 231
Christianity, 13, 21, 35, 48, 52, 78, 81, 82, 97, 103–4, 133, 171, 180, 183–94
  as anthropological phenomenon, 49

  as foreseeing its own failure, 174
  history in Japan, 7, 68–72
  as the religion of the end of religion, 21
  as revelation, 22
  truth of, 8, 67, 83
Clausewitz, Carl von, 60–61, 173, 184, 246
  On War, 173
Clinton, Bill, 29
Cold War, 20
Colloquium on Violence and Religion (COV&R), 2
Colombia, 15, 245–52
  Corporación Desarrollo Soidario, 252
  music of, 251–53
communality, 102
community, 46–47, 55, 62–63, 81, 109–10, 114, 144, 179, 183, 200, 253, 257
conflict resolution, 247–50
conflict transformation, 248
  desert as part of, 254
conversion, 10, 15, 60, 67, 90, 101, 118–19, 124, 125, 128, 131–33, 166, 257
Creon, 92

Davis, Mike, *Planet of Slums*, 137–38
decadence, 11, 47, 52
  Japan's fall into, 129–30
Decalogue, 229
deferral of violence, 4, 12, 14, 47, 159
  firstness as mode of, 51
  as humanity's most fundamental operation, 46
Derrida, Jacques
  parergon, 145
  supplement, 34, 145

desert, 16, 254
desertification, 11, 138, 145
desire, 66
   mediated, 100–101
   metaphysical, 62–63
   rivalistic, 77
   See also mimetic desire
dialectic
   for discovery of sequential types, 190
   of fate and accident, 34–35
   of imitation and authenticity, 153
   of near and far, 221
Dionysian, 9, 49, 64, 92, 97–98
Dionysus, 91, 96–98
distance, 14–15, 16, 34, 57, 103, 221–22, 224–27, 228–29, 231, 233–34
Don Quixote, 91, 100–104
Dostoyevsky, Fyodor, 233
Dr. Strangelove, 46
drums, 249
duel, 44, 60
Dumouchel, Paul, 3, 246–47
Dupuy, Jean-Pierre, 3, 4–6, 7–9, 10
   on paradox of nuclear deterrence, 46

earthquake, eastern Japan, 2, 95
efumi (stepping on an image of Christ or Mary), 69
escalation to extremes, 60

FARC. *See* Revolutionary Armed Forces of Colombia
Fayolle, Yoko Irie, 7–8
fiction, functioning of, 195
firstness, 47, 50
   Jewish, 48
   as mode of deferral, 51
   West's historical status of, 51

The Fog of War, 25, 29
forgiveness, 15, 257
Foucault, Michel, 173
Fukushima, 37, 83, 232

gaita, 251–54
game theory, 22
Gans, Eric, 3, 4, 5–6, 12, 158
generative anthropology, 3, 4, 41
Gifu prefecture, 106
Girard, René, 9, 14, 16, 66, 89, 131–32, 139, 155, 183–84, 216, 253
   and apocalyptic texts, 174
   Battling to the End (*Achever Clausewitz*), 6–7, 55, 60, 63, 172–74, 183, 245, 246
   as completing Heidegger, 217, 228
   concept of silence, 245, 248
   Deceit, Desire, and the Novel, 2, 89
   on Heidegger, 131–32
   I Saw Satan Fall Like Lightening, 43, 48–49
   and Japan, 2–3
   on meaning of apocalypse, 187
   on meaning of the Bomb, 20–21, 43–47
   on meaning of the Holocaust, 47–50
   "The Mimetic Theory and Theology," 217
   on pseudo-narcissism, 155
   The One by Whom Scandal Comes, 3
   The Scapegoat, 2
   A Theater of Envy, 3
   Things Hidden since the Foundation of the World (*Des choses cachées depuis la foundation du monde*), 2, 6, 10, 20–21, 22, 43, 55, 60, 216

view of Dionysus, 97
Violence and the Sacred, 144
When These Things Begin, 3
Goodhart, Sandor, 13–14
Goroubei, 110, 111–12
   role in the village, 113–14
Gospel, 19, 44, 45, 59, 61, 103, 133
   Synoptic Gospels, 174, 181

Habershon, Ada, *Study of the Types*, 187
Handa, Haruka, 139
Heidegger, Martin, 15, 33, 131, 225, 229, 233
   Being and Time, 218–21, 222–24, 226–27, 231
   "Building Dwelling Thinking," 221
   "A Dialogue on Language," 221
   Hermeneutics of Facticity, 223
   An Introduction to Metaphysics, 220
   Kant and the Problem of Metaphysics, 227
   "Origin and the Work of Art," 220
   "The Thing," 221
   "Time and Being," 221
Hidden Christians (*Kakure-Kirishitan*), 7–8, 68, 70
hierarchy, 80, 122–23
Hikaru, 90–91, 104
Himiko, legend of, 160–61, 162–63
Hiroshima, 2, 4, 5, 9, 23–25, 35, 36–38, 42, 76, 246
   as necessary evil, 24
   revisionists' interpretation of, 26–28
   as symbol of Japan's loss of the war, 53
   See also Anders, Günther
Hiroshima mon amour, 52–53
Hitler, Adolph, 48

Hitlerism, 49–50
Holocaust, 5, 41–42, 178, 256
   as substitute for "shoah," 36
hominization, 165
Hurricane Katrina, 38
Husserl, Edmund, 194

idolatry, 255
Illich, Ivan, 39
Ingarden, Roman, 197
Iran, 50, 52
Isaiah, Book of, 175, 176, 177
Islam, 50, 52
Iwakiri, Shoichiro, 9

James, Williams, 119
Japan, 1, 7, 13, 15, 37, 39, 67, 70, 75, 83, 89, 92, 95–96, 106, 109, 115, 129, 131, 139–41, 149, 153, 156, 166
   and Lolita, 153–54
   political system, 122
   prohibition of Christianity, 68–69, 71, 78
   and snobbery, 78–80
   and World War II, 2, 25–26, 41–42, 53, 74, 128
   See also Girard, René, and Japan
Jesus, 10, 21, 66, 75, 81, 81, 97, 132, 180, 181–82, 183, 203, 216, 257
   forgiving death of, 257
   Passion, 49
   revelation of, 45–46
Jews, 5, 23, 26, 42, 48, 120, 179
Job, 94, 176
   Book of, 176, 178
Jonah, Book of, 175–76
Jonas, Hans, 232
Judaism, 13, 48, 171, 181, 183, 184

Kamikaze Girls (*Shimotsuma Monogatari*), 12
   comparison with *2001: A Space Odyssey*, 163–65
   and Japanese subcultures, 149, 151, 159
Kant, Immanuel, 188, 190–92, 193, 219
   Critique of Judgment, 190–91
karakuri, 10, 119, 131
   construction of, 120–21
   emperor system as, 120, 121–22, 124
Kataoka, Chizuko, 76
Kavka, Gregory, 32
Kawasaki, Mizuho, 9–10
kegare (impurity), 69, 76–77, 80
kenosis, 230, 233
Kingdom of God, 20, 67, 127, 200
Kiritsubo, 90
Kojève, Alexandre, 67
Kubrik, Stanley, *2001: A Space Odyssey*, 150, 163–64

Laius, king, 93
law, 32, 137, 139, 143, 181
   abandonment to, 137, 143
   empire of, 247
   Talmudic, 181
Lederach, John Paul, 248
Levinas, Emmanuel, 218
Lévi-Strauss, Claude, 56
Lewis, David K., 32–33
logic
   of ideal types, 193
   of mercy, 8
   of place/social emplacement, 217, 228–29
   of the sacred, 21
   of sacrifice, 8, 75–76
   of violent inclusion and expulsion, 253, 257
   of war, 250–51
logos, 4
   of peace, 6, 52
   of violence, 6, 52
Lolita
   desexualized, 154
   fashion, 150, 152
   figure of, 12
   in Japan, 153–54
Lonergan, Bernard, 119
loneliness, 137
Lorein, G. W., 189

MacIntyre, Alasdair, 223–24
manifold, Husserlian notion of, 188, 194
Marie Antoinette, 155–56, 158
martyrs, Japanese, 8, 68–69, 71, 74, 81–82
McKenna, Andrew, 3
McNamara, Robert, 25, 29
   Memoirs, 34
méconnaisance, 4, 8, 11, 21–22, 52, 80
   Japanese snobbery as form of, 78–80
   of Japanese society, 72, 83
mediation, 90, 157–58, 167
   external, 57, 59, 79–80, 82
   hidden, 12
   internal, 57–58, 79, 90
mediator, 12, 66, 79, 107, 114, 115, 157, 248
   murder of, 107, 112
   Tengu as, 108, 109–10, 112
Melancholia, 53
Midas, 96

mimetic desire, 46, 66, 79, 82, 93, 100, 127, 131, 132, 145, 146
 triangular character of, 57
mimetic mechanism, 66
mimetic rivalry, 9, 11, 14–16, 66, 79, 93, 104, 123, 138, 142, 145–46, 188, 217, 218, 220, 225, 230, 233, 249, 257
mimetic theory, 2, 3, 4, 41, 67, 145, 157, 159, 164, 187, 202, 216, 221, 245
 and conflict resolution, 245
 and Japan, 9–13, 14, 16
 as necessary to complete Heidegger, 217
 and theology, 13–15
mimetic violence, 47, 66, 81–82
misrecognition. *See méconnaisance*
Motoshima, Hitoshi, 72
Muñoz, Francisco, 250
Murasaki, Shikibu, 89
Mutter, Michael, 138
myth, 12, 56, 80–81, 95, 103, 108, 110, 115, 150, 161, 165–67, 176, 183

Nagai, Takashi, 7–8
 The Bells of Nagasaki, 73, 83
 biographical background, 67
 funeral address, 73–75
 funeral address controversy, 75–77
 Leaving My Beloved Children Behind, 72
 role as Paraclete, 81
 We of Nagasaki, 82
Nagasaki, 2, 7–9, 23, 27, 37, 42
 dropping of bomb over, 68
 as nuclear Holocaust, 67, 74, 75
Nagasaki Shinbun (Nagasaki Newspapers), 76

Nagasaki-Urakami. *See* Nagasaki
Naito, Mikio, 71
Nakahata, Kunio, 10
Nakamura, Yūjirou, 111
Nakashima, Tetsuya, 149, 164, 166–67
Namiki, Koichi, 94
Nancy, Jean-Luc, 11, 136–37, 143
Naoya, Shiga, 130
narcissism, 12, 155
National Liberation Army (ELN), 245
Nazis, and reliance on Nietzsche, 47–50
Nietzsche, Friedrich, 43, 47–49, 137
 denying Jewish claim to firstness, 48
nihilism, 130
Nishida, Kitaro, 215, 230, 233
 "Basho" (Place), 217
 "Bashoteki Ronri to Shukyouteki Sekaikan" (The Logic of Place and the Religious World-View), 217
 "Watashi to Nanji" (I and Thou), 217
nuclear deterrence, 28–32
 fraught with paradox, 46
 and human intention, 35
 as structurally the same as primitive sacred, 35
 and "suspension of disbelief," 35

Oberprantacher, Andreas, 11
Oedipus, 93–95
Okamoto, Hiroyuki, 69, 76
Ozaki, Gakudo, 130
Ozaki, Yutaka, 160

Pacific War. *See* World War II
Paraclete, 81, 83
Patiño, Otty, 250
Perry, Matthew, 70
Petitjean, Bernard, 70

Plutschow, Herbert, 53, 157
Pol Pot, 256
postponing the apocalypse. *See* deferral of violence
prohibition, 19, 57, 59
prophetic, the, 13
  and the apocalyptic, 171
  Jewish conception of, 171–77
  strong and weak senses of, 180
pseudo-narcissism, 12

Qutb, Sayyid, 52

reciprocity, negative and positive, 58–60
  analogical relationship between, 61
  structural similarities between, 60–63
reflexive theory, 248, 256
religion, 14, 46, 48, 103, 104, 119, 165, 166, 174, 232–33, 234
  freedom of, 8, 68–72, 78
  sacrificial, 46
Resnais, Alan, 52–53
Revelation, Book of, 20, 173
Revolutionary Armed Forces of Colombia (FARC), 245
Rice, Condoleeza, 29
ritual, 6, 9–10, 19, 55–56, 59, 69, 80, 106, 107, 110, 112–15, 161
rivalry. *See* mimetic rivalry
Rodríguez, Mario Roberto Solarte, 15–16
Romer, Paul, 143
The Rose of Versailles, 12, 156–58
Rothberg, Michael, *Multi-directional Memory*, 42
Rousseau, Jean-Jacques, 38, 158
Ryba, Thomas, 13, 14

sacred, 4, 12, 19, 21–22, 35, 46, 75, 92, 109, 114, 118, 155, 164–65, 174, 165
sacrifice, 10, 12, 15, 64, 67, 74–76, 83, 106, 107, 109–11, 113–15, 127, 142, 143–44, 150, 162, 167, 175, 215, 216–17, 229–30, 232–33
sacrificial crisis, 11, 20, 142, 144–46, 164
sacrificial mechanism, 5, 21, 22, 45, 57, 146
Saito, Mokichi, 71
Sakaguchi, Ango, 10–11
  on being an individual, 132
  "Bungaku no Furusato" (The Birthplace of Literature), 128
  "Darakuron" (Discourse on Decadence), 118, 133
  "Zoku darakuron" (Discourse on Decadence Part II), 118, 133
  See also decadence
sakoku (closed country policy), 69, 139
Satan, 14, 19, 81–82, 97, 176
scandal, 62, 81–82, 226
scapegoat, 9, 11, 59, 62, 66–67, 79, 80–81, 83, 80, 112, 114, 132, 142, 145, 158–59, 160, 161, 165
scapegoat mechanism, 4, 11, 45, 55, 57–59, 63–64, 66–67, 79–82, 145, 159, 232
  apocalyptic doom in the absence of, 59
scapegoating, 12, 45, 47, 150, 158–59, 161–62, 233
Schell, Jonathan, 31
Schelling, Thomas
  "rationality of irrationality" theory, 33
  Strategy of Conflict, 33

Schenk, Richard, 14–15
Schmidt, Carl, 246
Schwager, Raymund, 216, 229, 233
Scotus, Johannes Dun, 223
Seaford, Richard, 92–98
servant of Yhwh, 178–79
Shinto, 69, 71, 166
Shishi (lion), 106–7
silence, 255
Silenus, 96
Sloterdijk, Peter, 231
snobbery. *See* Japan, and snobbery
Sophocles, *Oedipus tyrannus*, 92–93
Sori, Fumihiko, 139
state of abandonment. *See* abandonment, state of
Stendhal, *The Red and the Black*, 99–100
Sugoishishi, ritual dance, 10, 106, 110
Snyder, Timothy, 42

Tale of Genji, 9, 89, 103–4
  moments of conversion in, 91
Takahashi, Shinji, 75
Takahashi, Tetsuya, 75
  Kokka to Gisei (State and Sacrifice), 75
Takemoto, Novala, 149, 156, 158, 163
tamboras, 252–53
Tanabe, Hajime, 217
Tanaka, Kouichi, 113
Taylor, Matthew, 12–13
Tengu, 107–8
  as mediator, 108
  similarity with Hermes, 109
Thebes, 95–96, 141
Tiresias, 93
Tokugawa, Ieyasu, 69
topology, 218, 228–34
Toyotomi, Hideyoshi, 68

Traylor, Anthony, 6–7, 11
Truman, Harry, 26
tsunami
  atomic bombing in Japan as, 36
  of Christmas 2004, 38
  Lisbon earthquake of 1755, 38
  of March 2011, 2
  "shoah" as signifying, 36
type, 14, 188–90
  antitype, 198
  apocalyptic, 201
  common characteristics, 189–90
  in contrast to fiction, 196
  hypotype, 188, 190–92, 195
  ideal, 188, 190, 193–94
  streptotype, 198, 201
typology
  apocalyptic, 187–88
  Christian, 188
  as truth-expressive biblical communication, 187

Ukifune, 104
undifferentiation, 6–7, 11, 63, 145–46
  as apocalyptic melting point, 58
  dangers of, 60
  as means of reconciliation, 55
  as means toward re-differentiation, 55
  states of, 146
  telos of, 63
  two kinds of, 58
Urakami Cathedral, 67, 73
Urakami Punishment Theory, 72–73
Urakami Yonban Kuzure (fourth oppression of Urakami), 71, 72
Uribe, Àlvaro, demobilization program, 250–51
Ushijima, Nobuaki, 102

Vattimo, Gianni, 15, 216, 224, 228–33
Versailles, as aesthetic model, 151, 155
Vexille, 11, 139
  plot summary, 139–41
victim, 4, 5, 8, 9, 12, 21, 36, 39, 41, 51, 53, 74, 80, 232
  care for, 6, 43, 47–48, 50, 59, 89, 91, 109, 114, 125, 126, 157–59, 229, 232–33, 246, 248, 251, 253, 256
  care for rooted in Jewish monotheism, 48
  care for rooted in resentment, 49
  community as double of, 62–63
  innocence of, 81–83
  Nazis as combatting care for, 48, 49
victimage mechanism, 21–22
victimary logic, 50–52
violence, 3, 6, 7, 9, 11, 19, 20–22, 33–35, 36, 42, 44–46, 51–52, 58, 59, 61, 62–64, 66, 77, 79, 80, 89, 94, 97, 142, 144–46, 155, 165, 174, 179, 181, 217, 225, 246–49, 251, 252–54, 256–57
  generative, 10, 59, 107, 109–10, 112–16
  See also mimetic violence
von Rad, Gerhard, 186, 189, 190, 192
von Trier, Lars, 53

Weber, Max, 193–94
Weil, Simone, 133
Whitehead, A. N., fallacy of misplaced concreteness, 196
woman caught in adultery, 47, 50, 180–81
World War II, 4, 10, 119, 125, 127–28, 256
  living in its shadow, 41

yakubarai, 69
Yamaguchi, Masao, *Folklore of the Clown*, 108
Yamamura, Satobei, 110
Yonban Kuzure. See Urakami Yonban Kuzure

Jeremiah L. Alberg is professor of philosophy and religion at International Christian University, Tokyo. He is the author of a number of books, including *Beneath the Veil of the Strange Verses: Reading Scandalous Texts.*

www.ingramcontent.com/pod-product-compliance
Lightning Source LLC
Chambersburg PA
CBHW070401100426
42812CB00005B/1587